ROME AND JUGURTHA

D0814288

SALLUST

ROME AND JUGURTHA

EDITED WITH INTRODUCTION, NOTES
AND VOCABULARY

BY

J.R. HAWTHORN

Bristol Classical Press

This impression 2009
This edition published in 1979 by
Bristol Classical Press
an imprint of
Gerald Duckworth & Co. Ltd.
90-93 Cowcross Street, London EC1M 6BF
Tel: 020 7490 7300
Fax: 020 7490 0080
info@duckworth-publishers.co.uk
www.ducknet.co.uk

First published in 1969 by Macmillan Education Ltd.
© 1969 by J.R. Hawthorn

A catalogue record for this book is available
from the British Library

ISBN 978 1 85399 718 1

Printed and bound in USA by
IBT Global, Troy, NY

Contents

List of Maps

Preface

THERE are three ways of reading the *Jugurtha*. The first is as a swift-moving narrative, the scene now Rome, now North-Africa, the language terse and pointed, quite different from the grand verbosities of Livy and Cicero. On this level alone the *Jugurtha* is a masterpiece, and we shall not enjoy it to the full, or be fair to the author, unless this is in the front of our minds. The second is a study of Roman affairs of state, itself twofold – the conflict between the senate and its opponents in the late Republic, and the attempt to keep the peace on the fringes of the empire. The third is a literary study, for Sallust has a distinguished place in the line of ancient historians, the line which stretches from Herodotus to Tacitus, and such a study will deepen our understanding of them all.

In this book I have tried to make it possible to do any of these things, or all of them. For the first, I have reduced the *Jugurtha* to a length which I hope can be read in the time usually available, including not very much more than half of the total. I have also used the notes to give considerable help to the translator, aiming to give what I think would be needed by students who have graduated in the school of the Gallic Wars. The vocabulary is not literally complete – I do not insult the reader by translating *enim* or *res* for him (the one too easy, the other too difficult) – but if in doubt about a word I have usually put it in.

The shortening of the text has necessitated some difficult decisions. It is necessary to do this, since too many people have been put off the *Jugurtha* by its great length – if we start at the beginning and faithfully plough our way through, time will fail us and we shall not even have reached the appointment of Marius; just as many have read the *Catiline* and never got past the Milvian Bridge. But inevitably some things had to be omitted. No one will miss the boring and wildly inaccurate digression on the geography of Africa, or the irrelevance on the people of Lepcis. The omission of the Prologue will surprise those who think of Sallust as an original moralist, but I am sure that it is right; he was better at writing history than at writing about history, and if we do want to pause over his ideas on virtue, our first few days of Sallust are not the time. For purposes of discussion I print it as an appendix, with a full translation, and indicate in the notes the line I think the discussion should take. I have more regrets that some of the speeches have had to go; they are all good, but they are long. I have included the two most important, those of Memmius and Marius addressing the people.

For the second and third purposes, the study of the topics, I have tried in writing the notes to direct attention to the historical problems involved, but without unduly slowing down the narrative. More detailed discussion is reserved for the Introduction, which, like all introductions, should be read after the text. I have tried there to fill in the literary topic as well as the historical; Roman writers had a great, perhaps excessive, respect for their literary tradition, and unless we take account of this we shall never fully understand what they are doing. The two topics cannot be entirely separated, but I hope that the headings will act as adequate guides. The geography of Numidia was difficult to handle; it makes a kind of introduction to the Introduction, and I have set it apart as a separate note.

Bibliographies frighten me – they look so learned. Nor are they easy to use; many of the books and articles listed are likely to be difficult to find, and we are not always sure, if we do run them to earth, whether the prize will be worth the labour. For Sallust, too, a complete bibliography would be mostly in German. Those who want one will find it (down to 1962) in Professor Syme's *Sallust*, a work to which we all pay our respects. I have limited mine to what is in English, and what I have found valuable; I have added to each a short statement of what it is about, so that the reader who does not have access to it may know what he is missing, and he who could have may decide whether, for him, the search will be rewarded. To the authors I apologise, knowing that my few words cannot do justice to their great learning; but the purpose of a bibliography should be to serve the reader.

Introduction, Note, Bibliography; we print them together and since the Introduction is supposed to introduce they come before the text. For their length I make no apology, for there are a number of subjects involved and all are important. We are all of us learning these days that in reading a classical text we should look beyond the words in front of us, and study also the circumstances of the author and the people he is writing about. To this more enlightened method I hope this book may make some contribution.

But those whose desire is for a good story can pass them all by and go straight to the text. And perhaps they will have the best of it; for this, after all, is the story of Jugurtha, and, like the undergraduate at his Divinity *viva*, translating the shipwreck of St Paul, we 'want to find out what happens to this interesting fellow'.

J. R. H.

The chapters of Sallust, *Bellum Iugurthinum* included in this selection are as follows:

I Numidian Civil War and Appeal to Rome: V–VI, XII–XIII, XV–XVI, XX–XXVI.

II Limited Intervention: XXVII–XXXI, XXXIX–XLI.

III Outright War: XLIII–LV, LXIII–LXIV, LXXIII, LXXX–XCII 4, XCV–CII 4, CXI–CXIV

The text is based on that of Merivale (Macmillan: Classical Series), but in some places I have preferred the readings of Rolfe (Loeb Library). For the maps I have made most use of those of Holroyd in the *Journal of Roman Studies*, 1928.

List of Abbreviations

AJP	*American Journal of Philology*
CAH	*The Cambridge Ancient History*
CP	*Classical Philology*
JHS	*Journal of Hellenic Studies*
JRS	*Journal of Roman Studies*
TAPA	*Transactions and Proceedings of the American Philological Association*
Symb. Os.	*Symbolae Osloenses*

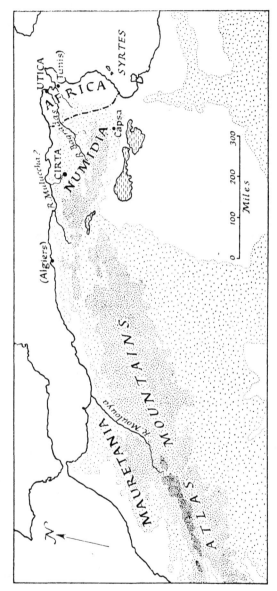

North-West Africa at the time of the Jugurthine War

Introduction

I Africa

The Client Kings

MAPS which are printed to illustrate the Roman Empire usually show a frontier clearly marked with a thick black line, and give the impression that if you were on one side of the line you were inside, and if you were on the other you were outside. The reality was not as simple as that. There were the provinces, of course, for which the Romans accepted some degree of administrative responsibility (as little as possible, in the period we are concerned with), and to which they sent Governors and in some cases garrison troops. But beyond the provinces, outside the tidy black lines on our maps, they were at pains to make alliances with the native rulers, so as to secure their loyalty or at least their acquiescence. For the understanding of Roman foreign policy it is more important to follow the relations between Rome and the native dynasties than to learn the dates of the annexations of provinces.

This relationship might begin, outwardly at least, as one of equality: two allies with a common interest and a purely voluntary agreement. But as the power of Rome grew with the growth of the Empire, that equality was not likely to endure. If the king broke off the alliance, or embarked on a policy likely to endanger the security of the province, the Romans could bring pressure to bear, in one way or another, and could very likely see to it that he was deposed; if one king was obstinate, another could be found to take his place;

while in the background was the possibility of invasion by the most formidable army in the world.

In our vocabularies the Latin for 'ally' is always 'socius', and before Rome had an empire this was adequate enough. But when provinces were annexed it was not usually by simple conquest, and the inhabitants of the provinces, whom we call 'provincials', or even 'subjects', were by the Romans called 'socii'. A more honourable term had therefore to be found for the native kings beyond the frontiers, and the Romans, always ready to concede the appearance of power as long as they held the reality, gave him the title of 'amicus'; sometimes 'socius et amicus'; or, more splendid still, 'amicus populi Romani'. As early as 122 B.C., some ten years before the war with Jugurtha, a law of Rome (the *lex Acilia*) speaks of those who are within the *amicitia populi Romani*.

'Amicus' he might be in name, but it did not do to presume too much on this relationship. The interests of Rome must be served. So long as he kept the peace, acting in fact as the first line of defence of the empire, and did not lend encouragement to any discontented men there might be in the province, the Romans would support him, and if his position was threatened by a usurper they might intervene actively on his behalf. But when in 58 the German Ariovistus, recently styled by senatorial decree *rex et amicus*, presumed to treat with Caesar as an equal, he was quickly taught a lesson. And when a king got into difficulties and appealed for help to his great ally, the Romans decided, in accordance with their own interests, whether to come to his aid or leave him in the lurch. The relationship was not really one of ally with ally but of client with patron; a pattern familiar in Roman society, and imported by them into their dealings with foreign rulers because it was in accord with the facts of power. On the edges of the empire, between the provinces and the truly independent foreigners, the client kings maintained their uneasy existence, kept in power so long as they served the interests of Rome.

Numidia

In the year 203, the year before the defeat of Hannibal at Zama brought the Second Punic War to an end, a parade of the Roman army was held in Africa. In view of the troops

THE NUMIDIAN ROYAL FAMILY

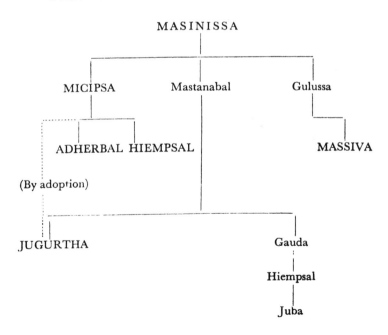

the Roman general, Scipio Africanus, decorated Masinissa with the highest military honours the Roman state could bestow, including the staff, cloak and tunic normally worn by a victorious Roman general in his triumphal procession through the streets of Rome. This Masinissa was the chieftain of a tribe of Numidians, the western neighbours of Carthage, and had been an ally of Carthage. He was won over to the Roman side by Scipio, and in the final African campaign he brought his cavalry to help the Romans. He assisted in the rounding up of Syphax, ruler of most of Numidia, and played an important part in the battle of Zama itself. For these services, and in order to create in Africa a power which would prevent the revival of Carthage, the Romans made him king of Numidia, promising him all the lands which his ancestors had possessed.[1]

The new king was a man of energy, and in his long reign of over fifty years he united and strengthened his kingdom, and under the protection of Rome he annexed, piece by piece, outlying portions of the territory of the defeated Carthage. He kept the approval of Rome by sending gifts of corn to Roman armies, and detachments of cavalry and elephants to help them in Spain, while he skilfully played on their almost pathological fear of a Carthaginian revival. At length he provoked the Carthaginians too far, they resisted, and Rome intervened – against the Carthaginians. Before this war, the Third Punic War, was over, Masinissa had died, at the age of ninety. For nearly sixty years he had assisted the Romans, and though we can see that he skilfully used their support for his own ends, later generations of Romans looked back on him as one of the great *amici populi*

[1] The extent of Masinissa's kingdom is discussed in the 'Note on the Boundaries of Numidia', p. liv.

Romani on whose goodwill the empire depended. It is for this reason that he appears in Cicero's 'Dream of Scipio'.

We must now follow in outline the tortuous history of the house of Masinissa. On the death of the old king, his kingdom was divided between his three sons, but the two younger ones soon died and the eldest, Micipsa, became king of a united Numidia. When, in 146, the territory of Carthage became the province of Africa, Numidia was its neighbour on the West and South. Micipsa had owed his throne to the Romans and remained their loyal ally, sending troops to support Scipio Aemilianus in the last years of the Spanish War.[1]

Civil War and Roman Interference

Among these troops was the king's nephew, Jugurtha, an able and energetic young cavalry officer who gained the approval of the Roman commanders. Impressed by a letter from Scipio, which was almost a command, Micipsa adopted him, and at his death divided the kingdom between Jugurtha and his own two sons – both younger than Jugurtha. The struggle for power which followed – Hiempsal murdered, Adherbal threatened – is told in our first section. Jugurtha had no intention of sharing the kingdom with his young brothers, and thought that his services in Spain had made him the favourite of the Romans[2]

---

[1] This double involvement of the two great Scipios in the affairs of Africa gave their family the status of patrons of the area. Jugurtha, as the protégé of Aemilianus, was to benefit from this.

[2] In fact there is an interval of silence between the fall of Numantia (133) and the death of Micipsa (118); Jugurtha's adoption must have been about 121.

But if Jugurtha could fancy himself as a client of Rome, entitled to expect support, so could Adherbal, and when worsted in battle he went himself to seek help from the protecting power. Jugurtha on his side sent a deputation, and both sides were heard by the senate. At this point Sallust is guilty of making things too simple: to him it was a clear case of the justice of Adherbal and the money of Jugurtha. The senate took a different view: they had no interest in a squabble between the native princes except as it affected Rome, and certainly had no desire to be involved in a war for one against another; they were not the world's policemen. They sent an embassy which divided the kingdom between the two cousins and naturally hoped that that had settled the matter.

Unfortunately, Jugurtha's ambition could not be satisfied with anything less than the whole kindgom, and they had allotted to him the poorer part of it, as the 'Note on the Boundaries of Numidia' will show. He thought his friends at Rome were still on his side, invaded eastern Numidia and blockaded Adherbal in his capital of Cirta. Now the Romans began to act. The senate decreed, and the people passed a resolution ordering Jugurtha to stop fighting, and in effect making it possible for the senate to declare war if he disobeyed. Three young senators were sent out to present this demand, but were put off by his assurances of loyalty to Rome and his promise to send a deputation to explain. This was in fact the first stage in the cumbrous Roman machinery for declaring war.[1] Then, when it was discovered that he was not mending his ways, a desperate letter from Adherbal having been read

---

[1] The apparently futile embassies of this year have been elucidated by Oost, in *AJP* lxxv 147. As narrated by Sallust, they seem quite pointless. See especially the note on XXI 4 p. 62.

in the senate, a more senior deputation was sent out, headed by an ex-consul, with more insistent threats – this was the second stage. It was now possible for the senate to declare war at any time if they wanted to, and in spite of their reluctance two things drove them to it: the first was popular agitation, led by the tribune-elect Memmius, the second was the sack of Cirta, in which not only Adherbal but also the entire resident community of Italians were massacred.

Now there was an outcry at Rome, war was declared, and an army was sent to Africa under the command of the consul of 111, Calpurnius Bestia. The attack on Jugurtha began. The invasion at once brought home the realities to both sides: Jugurtha realised that the Romans meant business, while the Roman generals discovered the extreme difficulty of campaigning in Africa; the strength of their army was its heavy infantry, admirable in Italy against an enemy who would stand his ground and defend his city, but not equipped for chasing elusive mobile troops who would retreat to fight again.[1] A negotiated peace was in everyone's interest.

Negotiations accordingly took place; the terms agreed upon were that Jugurtha should surrender, acknowledge the overlordship of Rome, pay a war indemnity (silver and thirty elephants were mentioned), and in return be installed as the king of all Numidia. Unfortunately for this sensible arrangement, Roman generals were not entitled to make peace; the only way it could be done was for Jugurtha to surrender unconditionally, on the understanding that Bestia

---

[1] The terrain of Algeria has been described by Sherwin White, *JRS* xxxiv (1944) 1; neither the forests of the north nor the steppes of the interior would be favourable to Roman armies.

and Scaurus would use their influence to persuade their government to ratify the terms.[1]

This the senate might have done. The whole incident would have been closed, with Roman dignity satisfied and a strong client king on the throne of Numidia. Bestia and his *legatus* had deserved well of the Republic. Again their plans were upset; Memmius challenged the genuineness of the surrender, and insisted that Jugurtha be brought to Rome to testify against the nobles. Jugurtha came – thus proving that the surrender was genuine – but while there he found a cousin of his, Massiva, who was being encouraged to claim the throne of Numidia, and promptly had him murdered. He soon found out that murder in Numidia was one thing, murder in Rome another; he was ordered to leave, and the new consul Spurius Albinus (it is now 110) resumed hostilities. But the Roman commitment was still less than whole-hearted. While the consul marched about in search of a battle, Jugurtha avoided a direct confrontation; it was still possible that, as they realised the difficulties of a war in Africa, the Romans would settle for peace on any terms which they could persuade themselves were honourable, and that Jugurtha would get his kingdom. But now came the final break: while the consul was in Rome holding the elections, his brother, left in temporary command, tried to win the war by an attack on Jugurtha's base at Suthul. His army was surrounded, and as they were at the enemy's mercy he was compelled to make an agreement to evacuate Numidia. As a symbolic gesture, Jugurtha borrowed an old Italian custom, and made the Roman soldiers file under the yoke, a mark of surrender. Now there could be no more compromise. The

---

[1] Von Fritz's article in *TAPA* LXXIV 134 concentrates on the problems surrounding this 'peace'.

honour of Rome had been openly insulted, for all the world to see, and at whatever cost there must be vengeance. The *dignitas* of the imperial power demanded it.

This period of increasing Roman intervention, from Jugurtha's attack on Cirta to his defeat of Aulus Albinus, is the subject of our Section II. When, after a conflict, you look back, in the light of the decisions taken, on the preliminary period of attempted compromise, it is bound to appear unsatisfactory, indecisive, perhaps culpable. Sallust has seized on the negotiations with Jugurtha to bring an indictment of wholesale corruption against the Roman nobility, and loses no opportunity of adding to the charge. There may well have been money involved, and there is no lack of other evidence that at this time the Roman nobles were mismanaging the affairs of their country. But some of Sallust's charges are patent fiction, as we shall see, so that we must suspect exaggeration throughout. We must also reckon with the possibility that Jugurtha's services in Spain had convinced some of the Roman nobles that he could make a good loyal king of Numidia. And if they realised that a war in Africa would be long, arduous and costly, the sequel showed how right they were.

The Fight to the Finish

The Romans were now fully committed to war, but it took four long years of fighting and a successful intrigue to finish the job. Two generals and an enterprising quaestor share the honours, and in the text which follows we give them a section each. All the time the elusive Jugurtha lurks in the background, difficult to bring to battle, erupting whenever he sees an opportunity.

First, Quintus Caecilius Metellus, the most distinguished of a distinguished family, who transformed the character of the war: he had to begin by disciplining the Roman army, which had become lax and demoralised. That done, the initiative was with the Romans. Since it was useless to march about in search of the enemy, Metellus concentrated on winning over the population by a show of strength and attacking the towns, in the hope that Jugurtha would think it necessary to fight for them. This brought considerable success, and put Jugurtha on the defensive, but after two years the war was still not won, and patience at Rome was wearing thin.

Sallust reserves his highest praise for Metellus, going out of his way to do him honour three times, at his appointment, when he disciplined the Roman army and on his return to Rome. Not so for his successor. Marius may have been the people's hero, but he was not Sallust's. There is no attempt to gloss over the intrigues by which the *legatus* undermined the authority of his proconsul. But once elected, Marius solved the problem which was hamstringing the foreign policy of the Republic – the shortage of troops. The ultimate result of this in the history of Rome is well known, but its immediate effect on the Jugurthine War is not always appreciated; Marius' strategy was that of Metellus, but with a larger and more professional army he was able to increase the pressure on Jugurtha and extend the area of operations, until Jugurtha was compelled to apply for help to his western neighbour, Bocchus of Mauretania. Roman victories over their combined forces then convinced Bocchus that the alliance with Jugurtha was a mistake.

At this point Sulla comes on the scene. He was Marius' quaestor and then proquaestor, a young man barely turned thirty, but Sallust has already decided to write a full-scale history of Rome from the death of Sulla (only fragments of which survive) and takes this opportunity of introducing the future dictator. He gives a highly favourable account of his gifts, both military and diplomatic, so that it seems natural that, when Bocchus sends emissaries to the Romans, the negotiations should be entrusted to Sulla. At last the war was ended by the surrender of Jugurtha, and the book ends abruptly, as if Sallust, having said what he had to say, had no interest in the final settlements.

II ROME

So far we have been concerned with what happened in Africa. It is time to turn to Rome, where most of the major decisions were made. We may in fact suspect that though the greater part of the book is narrative of war – and very well told it is – it is the effect of the war on the home front, or at least the interaction between the two, which is Sallust's main concern. What gives the *Jugurtha* its importance is that it is not an account of an isolated affair on the fringe of the empire, but a study of things central to the whole history of Rome. The Roman nobility were on trial, and their accusers could point to Spain, Gaul and Asia as well as Africa. There were military disasters in Spain, especially the failures of Galba in 151 and Mancinus in 137; worse still, defeats in the North under Carbo in 113, Silanus in 109, Longinus in 107, and most culpable of all under Mallius and Caepio in 105; accusations of corruption, difficult to prove, but plausible, in the handling of large sums of foreign money – the same Caepio accused of embezzling the treasures of Toulouse; Aquilius, head of the Commission which organised the new province of Asia, acquitted by the jury but not by public opinion; stories of the arrogance of Roman magistrates and recruiting officers, like that told by Gaius Gracchus of the consul passing through Teanum.[1] If the negotiations with Jugurtha are set against this background the indignation which they caused will be more readily understood. There had been assaults on these malpractices before – the establishment of the extortion court by Calpurnius Piso in 149, its strengthening by Gaius Gracchus in 122; growing exasperation now produced the Mamilian tribunal of 110 (p. 19) which condemned some of the guilty men, and the treason court started by Saturninus in 103 which condemned some more; and in 108 the people took the unprecedented step of themselves appointing a commander from outside the discredited circle to finish off the war against Jugurtha. Sallust has two main themes, which appear also in his book on Catiline but are seen more clearly in the *Jugurtha*. One is the decline of political morality at Rome, the other is the nature of the party struggles which followed. We must examine them in turn.

The Fall

The standard picture of Roman morality is that a hardy, frugal, peasant people, brimful of virtue, by sheer persistence conquered the world; that once they were masters of the Mediterranean they threw virtue out of the window and devoted themselves to the enjoyment of the fruits of victory. Now in the first place common sense should make us careful; a poor society has its vices as well as its virtues, only they are different from those of a rich society. In the second place

[1] Gellius, X 3.

this is a conventional complaint of moralists in any affluent society; it would be easy to find the same kind of thing in the literature of western Europe in the nineteen sixties. In Roman history there were special forces at work strengthening the contrast: it suited Augustus and the architects of his patriotic revival to hold up the heroes of early Rome as the patterns of virtue; this reaches us through Horace and the early books of Livy; even Cicero, who would have hated to live in a primitive society, sometimes goes back to those innocent days for his *exempla*; the appeal to the *mos maiorum* is his favourite argument. And there was Sallust. Not a success as a politician, not renowned as a general (see page xxx), he turned his acute brain to the exposure of fraud with a zeal which led him to condemn vice where others would take a more charitable view. His influence with succeeding generations was great; he stood head and shoulders above the other historians of his time, and echoes of his phrases occur in Livy as well as Tacitus.

The most remarkable thing about Sallust's account of the decline is the certainty with which he fixes its date – 146 B.C., the destruction of Carthage; only a few years before the Jugurtha episode. He names 146 as the beginning of party strife, with a bluntness which is simple to the point of being naïve. The reason is given with equal certainty – abundance of the good things of life had produced luxury and arrogance, but up to that time the fear of Carthage kept the Romans virtuous. In this case we can see reflected the arguments of contemporary Romans who had opposed the destruction of Carthage on the curious ground that it was good for Rome to have a rival. Sallust was not the only one to search for a symbolic date; Calpurnius Piso, the consul of 153 whose censorious *annales* were justified by his own practical integrity, fixed on the censorship of 154. If there is any virtue in picking on a date, it would not be difficult to argue that it should be earlier still; the complaints of the Spanish provinces in 171, or the return of Manlius Vulso's army from Asia in 187.

The Political Parties

Luxury and arrogance, these are upper-class virtues; senatorial morality is Sallust's target. Not that 'the people' come off any better – when they have the upper hand for a moment, and nobles are put on trial before the Mamilian tribunal in 110, Sallust's language is equally damning (*violenter, ex lubidine, insolentia*, p. 19). But it is senators who count; they claim to command the armies and make the decisions, and men who put themselves on pedestals must expect to be criticised. Nor will Sallust distinguish among the nobility between the new families and the old. True, he allows Marius, in his election speech (LXXXV) to contrast the *novus*, who relies on his own virtues, with the *nobilis*, who relies on the virtues of his ancestors, and gives him vigorous and telling language. We are almost carried away, until we remember the intrigues with which Marius won his election, and realise that in his Prologue Sallust says roundly that the new men 'now gain military and political distinction by deceit or malpractice rather than by honest excellence'. In Sallust's Senate those who put the public interest above their own profit are a small minority, the rest are corrupt, and vulnerable to the bribes of Jugurtha. In this conflict corruption always wins, so easily that it is not worth while to identify the minority.

Nowadays we do not think it as simple as that. Historians

are searching for evidence of competition for power between rival factions within the nobility, where marriage alliances were a political bond; the important words were not *pauci* or *boni*, but *amici* and *inimici*. It is a pity that Sallust has so little to say about this; but he is writing about a moment when, in face of the attacks of Memmius and his friends, the bulk of the nobility closed their ranks. For him the conflict which is real, and at the heart of Roman political life, is that between the nobles and the people. The nobles provide the consuls and generals and monopolise the spoils of office; the people are the poor in Italy, the overworked soldier in the ranks, weak because without organisation, protected only by tribunes.

The people are powerless on their own, and nothing effective is done for them until they are championed by honest men from the ranks of the nobility – the Gracchi, and, by implication, Memmius. It is a pity that having recognised the salient fact, the ineffectiveness of the *plebs*, Sallust did not go on and penetrate deeper into the political conflicts of the time, but after a few trite remarks about the Gracchi, he returns to his narrative. Later, when writing the *Histories*, and referring to the civil war which led to the dictatorship of Sulla, he sees through the pretensions of those who claimed to be the champions of the *plebs*: whatever they said, the real aim of both sides was their own domination.[1]

That Sallust was interested in the choice of the telling word is obvious to the most casual reader. He was also alert to words with political associations, the propaganda words, though whether they belong to the time of Marius or of Sallust himself it is not easy to say. The words of approval

[1] The *Speech of Macer*, § 11, *certatum utrimque de dominatione*.

occur, *auctoritas* and *dignitas* of the nobility, *libertas* of the people: *boni* of those who are politically 'sound'; *optumus quisque*, even, though he avoids, except in the speeches, most superlatives (*optimates* does not occur in our pages). *Virtus* is the aristocratic ideal, achieved by *bonae artes*: in the *Jugurtha* it is applied to the nobles of the good old days: after 146 not even to Metellus, though he is *acer*, which seems to be its adjective: Marius claims it for himself. Jugurtha has *virtus*, since moral standards for an African need not be so high.

But it is natural that the words of disapproval, the words men used of their opponents, should bulk larger. In this, too, the *plebs* do not escape: their tribunes are *seditiosi*, *lubido* is used of them as well as of the nobles, and so is *insolentia*. But it is the nobles who are the chief target. They are the *pauci*, a *factio*, their power is *potentia*, not *potestas*, their besetting sins are *superbia* and *avaritia*, they aim at *dominatio*; Marius uses of them the derisory phrase *globus nobilitatis* (Vatinius, tribune of 59 and Cicero's *bête noire*, meant the same thing when he spoke of the *natio optimatium*); the presents they received from Jugurtha call down on themselves the full resources of the Latin language – they are *pecunia*, *praemium*, *largitio*, *gratia*, *divitiae*, all (with *aurum* and *argentum* and the gerund *largiundum*) in the course of two chapters. It has not escaped Sallust that the same thing may be described in different words by different people, in the way that our soldiers are gallant and the enemy's ferocious. So Memmius: what among good men is *amicitia*, among bad men is *factio*. In a tribune's speech in the *Histories* it is pointed out that a state of tranquillity suits the men in power and they call it 'peace', but it is only obtained by the servility of the masses: 'Do not', says Macer to the people, 'pervert language to justify your cowardice, and describe as "peace" (*otium*) what is really slavery (*servitium*).'

III SALLUST

The Politician

Sallust's family came from Amiternum, in the Sabine country in central Italy, traditionally a hardy peasant people, frugal and dour.[1] Hence perhaps the moralising streak. As an aspirant for honours at Rome he was a *novus*, and though he knew well the means by which in his own day such a man must rise to power, it adds point to Marius' great speech when we remember that it is one *novus* being reported by another. Sallust himself is first heard of as one of the riotous tribunes of 52, the year of Clodius' death and Pompey's purge; he knew about the violence of 'popular' tribunes – *seditiosi* is his word, and *seditio*; he was a connoisseur. He seems to have been on the side of Clodius, but unlike others he was not a victim of the prosecutions which followed. In 50, however, the censors, the stronger of whom was the diehard Appius Claudius Pulcher, set out to complete the job, and Sallust was expelled from the senate. Both his escape and his expulsion are more easily understood if he was already a partisan of Caesar, who still had influence with Pompey in 52 but was the target of the nobility in 50. Certainly Sallust went to Caesar, and served in his armies in the Civil War. Not with great distinction – Caesar had

[1] Sallust's early career is discussed by Earl in *Historia*, xv (1966) 302, who estimates the practical importance of being an Italian and a *novus*. He also makes the interesting suggestion that at the time of the conspiracies of Catiline Sallust was serving in Pompey's army in Asia.

better soldiers at his disposal – but in the African campaign of 46 Sallust was in charge of transport. Suddenly came promotion, to be the first governor of the new province which Caesar made in the territory of Numidia, *Africa Nova*. The moraliser now had the opportunity of showing how he would meet the greatest temptation of the Roman nobility – the almost absolute power of a provincial governor. If our late source is to be believed, Sallust was no better than the rest of them, and had to face a prosecution on his return from Rome – though he does not appear to have been condemned.

Caesar had advanced Sallust to the praetorship, and so back into the senate; but that was the end. If Sallust had any hope of a consulship, which is by no means certain when Caesar's *clementia* was bringing his old opponents back into office, they were dashed by the Ides of March. Then, or soon after, he made the descision, which he justifies in the prologue of the *Jugurtha*, to retire from politics; magistracies, military commands, in fact all political activity have ceased to be desirable, since office is not given to merit, and when given illegally brings neither protection nor distinction; force is paving the way for murder, exile and the horrors of war (*caedem, fugam, aliaque hostilia*). This was a fair description of the year 43, disastrous for the Roman Republic.

The Historian

If not politics, what then? Some had retired to their fish-ponds and their hunting-lodges.[1] This would not satisfy a man of Sallust's energy, and was, too, something of a dere-

[1] Cicero described these men, disparagingly, as *piscinarii*.

liction of duty. One activity remained, which had always been thought worthy of a senator and almost a duty, the writing of history; this would bring both distinction and a sense of purpose. In Rome history had always been written by senators, men of affairs who had known how history was made before they came to write it. Sallust was exceptional only in that he retired from public life to write at an age when a man could still hope for further advancement. There were three ways of writing history: you could write your memoirs, like Rutilius Rufus, Aemilius Scaurus, Sulla, Caesar, like the generals of the Second World War; these were *commentarii*, the raw material of history. Or you could write a continuous history, like the *Annales* of Calpurnius Piso, the *Historiae* of Sisenna or the *Origines* of Cato the Censor. There was also a third way, the monograph, or history of a particular topic. Polybius had written a biography of Philopoemen, and a separate account of the Numantiine War, separate from his main history. In the monograph the sterner rules of history were relaxed, as we shall see later, less detachment was expected, and more colour. This suited Sallust; he could take a single episode, and describe it in detail in such a way as to throw a searching light on society and politics. His first choice was the conspiracy of Catiline in his own lifetime; for the second he went back a generation to the war against Jugurtha. Each has a strong biographical element, the hero an enemy of the state who is ultimately destroyed. But in each case, beside the traditional pattern of the rise and fall of the hero, the established order is on trial: in the *Catiline* the wounds inflicted on Italy by the proscriptions of Sulla, in the *Jugurtha* the arrogance and avarice of an aristocracy exposed to unprecedented temptations. Nor can it be claimed that he was impartial; in this trial of the nobility he was prosecutor rather than judge, and it is as speeches for the prosecution that we should regard the monographs. The *Catiline* was a good beginning, the *Jugurtha* is a masterpiece, with its mingling of the two themes of foreign war and urban corruption, the scene itself an added attraction to the ex-governor of *Africa Nova*. After these two monographs the seam for Sallust was worked out. An episode from the forties, the Ides of March for instance, *Bruti Coniuratio* or *Coniuratio in Caesarem*, would have been fascinating, but too dangerous with the triumvirs in power. Anything else in the previous hundred years would have been repetition, and the alternative, early Roman history, does not seem to have interested him. But he had found a talent for writing, and before finishing the *Jugurtha* was already planning a continuous history starting from the death or abdication of Sulla. He died, apparently in 35, the work uncompleted. Four speeches and two rhetorical letters have survived; of the narrative nothing but odd phrases quoted by grammarians. It is a tragedy that for the last phase of the Republican history accident has deprived us of Sallust as well as Livy. Plutarch used him for his lives of Sertorius and Lucullus, but we should have learned more of the interplay of war and politics from the original. However, a continuous narrative demands virtues of accuracy, completeness and detachment in which Sallust did not excel and it is likely that what we have is the best part of his work.

The Latin

Caesar set out to write a factual account of what he and his commanders did in Gaul, to tell the world exactly what happened, with the Olympian pretence that he did not care what they thought about it. The Latin is therefore clear, factual, unadorned, with no appeal to the emotions. Cicero was a barrister, to whom words were a means of persuading, and though he could tell a tale supremely well he told it with a purpose, the language rich in ridicule or patriotic fervour. Though he could attack individuals with violence when the occasion demanded – the *Verrines* for instance, or the *Philippics* – he preferred to make friends, and most of his speeches are for the defence. He was on the side of the established order, justifying the Roman constitution, auspices and all. Hence the language of idealising, rolling and sonorous, with its many superlatives, and honourable epithets for honourable men (*vir summae constantiae, singulari virtute* and the rest). The letters do show that there was another side, intrigues and disappointments, gossip and informality, but his style was formed in his early optimistic days, and when there was no use for it in politics he transferred it, with no more than the necessary adjustments, to his technical writings. He wrote so much and so well that he dominated the literature of the Republic in his own time, and has continued to do so ever since.

This would not do for Sallust. A new man like Cicero from an Italian town, he chose a different way of making his name at Rome – sedition, hostility to the establishment, and the support of its enemies. He turned to literature when politics proved a dead end, to describe the class which had not accepted him. The style could not be that of Cicero; Sallust is sharper, more wounding, not mounting an attack with massive sentences, but deflating, exposing, harrying. His sentences are shorter and more vivid, the narrative carried along swiftly by groups of historic infinitives. To match the old-fashioned morality, he uses old-fashioned words and old-fashioned spelling – the letter *u* in superlative and gerund (*optumus, capiundum*), also in *lubido, lubet*; according to an ancient historian he copied the vocabulary of Cato the Censor, who had written more than a century earlier.

For language, Cato and the old Romans could suggest to Sallust what he needed; for historical composition they had nothing to offer – he must look back to Greek literature, which provided examples of great variety. Inevitably it was not to the Hellenistic historians that he turned, trained in the flowing, musical, verbose school of Isocrates, not to Herodotus, historian of the great triumph of Greece, but to Thucydides. Thucydides and Sallust have much in common, both historians of greatness in decline (as they thought), both going behind the public facade to the heart of the matter, both interested in the contrast between words and things, both men who had held office themselves, and who turned to their enduring work after political failure. Thucydides had the style which suited Sallust, clear and rapid in narrative, abrupt and compressed in judgement. The ancient writers saw the similarities, and to compare the two became a commonplace, all the more popular because it tickled Roman vanity to think that they could compete with the great Athenian. In this way they flattered themselves; we have not the text of the *Histories* of course, but from what we have it seems clear that Sallust was not prepared to do the arduous research which lay behind the history of Thucydides; he wrote more quickly, and his range was narrower. In the monograph, where he could choose what interested him and omit what did not, he found the type of writing which suited him.

Sallust had a model; he also had an imitator. Sallust described the moral decline of the nobility, Tacitus described their fall from political power – and their physical extinction. He began in much the same way as Sallust – first the *Agricola*, the biography of his father-in-law, for the most part a success story but ending in disappointment and criticism of the régime; then the *Germania*, a kind of armchair travelogue, a regular literary type by that time, but conveying an implied attack on Roman society by comparing it with the life of the simple Germans; then the *Histories*, a connected narrative of the Civil War and the Flavian reigns, of which only the beginning has survived. So far, a close copy of Sallust and no great superiority of pupil over master; but Tacitus lived to finish his *Histories*, and went on to write his most mature and powerful work, the *Annals*, by which he is usually judged. He wrote some hundred and fifty years after Sallust, and all that had happened in the interval, in society, politics and literature combined to accentuate the individuality of the style. The rhetorical element in Sallust still belongs to the time of open oratory, when public speaking could influence policy. His was terse and sharp, and pointed the way to the future, but it was not yet the age of the continuous barbed innuendo, the society which has been described as 'despotism tempered by epigrams'.

IV THE LITERARY HISTORIANS

In discussing any form of literature it is difficult not to start from Aristotle, but this time Aristotle leads in the wrong direction. His remarks are to be found in the *Poetics*, where he is concerned with the subject and spirit of tragedy and epic, and for his purpose he compared them with a colourless chronicle which he calls 'history', or 'the usual histories'. Had he written a treatise about prose writing and treated the subject of history in depth, we should no doubt have had something more satisfying, including a distinction between chroniclers and the literary historians; and then much modern writing on Thucydides might not seem so modern.

However, to turn to what Aristotle did actually say: tragedy he tells us,[1] is more serious than history, because tragedy tells us 'the sort of thing which is likely to happen', which is important, whereas history only tells us what actually did happen, which is accidental and may even be trivial; tragedy is general, and of general interest, history is only particular. Consequently[2] both tragedy and epic are superior, because they have a beginning, a middle and an end, and a connected theme, while poor slighted history deals with all the miscellaneous events which have occurred in a given period of time. The inferiority of Aristotle's history is that it lacks a serious connected theme of general interest.[3]

It is possible that there were historians of this kind before Aristotle's day, and we can collect the names of some known to us, and speculate on which of them deserved to be so belittled. But, fortunately, there were some who took a different view, even in Aristotle's time, and who regarded history as a part of literature, with artistic as well as factual standards; strongly influenced by other forms of literature, they rescued it from the pedantic path which Aristotle had mapped out for it. Not surprisingly, the sterile chronicles have mostly perished whilst the literary historians, have, though with tantalising gaps, survived. The most fruitful influences on the historians were those of tragedy and oratory and to these we must now turn.

---

[1] *Poetics*, IX 3.   [2] *Poetics*, VII 3.
[3] Polybius is no help; when he writes of history as 'tragic' he really only means sensational, e.g. III 48, 8.

Tragedy in History

Cornford long ago pointed out[1] that the great history of Thucydides, which had once been taken for straightforward narrative, had underlying it a dramatic structure. It is not difficult to recognise Athens as the hero, led, like Xerxes or Agamemnon, to acts of pride and arrogance, and being like them struck down in consequence. No wonder Aristotle, for his purpose in the *Poetics*, did not mention Thucydides.

Of course it was easier to perceive this sort of pattern in events (or to impose it on them) if the subject was comparatively short; in a universal history the brute mass of facts is likely to defy the arranger, and, if he succeeds, the patterns are likely to be of his own making and sometimes capricious. There grew up, therefore, a more or less recognised distinction between the general history and the monograph, with recognisably different rules, the one aiming at truth and utility the other at artistic satisfaction.[2] Not that the general historians always obeyed these rules; emotional non-factual appeals were common enough in the Hellenistic historians, and in the Roman annalistic historians there are often episodes which are treated dramatically: the Hannibalic books of Livy are set apart from the rest by their special preface[3] which closely echoes the opening chapters of Thucydides; even the sober Polybius made the story of Philip V of Macedon into a tragedy.[4] But it is in the monograph that we really see the invasion of history by drama. The subject – be

---

[1] In the second half of *Thucydides Mythistoricus*.
[2] Ullman has collected details of this in *TAPA* LXXIII 25.
[3] Livy, XXI 1.
[4] Walbank, *JHS* LVIII 55. Motives of Philip and his downfall are seen by Polybius as Aeschylus might have seen them.

it a war, a man, or a conspiracy – could be viewed as a whole, and could have what Aristotle missed in 'the usual histories', a beginning, a middle and an end; the Peloponnesian War, described by Thucydides, the Sacred War of 356–346 described by Callisthenes and others, the Numantine War by Polybius, who also wrote a biography of Philopoemen.[1] We have a letter from Cicero to his friend Lucceius the historian,[2] in which he asks him to separate the Catilinarian conspiracy and its aftermath from the history he is compiling, and to write a separate book on Cicero's great triumph; and he writes quite openly that he expects Lucceius to waive the rules of history and to write a little more enthusiastically even than he feels; he uses the language of the theatre – *hanc quasi fabulam* – *habet varios actus* – and there is no doubt who is to be the hero of the drama.

Dramatic effect, appeals to the emotion, shaping the story, relaxation of the strict rules of evidence – all these things suited Sallust. For his first work he took a limited theme – the great conspiracy which Cicero had asked Lucceius to exploit. It centres round the villain-hero, and takes him from his dubious youth, through his dangerous ascendancy to violent and almost tragic death. Sallust would have appreciated the modern historian's vision of the hills round Rome as the seats of a Greek theatre, 'as if Rome were a stage on which their looks were centred.'[3]

After Catiline, Jugurtha; a more complex story, with greater dramatic as well as social possibilities. The conflict

---

[1] If these two works had survived the reputation of Polybius today might have been different.

[2] *ad Fam.* V 12. The whole letter is worth careful reading.

[3] G. M. Trevelyan, *Garibaldi's Defence of the Roman Republic* (1907). Introduction.

began slowly and uncertainly, became by stages more deadly, and finally rose to a climax when after hard-won victories by Roman arms it was until the last moment doubtful whether the king of the Moors would surrender Jugurtha to Sulla, or Sulla to Jugurtha; one in which the fortunes of Jugurtha himself rose from promising – and virtuous – beginnings, until arrogance and avarice led him to commit the fatal crimes which brought about his downfall. As with Xerxes in the Persae, the reader is not sure whether to regard the end as triumph or disaster. There is even something in the *Jugurtha* of the formal structure of Aeschylean tragedy, the digressions (Africa, Roman political parties) acting as the choruses which separate the episodes and fill in the background. One element is missing, the lamentation at the end, and even if we are not consciously thinking in terms of drama, Sallust's abruptness here strikes us as a serious fault.

Rhetoric in History

That there was a strong rhetorical bias in Roman higher education is evident from the writings of Quintilian, the man who came nearest of any Roman to being a Regius Professor. The effects of this education go far beyond the choice of words and the structure of effective sentences. Much of the Roman undergraduate's time was spent composing speeches for an imaginary audience – or a real audience of his fellow pupils – and the effect he was making on them was in the front of his mind. The result was efficiency of presentation, orderliness of thought and craftsmanship in words; the expertise of the Roman literary man was remarkable. But as with any debating society, the standard subjects could become stereotyped, his range limited, his facts secondhand;

there was not much new to be said on the subject of whether Hannibal should have marched on Rome after Cannae, or – another stock subject of the *declamatio* – the rights of the father who disinherited his disobedient son.[1] To the critics of the ancient world *inventio* meant, not, as we might expect, the free use of individual imagination, but the discovery of what ought to be said[2] which is a very different, and more conventional thing.

It is certain that Roman orators acquired a stock of pre-fabricated general passages which they could – and did – incorporate in their speeches with a little adaptation when they became relevant. Nor was this confined to orators. Historians also searched out' what ought to be said', and drew on their repertoires in the same way; battle scenes were filled out with details which were likely to have happened, judged by their suitability and effectiveness as narrative more than by their truth; speeches contained what the historians thought would have been suitable arguments; descriptions of character contain contrasts which are more neat than credible.

We must not exaggerate: the Roman historian was allowed freedom with the details in order to present the main story more effectively, not to alter it; to improve the record of what was actually said – which might have been dis-appointing – by the insertion of 'what ought to have been said'. 'What did happen' (to use Aristotle's language) might be less illuminating than 'what would happen'. True, Aristotle was saying that it was poets who were concerned with 'what would happen' while historians were limited to what did happen and were therefore inferior; but in Rome at

[1] S. F. Bonner, *The Education of a Roman* (1950) p. 18.
[2] D. A. Russell, *Greece and Rome* xiv second series (Oct. 1967) p. 135.

least, the literary historians took for themselves something of the license of the poets. Time has vindicated their judgement. Sallust and Livy have survived in bulk, Cato's *Origines* only in fragments.

We must now consider the practical effects on Sallust of this rhetorical training.

Battle Scenes

Sallust's staccato, excitable style is admirably suited to the description of sudden and violent action, and the battles and murders of the *Jugurtha* provide scope for its use. That can be judged from a simple reading of the book. What is here at issue is how much is 'stock' description, which could be applied to almost any battle, and how much is genuine authentic account of the one being described. The two most important battles which are included in this text, Metellus at the Muthul (XLVIII) and Marius near Cirta (C), come well out of the test. Both are full of individual details, and unless an imaginative style is itself a crime no charge of rhetorical invention can reasonably be made. The first of these has an exceptional account of geographical and tactical detail, so that we suspect that Sallust is following an eye-witness account by a professional soldier; we also note that one of the officers present subsequently wrote his memoirs – and that was Rutilius Rufus, who spent the next year training the new Roman army in Italy. The other comes from the part of the book in which Sulla was prominent, which by its length reminds us that Sulla's memoirs were also available to Sallust.

Other battle scenes are vaguer and more general, and we can be less sure that Sallust is not filling in the picture

himself for lack of authentic material. Certainly, in the long
account of the siege of Zama the description of the inhabitants standing on the walls and following the fortunes of the
battle going on before their eyes (LX) has always been
recognised as an imitation of Thucydides' description of
the Athenians on the shore of the Great Harbour at Syracuse (VIII 71); while the trick by which the fort on the
Muluccha was captured (XCIII) is such a traditional one –
the Ligurian finding the unguarded path and leading the
chosen party up the cliff in the enemy's rear – that the story
is bound to be regarded with some suspicion, especially
when we realise how thin the story would be without it.
Rutilius had left Africa, Sulla had not yet arrived, Marius left
no written record; Sallust could be short of hard fact.

At one point we can catch him out — the siege of Cirta
(Ch. XXIII). Sallust records that Jugurtha *vallo atque fossa
moenia circumdat*. Now we should in any case have doubted
whether a Numidian army was technically or psychologically
capable of completing a continuous earthwork of this length
(how many spades would be needed? how many hours'
digging? it is more than a doubt); but in fact, if Cirta is
as we presume Constantine, its situation, close inside a
semicircle of river, rules out any such thing. Attempts to re-
interpret *circumdat* are beside the point; Sallust knows that
Jugurtha made repeated attacks on Cirta, thinks of this,
reasonably, as a siege, and then fills in, from stock, the
details of Roman siege warfare. He had not been to Cirta.[1]

But on the whole, and with few reservations, Sallust's
battle scenes seem to be honest enough. They are not full,
like Livy's, of generals keeping their heads when all about

---

[1] But see suggestion 3 on p. lvii.

them were losing theirs, like Flaminius at Trasymene (XXII 5), or panic-stricken soldiers looking at each other in despair and arguing in conventional terms about what to do next, like the legionaries at the Caudine Forks (IX 3). Comparing them with Caesar's, we miss the accuracy of the eye-witness and the matter-of-factness of the professional soldier, but those are limitations we must expect. If we miss the imaginative power which we find in Tacitus' description of the army of Germanicus, surrounded in a German forest or trapped by the tide near the mouth of the Visurgis (*Ann.* I 65, 70, and how much of that is rhetorical embroidery?) at least no gods or heroes appears to guide Marius through the desert, like those who in historians unnamed by Polybius helped Hannibal over the Alps.

The Speeches

Apart from the general influence of rhetorical style, the actual reporting of speeches by ancient historians calls for a word of comment. The most immediately noticeable feature is that they are not *verbatim* reports; they were part of an artistic whole, and were regarded as its chief ornaments, so that if an author had just inserted another man's words he would not only have failed his readers but also missed his greatest chance.

They may have a dramatic purpose, as in Herodotus: at the moments of great decision Miltiades appeals to the Athenian commander-in-chief before Marathon, Themistocles to the Spartan admiral before Salamis; Artemisia gives advice to the Persian king. Good, stirring stuff. Thucydides used the speeches for another purpose, and evolved for this a different type of Greek: they do not so much highlight a particular moment, or a particular person (in fact they are sometimes put into the mouths of nameless ambassadors), as express what in Thucydides' opinion were the arguments for or against a course of action.[1] The style of the speeches was all his own – no one could ever speak quite like that – and the arguments were influenced by his own reflections: not only what was said, but what was likely to be said. Often he reports speeches by both sides in a dispute, putting both cases with careful impartiality.

Sallust's speeches were influenced by both types of writing. Micipsa to Jugurtha, asking him to look after his step-brothers, Adherbal to the Senate pleading for help, are in the tradition of Herodotus, drama to enliven the narrative.

Marius' great speech, on the other hand, probably keeps quite closely to the original; it was a famous speech, and is marked by a blunt sarcasm which may well have been Marius' own; but we can see in it too the conventional opposition of *novus* to *nobiles*.[2] When reporting Memmius, Sallust has a number of similar speeches to choose from, and picks the one which suits his purpose best; it is not tied to a particular occasion, but an instance of his usual eloquence; in fact, a typical example of tribunician agitation. In the *Histories* he seems to have gone further; it is not likely to be by accident that what has survived of them is a collection of speeches (and letters which are in fact speeches): the manifesto of Lepidus, consul of 78 and rebel against the system of Sulla, a letter from Pompey in Spain and one from Mithridates in

---

[1] In fact there is more of this in Herodotus than is sometimes realised; the drama tends to conceal the exposition.

[2] For discussions of this speech see Bibliography and the note on page 98.

Asia (a second and more powerful Jugurtha), and another example of tribunician agitation, this time Macer in 73 – which is a speech of Memmius brought up to date.

Not surprisingly, the Latin is no longer that of the narrative. The Roman literary man tried his hand at various styles, and was expected to be proficient in more than one. It was accepted that different styles were best for different types of book, so that writers were accustomed to varying their style to suit their subject. This has been put more drastically: 'Latin . . . is a literature in which *genre* determines style.'[1] So in Tacitus' biography of Agricola, the philosophical introduction and conclusion recall Cicero, while the central historical section is nearer to Sallust. In Sallust's dramatic speeches, the historic infinitives disappear, the sentences become longer and more measured, and superlatives, almost absent from Sallust's narrative, occur, though not in Ciceronian profusion; Adherbal is made to describe Jugurtha as 'homo omnium quos terra sustinet sceleratissumus'. The propaganda speeches show the influence of Thucydides: the clear antithesis – 'dominari illi volunt, vos liberi esse' – the general principle in the middle of a particular argument – 'exercitum supplicio cogere, id est dominum, non imperatorem esse'. But taking the speeches as a whole, the philosophical element does not predominate; there was too much of the dramatist in Sallust for that.

In Tacitus, the speeches also have taken a further step. By this time public oratory has lost its old importance, since it seldom determines policies, and Tacitus' use of speeches is different. A few rhetorical set pieces remain, but more characteristic is the expression, in indirect speech, of the policy

[1] Ogilvie and Richmond (eds), Tacitus, *Agricola*, p. 16. Biography is itself a specialised genre. On the *Agricola* see also below p. l.

or the views of a group of people. The anonymity, both of speaker and occasion, gives the author greater freedom in developing his arguments, greater opportunity, in fact, of conveying his own ideas; and we must allow, too, for what has been called his 'innate distaste for the more obvious flourishes of ordinary rhetoric'. In the first book of the *Annals*, for instance, there is a piece of sentimental rhetoric in the mouth of Germanicus, and another by a German prince: ornament, no more; Herodotus could have done as well, or Sallust. But there are also two long chapters of indirect statement, giving two different views of the reign of Augustus, each packed with propaganda and innuendo, and it is these, and their like, which remains in the mind.

Character-sketches

In any history which is not just a chronicle, the characters of the leading men are bound to be important, and historians have found various ways of bringing them to life. Herodotus used the revealing anecdote – Pisistratus dressing up a local girl as Athena and marching in procession behind her; Darius getting his groom to make sure that his horse was the first to neigh. Thucydides, in this as in so many things quite different, gives us only what is strictly relevant in a few compressed words – Cleon is 'persuasive' and 'violent', Hyperbolus is 'abominable'; only the two pre-war heroes, Themistocles and, of course, Pericles, receive lengthy notices.

Of Sallust's Roman predecessors, we can guess what Cato did: he is said not to have even mentioned the names of the generals, since he was writing about Rome not about individuals. Caesar avoided personalities, except by implication, which explains the colourless competence which is all we remember of Labienus. Of the others we do not know, but in Sallust we find a well-developed technique, so well developed that we suspect that it is not a new invention: at the first mention of one of the important characters, we are given any thing from two lines to a whole paragraph, describing his family, physique, youth, qualities and activities. Another *genre* has been born, and as we should expect it brings with it its own stylistic peculiarities. First in order of writing came the description of Catiline (Sall. *Cat.* V), still one of the most famous; Catiline was followed by the emancipated woman Sempronia (Sall. *Cat.* XXV), whose personality is emphasised by her appearance in this gallery of men. Next Jugurtha himself (Sall. *Jug.* VI), with the added attraction that he is the unsophisticated child of nature. Of the other leading figures of the *Jugurtha*, Metellus is given two lines – he is all virtue, and Sallust finds virtue less interesting; Marius is described at some length in Ch. LXIII, where, though the pattern is slightly disturbed (it is not his first appearance in the book), the elements are all present. When he comes to Sulla (Ch. X CV) Sallust explains his reasons for inserting the portrait at this point, signalling clearly his intention of writing a character-sketch.

For all the differences between them, Livy owed a debt to Sallust, as well as to the other historians whom they had both read and we cannot. His subject is the whole sweep of Roman history, politics and wars loom larger in his mind, his interest in individuals is less intense; but by now the character-sketch is a recognised part of a history, and when the moment arises Livy is not wanting. The famous description of Cato the Censor (XXXIX 40) is in this tradition; it has less variety than Sallust's sketches, as Cato, as represented in the legend, was a less varied person, but the stylistic peculiarities are the same.

In Tacitus we find the same kind of development which we found in the use of speeches; at first the now traditional method: the description of Agricola begins in the usual way (Tac. *Agr.* IV) – birth, family, education: his exploits then develop into full biography including the history of Roman Britain, and then in Ch. XLIV we are back again in the recognisable style. The whole book is a character-sketch, with the central section enlarged. Early in his next work, the *Histories*, is a ten-line description of Mucianus, the kind of mixed character Sallust and Tacitus both delighted in (I 10) and in the second book a similar judgement on Antonius Primus (II 86); after that, fewer: compressed commendation of Vipstanus Messala (III 9) and Civilis (IV 13); rather more in honour of the future emperor Titus (X 1). Then, an interesting change: instead of describing the actor as he comes on to the stage, Tacitus waits for the moment when he leaves it. He was familiar, as Professor Syme has pointed out[1] with the pomp and ceremony of a Roman aristocratic funeral, with its formal *laudatio*, and he casts his estimates of character into the form of obituaries, compressed and candid, some with honour, more with malice. He began this in the *Histories*, with the famous descriptions of Galba (I 49) and Otho (II 50), and in the early books of the *Annals* it is his way of referring back to the reign of Augustus. It proved a more effective method, more final in praise or blame. Again Tacitus has turned a literary device to his own devastating purpose.

To return to the type; what the historian needed was a variety of ways of attaching a quality to a man, and this the

[1] 'Obituaries in Tacitus', *AJP* LXXIX (1958) 18.

Latin language could provide: a nominative adjective, standing alone at the beginning of a sentence, only distantly related to the eventual verb: the ablative or genitive of quality, frequently involving the nouns *ingenium, animus* or *ars*: the quality in the nominative and its possessor in the dative: active nouns in *-tor*: participles with objective genitive: striking antitheses, often in chiasmic order. Most of these can be found in the portrait of Sulla (Sall. *Jug.* XCVI), as they are found in Livy's portrait of Cato. The *genre* had its own style and it was a style particularly to the liking of Sallust.

Sallust obviously took a delight in his character-sketches, and so do we. They give greater depth to the narrative, and indicate that the forces at work then were forces which we know and can recognise. In general they assist and convince. If we start looking too closely, doubts begin to arise. The famous epigram on Catiline, for instance: *satis eloquentiae, sapientiae parum*: brilliant and penetrating – until we start to translate *sapientiae*; does it really say very much after all? Have we reached the stage where the language has taken charge and is dictating the judgement, instead of only expressing it?[1] Perhaps it is only that the Latin language is so good at conveying these sharp and telling contrasts that it encourages the writer to see things in this way. More serious doubts have been raised: when Marius is described (*Jug.* C) as foreseeing everything (*omnia providere*), and himself inspecting sentries, is this because Marius inspected the sentries, or because Marius is being featured as the Good Commander and this is one of the stock qualities of the part? Does Sallust, in fact, really mean *circumire*, or should we

---

[1] The character sketches of the *Jugurtha* are less open to this criticism— a mark of greater maturity.

interpret it as equivalent to *is esse qui circumiret?* Metellus also went the rounds of the sentries (Ch. XLV), but this is less suspicious in that his disciplinary measures contain elements which do not seem to be drawn from the type. The same doubts have been raised about the virtues of Agricola: did he really take his position at the head of his troops (Tac. *Agr.* 18, 2) or is he also being the Good Commander?

To the Roman way of thinking it did not matter. It was the atmosphere of the moment, the morality, which mattered, and provided the historian – or orator – got those right, only a pedant could find fault with his literal accuracy. With this licence, Sallust and the others could write with more confidence, without the perpetual niggling 'perhaps' and 'although' to which we moderns are condemned, and could make full and uninhibited use of the great talents which their rhetorical education had fostered. If we are to read the Latin historians with pleasure we must meet them on their own ground; knowing what they are doing, but accepting it as normal and legitimate. If we insist on a twentieth-century standard of factual exactness we shall be judging them by the rules of a game which they were not playing. We shall spoil our pleasure, and to little profit.

If we are to enjoy Sallust there are two quite different things which we have to swallow. First, careless inaccuracy of detail; this is the work of the impressionist, to whom half of the picture is not in focus. Second, and more difficult, deliberate distortion at the centre of the picture to compel the details to serve the major purpose. Until his consulship, Marius is the virtuous *novus*, rising by his own efforts in despite of the *superbia* of the nobles; so the inconvenient facts have to be suppressed, and when we find them we complain naturally of Sallust's misrepresentation. Yet, in the last resort, Marius' importance in history *is* as the *novus* who succeeded in battle, reconstituted the army and failed in politics. Sallust has quite certainly exaggerated the corruption of the nobility, and this is grossly unfair to individuals, Scaurus in particular; yet that they were corrupt is a major fact of the history of the period. The pictures are overdrawn, stylised, but as Professor Fraenkel once said of Tacitus, 'He may have got his facts wrong, but he told the truth.'

The Prologues

To end with the beginning, the Prologue. To each of his monographs Sallust has prefixed an introduction of four chapters on the subject of human nature in the abstract and the writing of history. This has surprised the critics, beginning with Quintilian who complained that Sallust's prologues had nothing to do with history (*nihil ad historiam pertinentibus*), and inevitably looked for a Greek precedent. Isocrates had begun his *Panegyricus* with a preface on the subject of virtue. In *genre* the *Panegyricus* was 'epideictic' (display oratory; we should call it a form of *belles lettres*), where a considerable licence in prologues was recognised. It was this leap from one *genre* to another which surprised Quintilian. Since then there have been varying estimates of the relevance and profundity of Sallust's prologues. They have a champion in Rambaud (*Revue des Études Latines*, 1946 – in French), who makes the valid point that since they are both very similar in structure and theme the author must have felt that he had something important to say. The *Catiline* came first, of course, but the *Jugurtha* repeats the scheme – two chapters on morality and two on the writing of history – and the general outline. It is the more reasonably argued of the two, and a full text and translation will be found on pages 121ff.

First, the morality, Chapters I and II. Sallust starts with the Greek idea that the nature of man is partly body and partly mind; these are so interpreted that all ordinary pleasures are attributed to the body, which is then responsible for all kinds of vice, while every virtuous activity must be activity of mind. So far, nothing original; there is a near ancestor in Plato, who wrote of the mass of humanity going about 'like cattle, with their eyes always fixed on the ground', but the idea became a common one, and could have come to Sallust from a number of sources. But when we follow up the activities of mind and body we find a distinctively Roman flavour. Virtue is the product of mind (*animus*, *ingenium*) working through *active* pursuits (*bonae artes*, which include such things as *industria* and *probitas*); there is no such thing as a life of virtuous contemplation; (the reward is *gloria* and *immortalitas*); the adjectives of commendation are those which imply energy – *strenuos*, *acer*. On the other side; proceeding presumably from the body, are nouns like *socordia* and *ignavia*, adjectives like *iners*, and all the language of self-indulgence – *luxuria*, *lubido*, *voluptates*. So in the story of Jugurtha we find that the heroes are *gloriae avidus* (Marius, LXIII 2) and *gloriae cupidior* (Sulla, XCV 3), while the villains are *cupidine caecus* (Aulus, XXXI 5) or *praemio inducti* (senators, XIII 8).

This belief that virtues and vices come from different sources, and therefore have nothing in common, goes well with Sallust's temperamental black-and-white morality; his view that a vast gulf divided the few who were above corruption from the majority who took Jugurtha's bribes (especially Ch. XV). If a man did not fit neatly on one side or other of the gulf a special reason must be found – Scaurus was 'clever at concealing his vices'.

The aim of virtue is glory, and this, for Sallust as for any other upper-class Roman of his time, could only be properly achieved in public life. The purely personal virtues of private life were seldom honoured in Roman society; *virtus*, in most Roman writers, was the prerogative of the political classes, and very nearly the prerogative of the hereditary nobility, in their capacity of leaders of the state.[1] This puts Sallust himself at a disadvantage, in that he had retired from public life voluntarily, and that at an age when he could have been a candidate for the consulship. He therefore devotes two whole chapters to his reasons for abandoning politics – as outspoken a criticism of the triumvirs as was probably safe – and to the theme that writing history was the next best thing to making it. In the language of the first two chapters, history was a pursuit of an energetic mind, a *bona ars*, unlike gentleman-farming, for instance, and in the division between mental virtues and corporeal vices it fell on the right side of the line.

With this most Romans would agree. The picture of Fabius and Scipio, the two heroes of the Hannibalic War, contemplating with profit the busts of their ancestors, may strike us as sentimental rhetoric, but it represents a seriously held Roman belief. History to them was a storehouse of the great *exempla*, in which the virtuous deeds of the past (mostly done by Romans) and the vicious deeds (mostly done by foreigners) were held up for emulation or avoidance. To this moral education it seems the *Jugurtha* was to contribute.

[1] Marius claimed it for himself, though a *novus*, but the claim was unexpected, and, to right-thinking men, outrageous. On this subject see Earl, *The Political Thought of Sallust*.

·*Note*

THE BOUNDARIES OF NUMIDIA

I T might be expected that after reading a book of this length on a war for Numidia, written by a man who was himself proconsul of part of it, we should know what Numidia was. Yet the surprising fact is that we are still in doubt. The Numidians were traditionally a wandering people, living up to their name, which is derived from the Greek word for a nomad. Add to this that Sallust was interested in morals, not geography, to such an extent that a reader of the *Jugurtha* would never guess that he had ever set foot in Africa. Since, however, there are two moments in the story when our understanding is materially affected by our reading of the map, it will be necessary to make up our minds on certain points. For what follows, the maps on pp. xii and lxiv are essential.

On the east, though the exact line of the frontier with the province of Africa is not certain, the limits of doubt are not very wide. Zama had been Carthaginian, but as it is later known as Zama Regia it must presumably have belonged to Masinissa or Micipsa. The frontier cannot have been far from here.

The principal doubts centre round the western frontier, with which is bound up the identification of the river Muluc-cha. At the time of the Second Punic War, it appears that Mauretania, the country of the Mauri, lay entirely to the west of the Moulouya, and that this river was Livy's Muluc-

cha. The whole of the land between this and the territory of
Carthage was then inhabited by the two Numidian tribes,
the Massylii on the east, ruled by the family of Masinissa, and
the much larger Masaesyli on the west, ruled by Syphax.[1]
It used to be assumed that at the end of that war Masinissa was given the kingdom of Syphax in addition to his
own, and that therefore Jugurtha's Numidia extended all the
way to the Moulouya; Sallust's references to the Muluccha
as the Mauretanian frontier appeared to settle it.

A closer reading of the *Jugurtha* will show that this must be
wrong. It is argued on page 109 that Marius cannot possibly
have marched to the Moulouya; nor could Bocchus have
played the decisive part in the war if he had been king of a
small kingdom six hundred miles away. Sallust's Muluccha
cannot have been the Moulouya. There may have been a
Muluccha nearer to Cirta, or he may just have been confused – he was a careless geographer.

To return to Masinissa's kingdom: in addition to the
Massylii, he was given by the Romans not the whole of the
kingdom of Syphax, but 'Cirta and the other cities and lands
of the kingdom of Syphax which had come into the power
of the Romans'.[2] This would not take him far west of Cirta;
furthermore, Livy recorded that not long before 150 a grandson of Syphax, Ariobarzanes, was helping Carthage against
Masinissa with an *ingens Numidarum exercitus*, so that Masinissa cannot have ruled all Numidia. Certainly Walsh has
shown that his eyes were to the east, and that the evidence
of the agricultural prosperity for which he was famous does
not extend farther west than Saldae.[3] Since the river of
Saldae is about the distance which is credible for Marius'

[1] The boundary between them may even have been east of Cirta.
[2] Livy, XXX 44. See Sall. *Jug.* V.   [3] *JRS* LV (1965) 151.

westward march, and a distance from which Bocchus could intervene in the war,[1] the frontier cannot have been far from here and I have marked it as Sallust's Muluccha. The steps by which the Moors gained control of the bulk of the Masaesyli are hidden from us – it is possible that it was only completed during the Numidian Civil War – but by 106 there was no independent power between Jugurtha and Bocchus.

One further problem remains – the division of the kingdom between Jugurtha and Adherbal. It seems clear from Chapter XXI that Cirta was Adherbal's capital; it is also certain that he had eastern Numidia. What then did the senatorial commission allot to Jugurtha? We know beyond all doubt, whatever Sallust may say to the contrary, that Adherbal's portion was the richer of the two: apart from the greater fertility of the Bagradas valley (the Carthaginians had planted the lower reaches with fruit trees), Sherwin-White has shown (*JRS* xxxiv (1944) 1) that the natural lines of communication of Algeria run east and west, reaching the sea near the modern Bizerta and Tunis, not Algiers (see especially his fig. 3, *The Trend Lines and Folds in Algeria and Tunisia*). Adherbal's portion was not only richer in itself but was also the doorway into the interior. If the division was to be an equal one, Jugurtha would have to be offered something substantial. The map does not leave much room for this. There seem to be three possibilities:

1. At the time of the division (Ch. XVI) the Numidian kings still laid claim to land west of Saldae. Jugurtha was being encouraged to reassert this claim, in the hope that this task would fully occupy his energies, while Ad-

---

[1] One of the meetings between Bocchus and Sulla (Ch. CX) takes place *west* of the Muluccha.

herbal enjoyed the peaceful east. Instead, by attacking Adherbal, he allowed Bocchus to complete his advance to Sallust's Muluccha.

2. Jugurtha's main strength was not in the west but in the south – the Gaetulians and the old Carthaginian trading posts in the Emporia region, which appear to have been part of the kingdom of Numidia in 146.[1] This would also give more importance to Marius' march to Capsa. But if this is so Sallust is not guilty of carelessness but of downright cardinal error; nor is it easy to believe that the commission could have made such a division.

3. In later times Sicca was also known as Cirta Nova, and it probably had this name when Sallust was its governor and old Cirta (Constantine) was not in the province. It is just possible that to Sallust (but not to Livy, who in Book XXX followed Polybius) Cirta was Sicca. It would then be possible to believe in a less inequitable division of Masinissa's Numidia, since Sicca is on the Bagradas, over a hundred miles to the east of Constantine. Then the whole war is concentrated in eastern Numidia, and Cirta (Constantine) is not in the picture.

Whatever the truth, Sallust's claim that the commission favoured Jugurtha is not tenable. Their reasoning may have been that the western tribes needed the stronger ruler, but Jugurtha could see the rich and civilised Bagradas valley being handed over to his brother. It begins to look as if the senate was recognising Adherbal as the rightful king of Numidia, and allotting Jugurtha an outlying province. Opimius was really an opponent of Jugurtha,[2] and the bribery of Chapter XXI was a malicious invention.

[1] Appian, *Lib.* 70; Pliny, *Nat. Hist.*, V 25 3.
[2] Reading, with most editors, *in inimicis* in XVI 3.

Table of Dates

Some of the following dates are approximate.

Select Bibliography

O F the general histories of the period the best are by Last, *Cambridge Ancient History*, vol. IX, chapter iii, and Scullard, *From the Gracchi to Nero*, but any of the standard school history books will serve provided that Marius is not billed as an agricultural labourer with a Field-Marshal's baton in his knapsack.

The young historian who will soon be working from the periodicals could well make his acquaintance with this modern *genre* by reading the articles by Oost, Holroyd and von Fritz.

Allen, W. 'The Sources of Jugurtha's Influence with the Roman Senate', *CP* XXXIII (1938) 90. That after Numantia Scipio's friends were patrons of Jugurtha. 3 pages.

Badian, E. 'Marius and the Nobles', *Durham University Journal* (March 1964). The best account of its subject for those who can get hold of it.

— *Foreign Clientelae*, 264–70 B.C., 1958, especially pp. 192–203. Excellent for advanced historians; client kings, Italian recruitment, Marius' supporters.

— *Roman Imperialism in the Late Republic*, 1968. Pp. 25–9 have an acute discussion of the Roman motives in Numidia.

Bell, M. J. V. 'Tactical Reform in the Roman Republican Army', *Historia*, XIV (1965) 404. A long discussion of war in Spain, then pp. 415–22, clear account of use of cohorts, maniples, velites in Jugurthine War.

Carney, T. F. 'Once Again Marius' Speech After Election in 108 B.C.', *Symb. Os.* xxxv (1959) 63. A further development of Skard's article (see below).

Cary, M. *Geographic Background of Greek and Roman History*, 1949. Pages 220–9 describe the contours and cultivation of N.W. Africa.

Earl, D. C. *The Political Thought of Sallust*, 1961. Good account of the morality of the Prologues and its development in the narrative; the words *virtus, ingenium*, etc. followed up. Reviewed by Hands, in *JRS* LII (1962) 274.

— 'Political Terminology in Plautus', *Historia*, IX (1960) 235. The same aristocratic political vocabulary in popular Latin two generations before Jugurtha.

— 'The Early Career of Sallust', *Historia*, xv (1966) 302. Sound common sense about new men and Italians in the Roman Senate.

— 'Sallust and the Senate's Numidian Policy', Latomus 1965, p. 532. The Mamilian Commission a paying off of old scores.

— Review of Syme, 'Sallust', in *JRS* LV (1965) 233. Includes an effective criticism of Sallust on Scaurus and Marius.

von Fritz, K. 'Sallust and the Attitude of the Roman Nobility', *TAPA* LXXIV (1943) 134. An examination of the surrender of Jugurtha in 111. Clear and readable.

Hands, A. R. 'Sallust and Dissimulatio', *JRS* XLIX (1959) 56. Sallust misrepresented Scaurus because he despised adaptable politicians.

— Review of Earl. 'The Political Thought of Sallust', *JRS* XLIX (1962) 56.

Hawthorn, J. R. and Macdonald, C. *Roman Politics 80–44 B.C.*, 1960. Short essays on politics (tribunate, etc.);

Latin extracts with historical notes; index of the political vocabulary of the time between Jugurtha and Sallust.

Holroyd, M. 'The Jugurthine War. Was Marius or Metellus the Real Victor?', *JRS* xviii (1928) 1. Excellent account of the war.

Laistner, M. L. W. *Greater Roman Historians, Sallust,* 1947. A general account, useful to start with.

Ogilvie, R. M. and Richmond, Sir I. A. (eds). Tacitus, *Agricola,* 1967. Introductory remarks on biography as a *genre.*

Oost, S. I. 'Fetial Law and the Outbreak of the Jugurthine War', *AJP* lxxv (1954) 147. The embassies of 112. Clear and good.

Paul, G. M. 'Sallust', ch. iv of *Latin Historians,* ed. T. A. Dorey, 1966. An excellent survey; deals clearly in twenty pages with the chief points of Sallustian criticism. Arrived too late to be quoted in the text.

Rambaud, M. 'Les Prologues de Salluste et la démonstration morale dans son œuvre', *Revue des Études Latines,* xxiv (1946) 115. The connection of the prologue with the narrative. (The French is not difficult.)

Sherwin-White, A. N. 'Geographical Facts in Roman Algeria', *JRS* xxxiv (1944) 1. Forests, steppes and communications. Valuable for the understanding of everything which happened in Numidia.

Skard, E. 'Marius' Speech in Sallust's *Jugurtha* 85', *Symb. Os.* xxi (1941) 98. The speech a mixture of a 'common' personality and a 'common' philosophy – that of the Cynics. Short and clear.

Syme, R. *Sallust,* 1964. Two chapters on the Jugurthine War, and a sinister impression of the time when Sallust was writing. Reviewed by Earl, *JRS,* 1965.

Ullman, B. L. 'History and Tragedy', *TAPA* LXXIII (1942) 25. The monograph bridged the gap between history and tragedy. 'Isocrates triumphed over Aristotle.'

Walbank, F. W. Φίλιππος Τραγῳδούμενος, *JHS* LVIII (1938) part I, p. 55. Even Polybius writing an obviously dramatic biography. (Knowledge of Greek not essential.)

Walsh, P. G. 'Massinissa', *JRS* LV (1965) 149. Includes a discussion of how much of Numidia was ruled by Massinissa.

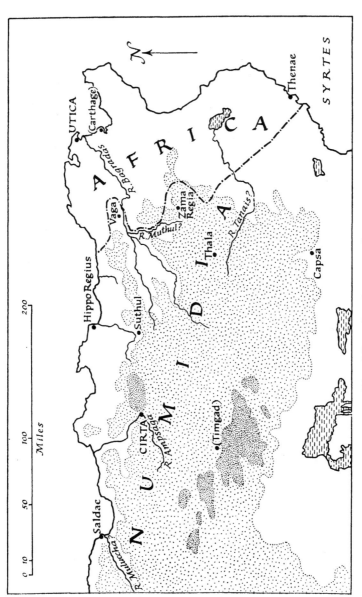

Numidia: the theatre of war

Sallust

THE WAR AGAINST JUGURTHA

PROLOGUE

[I–IV. The writing of history: men blame fortune for their own failings, though human nature is strong enough to overcome fortune. The things of the body are temporary, the things of the mind are permanent, and a life of pleasure, gratifying the body, is shameful.

Man has a duty to be active in mind, but, of the possible activities, a political career has lately become undesirable, since the rewards no longer go to men of merit, and violence is king. Of intellectual activities the most beneficial is the writing of history, and I shall devote myself to that. Those who think that this is idleness should blame not me but the present state of politics.]

The Prologue, with a translation, will be found on p. 121.

I NUMIDIAN CIVIL WAR AND APPEAL TO ROME

V–VI. *The early history of Numidia and the character of Jugurtha.*

V. Bellum scripturus sum, quod populus Romanus cum Iugurtha, rege Numidarum, gessit; primum, quia magnum et atrox, variaque victoria fuit; dein, quia tum primum superbiae nobilitatis obviam itum est; 2. quae contentio divina et humana cuncta permiscuit, eoque vecordiae processit, uti studiis civilibus bellum atque vastitas Italiae finem faceret. 3. Sed priusquam huiuscemodi rei initium expedio, pauca supra repetam; quo ad cognoscundum omnia illustria magis magisque in aperto sint.

4. Bello Punico secundo, quo dux Carthaginiensium

Hannibal post magnitudinem nominis Romani Italiae opes maxume attriverat, Masinissa rex Numidarum, in amicitiam receptus a P. Scipione, cui postea Africano cognomen ex virtute fuit, multa et praeclara rei militaris facinora fecerat; ob quae victis Carthaginiensibus et capto Syphace, cuius in Africa magnum atque late imperium valuit, populus Romanus quascumque urbis et agros manu ceperat regi dono dedit. 5. Igitur amicitia Masinissae bona atque honesta nobis permansit: imperii vitaeque eius finis idem fuit. 6. Dein Micipsa, filius, regnum solus obtinuit, Mastanabale et Gulussa fratribus morbo absumptis. 7. Is Adherbalem et Hiempsalem ex sese genuit, Iugurthamque, Mastanabalis fratris filium, quem Masinissa, quod ortus ex concubina erat, privatum dereliquerat, eodem cultu, quo liberos suos, domi habuit.

VI. Qui ubi primum adolevit, pollens viribus, decora facie, sed multo maxume ingenio validus, non se luxu, neque inertiae corrumpundum dedit; sed, uti mos gentis illius est, equitare, iaculari, cursu cum aequalibus certare, et cum omnis gloria anteiret, omnibus tamen carus esse: ad hoc pleraque tempora in venando agere, leonem atque alias feras primus aut in primis ferire, plurumum facere minumum ipse de se loqui.

2. Quibus rebus Micipsa tametsi initio laetus fuerat, existumans virtutem Iugurthae regno suo gloriae fore, tamen, postquam hominem adulescentem, exacta sua aetate et parvis liberis magis magisque crescere intellegit, vehementer negotio permotus multa cum animo suo volvebat. Terrebat eum natura mortalium avida imperii et praeceps ad explendam animi cupidinem, praeterea opportunitas suaeque et liberorum aetatis, quae etiam mediocris viros spe praedae transvorsos agit; ad hoc, studia Numidarum

in Iugurtham accensa; ex quibus, si talem virum dolis interfecisset, ne qua seditio aut bellum oriretur anxius erat.

[VII–XI. Thinking him a danger to his own sons, Micipsa sent Jugurtha to Spain, in command of a Numidian force which was to help the Romans at Numantia. Jugurtha distinguished himself, winning the approval of Scipio Aemilianus. The Roman nobles led him to believe that on Micipsa's death Rome would consider him a suitable king of Numidia.

Micipsa adopted Jugurtha, thus making him his eldest son, and on his deathbed begged him to protect his new brothers, Adherbal and Hiempsal. Micipsa died, and the three brothers met to divide the inheritance.]

XII–XIII, XV–XVI. *Jugurtha murders Hiempsal and attacks Adherbal. Adherbal and Jugurtha send ambassadors to Rome, where the Senate appoints a commission which divides the kingdom between them.*

XII. Primo conventu, quem ab regulis factum supra memoravi, propter dissensionem placuerat dividi thesauros finisque imperii singulis constitui. 2. Itaque tempus ad utramque rem decernitur, sed maturius ad pecuniam distribuendam. Reguli interea in loca propinqua thesauris, alius alio, concessere. 3. Sed Hiempsal in oppido Thirmida forte eius domo utebatur, qui, proxumus lictor Iuguthae carus acceptusque semper fuerat; quem ille casu ministrum oblatum promissis onerat impellitque, uti tamquam suam visens domum eat, portarum clavis adulterinas paret; nam verae ad Hiempsalem referebantur; ceterum, ubi res postularet, se ipsum cum magna manu venturum. 4. Numida mandata brevi confecit atque, uti doctus erat, noctu Iugurthae milites introducit. 5. Qui postquam in aedis irrupere, divorsi regem quaerere; dormientis alios, alios occursantis interficere; scrutari loca abdita; clausa effringere; strepitu et tumultu omnia miscere cum Hiempsal interim reperitur, occultans se in tugurio mulieris ancillae, quo initio pavidus et ignarus loci perfugerat. Numidae caput eius, uti iussi erant, ad Iugurtham referunt.

XIII. Ceterum fama tanti facinoris per omnem Africam brevi divolgatur; Adherbalem omnisque, qui sub imperio Micipsae fuerant, metus invadit; in duas partis discedunt; plures Adherbalem sequuntur, sed illum alterum bello meliores. **2.** Igitur Iugurtha quam maxumas potest copias armat; urbis partim vi, alias voluntate imperio suo adiungit; omni Numidiae imperare parat. **3.** Adherbal, tametsi Romam legatos miserat, qui senatum docerent de caede fratris et fortunis suis, tamen, fretus multitudine militum, parabat armis contendere. **4.** Sed ubi res ad certamen venit, victus ex proelio profugit in provinciam ac deinde Romam contendit.

5. Tum Iugurtha, patratis consiliis, postquam omnis Numidiae potiebatur, in otio facinus suum cum animo reputans, timere populum Romanum, neque advorsus iram eius usquam nisi in avaritia nobilitatis et pecunia sua spem habere. **6.** Itaque paucis diebus cum auro et argento multo Romam mittit, quis praecepit, primum uti veteres amicos muneribus expleant; deinde novos acquirant; postremo quemcumque possint largiundo parare ne cunctentur.

7. Sed ubi Romam legati venere et ex praecepto regis hospitibus aliisque, quorum ea tempestate auctoritas pollebat, magna munera misere tanta commutatio incessit, ut ex maxuma invidia in gratiam et favorem nobilitatis Iugurtha veniret; **8.** quorum pars spe, alii praemio inducti, singulos ex senatu ambiundo nitebantur, ne gravius in eum consuleretur. **9.** Igitur legati ubi satis confidunt, die constituto, senatus utrisque datur. Tum Adherbalem hoc modo locutum accepimus.

[XIV. Speech of Adherbal, complaining of the aggression of Jugurtha, who has killed his brother and is threatening him.]

XV. Postquam finem loquendi fecit, legati Iugurthae, largitione magis quam causa freti, paucis respondent: Hiempsalem ob saevitiam suam ab Numidis interfectum: Adherbalem, ultro bellum inferentem, postquam superatus sit, queri, quod iniuriam facere nequivisset: Iugurtham ab senatu petere, ne alium putarent ac Numantiae cognitus esset, neu verba inimici ante facta sua ponerent **2.** Deinde utrique curia egrediuntur. Senatus statim consulitur: fautores legatorum, praeterea magna pars gratia depravata, Adherbalis dicta contemnere, Iugurthae virtutem extollere laudibus: gratia, voce, denique omnibus modis pro alieno scelere et flagitio, sua quasi pro gloria, nitebantur. **3.** At contra pauci, quibus bonum et aequom divitiis carius erat, subveniundum Adherbali, et Hiempsalis mortem severe vindicandam censebant; **4.** sed ex omnibus maxume Aemilius Scaurus, homo nobilis, impiger, factiosus, avidus potentiae, honoris, divitiarum; ceterum vitia sua callide occultans. **5.** Is postquam videt regis largitionem famosam impudentemque, veritus, quod in tali re solet, ne polluta licentia invidiam accenderet, animum a consueta lubidine continuit.

XVI. Vicit tamen in senatu pars illa, quae vero pretium aut gratiam anteferebat. **2.** Decretum fit, uti decem legati regnum, quod Micipsa obtinuerat, inter Iugurtham et Adherbalem dividerent: cuius legationis princeps fuit L.

Opimius, homo clarus et tum in senatu potens; quia consul C. Graccho et M. Fulvio Flacco interfectis acerrume victoriam nobilitatis in plebem exercuerat. **3.** Eum Iugurtha tametsi Romae in inimicis habuerat, tamen accuratissume recepit; dando et pollicitando multa perfecit, uti fama, fide, postremo omnibus suis rebus commodum regis anteferret. **4.** Reliquos legatos eadem via aggressus, plerosque capit; paucis carior fides quam pecunia fuit. **5.** In divisione quae pars Numidiae Mauretaniam attingit, agro virisque opulentior, Iugurthae traditur; illam alteram, specie quam usu potiorem, quae portuosior et aedificiis magis exornata erat, Adherbal possedit.

[XVII–XIX. The geography of Africa and the origins of its peoples, taken from Carthaginian sources.]

XX–XXVI. *Jugurtha continues to attack Adherbal, although the senate sends two embassies to stop the war. Eventually Adherbal is killed at Cirta.*

XX. Postquam, diviso regno, legati Africa decessere, et Iugurtha contra timorem animi praemia sceleris adeptum sese videt, certum ratus, quod ex amicis apud Numantiam acceperat, omnia Romae venalia esse, simul et illorum pollicitationibus accensus, quos paulo ante muneribus expleverat, in regnum Adherbalis animum intendit. **2.** Ipse acer, bellicosus; at is, quem petebat, quietus, imbellis, placido ingenio, opportunus iniuriae, metuens magis quam metuendus. **3.** Igitur ex improviso finis eius cum magna manu invadit, multos mortalis cum pecore atque alia praeda capit, aedificia incendit pleraque loca hostiliter cum equitatu accedit; **4.** dein cum omni mul-

titudine in regnum suom convortit, existumans dolore
permotum Adherbalem iniurias suas manu vindicaturum,
eamque rem belli causam fore. **5.** At ille, quod neque se
parem armis existumabat, et amicitia populi Romani magis
quam Numidis fretus erat, legatos ad Iugurtham de
iniuriis questum misit; qui tametsi contumeliosa dicta
retulerant, prius tamen omnia pati decrevit, quam bellum
sumere; quia tentatum antea secus cesserat. **6.** Neque
tamen eo magis cupido Iugurthae minuebatur: quippe
qui totum eius regnum animo iam invaserat. **7.** Itaque
non, ut antea, cum praedatoria manu, sed magno exercitu
comparato, bellum gerere coepit et aperte totius Numidiae imperium petere. **8.** Ceterum qua pergebat urbis,
agros vastare, praedas agere; suis animum, terrorem hostibus augere.

XXI. Adherbal ubi intellegit eo processum, uti regnum
aut relinquendum esset, aut armis retinendum, necessario
copias parat, et Iugurthae obvius procedit. **2.** Interim
haud longe a mari, prope Cirtam oppidum, utriusque
consedit exercitus: et quia die extremum erat, proelium
non inceptum. Ubi plerumque noctis processit, obscuro
etiam tum lumine, milites Iugurthini, signo dato, castra
hostium invadunt; semisomnos partim, alios arma sumentis
fugant funduntque; Adherbal cum paucis equitibus
Cirtam profugit, et ni multitudo togatorum fuisset, quae
Numidas insequentis moenibus prohibuit, uno die inter
duos reges coeptum atque patratum bellum foret. **3.** Igitur
Iugurtha oppidum circumsedit, vineis turribusque et
machinis omnium generum expugnare aggreditur, maxume festinans tempus legatorum antecapere, quos ante
proelium factum ab Adherbale Romam missos audiverat.
4. Sed postquam senatus de bello eorum accepit, tres

adulescentes in Africam legantur, qui ambo reges adeant, senatus populique Romani verbis nuntient, Velle et censere eos ab armis discedere; de controversiis suis iure potius quam bello disceptare; ita seque illisque dignum esse.

XXII. Legati in Africam maturantes veniunt, eo magis, quod Romae, dum proficisci parant, de proelio facto et oppugnatione Cirtae audiebatur: sed is rumor clemens erat. 2. Quorum Iugurtha accepta oratione respondit: sibi neque maius quidquam neque carius auctoritate senati: ab adulescentia ita enisum, ut ab optumo quoque probaretur: virtute, non malitia P. Scipioni, summo viro, placuisse: ob easdem artis ab Micipsa, non penuria liberorum, in regnum adoptatum: 3. ceterum, quo plura bene atque strenue fecisset, eo animum suum iniuriam minus tolerare: 4. Adherbalem dolis vitae suae insidiatum; quod ubi comperisset, sceleri obviam isse; populum Romanum neque recte neque pro bono facturum, si ab iure gentium sese prohibuerit: postremo de omnibus rebus legatos Romam brevi missurum. 5. Ita utrique digrediuntur. Adherbalis appellandi copia non fuit.

XXIII. Iugurtha, ubi eos Africa decessisse ratus est, neque propter loci naturam Cirtam armis expugnare potest, vallo atque fossa moenia circumdat, turris exstruit, easque praesidiis firmat: praeterea dies noctisque, aut per vim aut dolis, tentare; defensoribus moenium praemia modo, modo formidinem ostentare; suos hortando ad virtutem erigere; prorsus intentus cuncta parare. 2. Adherbal ubi intellegit omnis suas fortunas in extremo sitas, hostem infestum, auxilii spem nullam, penuria rerum necessariarum bellum trahi non posse, ex his, qui una Cirtam profugerant, duo maxume impigros delegit, eos multa pollicendo ac miserando casum suum confirmat, uti per hostium munitiones noctu ad proxumum mare, dein Romam pergerent.

XXIV. Numidae paucis diebus iussa efficiunt; litterae Adherbalis in senatu recitatae, quarum sententia haec fuit: 'Non mea culpa saepe ad vos oratum mitto, Patres con- 2. scripti, sed vis Iugurthae subigit; quem tanta lubido exstin- guendi me invasit, uti neque vos, neque deos immortalis in animo habeat; sanguinem meum, quam omnia, malit. 3. Itaque quintum iam mensem socius et amicus populi Romani armis obsessus teneor; neque mihi Micipsae patris beneficia, neque vostra decreta auxiliantur; ferro an fame acrius urgear, incertus sum. 4. Plura de Iugurtha scribere dehortatur me fortuna mea; etiam antea expertus sum, parum fidei miseris esse; 5. nisi tamen intellego, illum supra quam ego sum petere, neque simul amicitiam vostram et regnum meum sperare: utrum gravius existumet, nemini occultum est. 6. Nam initio occidit Hiempsalem fratrem meum; deinde patrio regno me expulit:—quae sane fuerint nostrae iniuriae, nihil ad vos. 7. Verum nunc vostrum regnum armis tenet; me, quem vos imperatorem Numidis posuistis, clausum obsidet; legatorum verba quanti fecerit pericula mea declarant. 8. Quid reliquom, nisi vis vostra, quo moveri possit? 9. Nam ego quidem vellem et haec, quae scribo, et illa, quae antea in senatu questus sum, vana forent potius quam miseria mea fidem verbis faceret. 10. Sed quoniam eo natus sum ut Iugurthae scelerum ostentui essem, non iam mortem neque aerum- nas, tantummodo inimici imperium et cruciatus corporis deprecor. Regno Numidiae, quod vostrum est, uti lubet, consulite; me manibus impiis eripite, per maiestatem imperii, per amicitiae fidem, si ulla apud vos memoria remanet avi mei Masinissae.'

XXV. His litteris recitatis fuere qui exercitum in Africam mittundum censerent, et quam primum Adherbali subveniundum; de Iugurtha interim uti consuleretur, quoniam non paruisset legatis. **2.** Sed ab iisdem regis fautoribus summa ope enisum, ne tale decretum fieret. **3.** Ita bonum publicum, ut in plerisque negotiis solet, privata gratia devictum. **4.** Legantur tamen in Africam maiores natu nobiles, amplis honoribus; in quis M. Scaurus, de quo supra memoravimus, consularis et tunc in senatu princeps. **5.** Hi, quod in invidia res erat, simul et ab Numidis obsecrati, triduo navim ascendere; deinde brevi Uticam appulsi, litteras ad Iugurtham mittunt: quam ocissume ad provinciam accedat; seque ad eum ab senatu missos. **6.** Ille ubi accepit homines claros, quorum auctoritatem Romae pollere audiverat, contra inceptum suum venisse, primo commotus, metu atque lubidine divorsus agitabatur. **7.** Timebat iram senati, ni paruisset legatis; porro animus cupidine caecus ad inceptum scelus rapiebat. **8.** Vicit tamen in avido ingenio pravom consilium. **9.** Igitur exercitu circumdato summa vi Cirtam irrumpere nititur, maxume sperans diducta manu hostium aut vi aut dolis sese casum victoriae inventurum. **10.** Quod ubi secus procedit, neque quod intenderat efficere potest, uti prius quam legatos conveniret Adherbalis potiretur, ne amplius morando Scaurum, quem plurumum metuebat, incenderet, cum paucis equitibus in provinciam venit. **11.** Ac, tametsi senati verbis minae graves nuntiabantur, quod oppugnatione non desisteret, multa tamen oratione consumpta legati frustra discessere.

XXVI. Ea postquam Cirtae audita sunt, Italici, quorum virtute moenia defensabantur, confisi deditione facta propter magnitudinem populi Romani inviolatos sese fore,

Adherbali suadent, uti seque et oppidum Iugurthae tradat; tantum ab eo vitam paciscatur, de ceteris senatui curae fore. **2.** At ille, tametsi omnia potiora fide Iugurthae rebatur, quia penes eosdem, si advorsaretur, cogundi potestas erat, ita, uti censuerant Italici, deditionem facit. **3.** Iugurtha in primis Adherbalem excruciatum necat; deinde omnis puberes Numidas et negotiatores promiscue, uti quisque armatis obvius fuerat, interfecit.

II Limited Intervention

XXVII–XXIX. *In response to popular clamour the senate sends the consul, Calpurnius Bestia, with an army. Jugurtha surrenders and pays an indemnity.*

XXVII. Quod postquam Romae cognitum est, et res in senatu agitari coepta, idem illi ministri regis interpellando ac saepe gratia, interdum iurgiis trahundo tempus atrocitatem facti leniebant. **2.** Ac ni C. Memmius, tribunus plebis designatus, vir acer et infestus potentiae nobilitatis, populum Romanum edocuisset id agi, uti per paucos factiosos Iugurthae scelus condonaretur, profecto omnis invidia prolatandis consultationibus dilapsa erat: tanta vis gratiae atque pecuniae regis. **3.** Sed ubi senatus delicti conscientia populum timet, lege Sempronia provinciae futuris consulibus Numidia atque Italia decretae: consules declarantur P. Scipio Nasica, L. Bestia: Calpurnio Numidia, Scipioni Italia obvenit: deinde exercitus, qui in Africam portaretur, scribitur: **5.** stipendium aliaque, quae bello usui forent, decernuntur.

XXVIII. At Iugurtha contra spem nuntio accepto, quippe cui Romae omnia venum ire in animo haeserat, filium et cum eo duo familiaris ad senatum legatos mittit; hisque ut illis, quos Hiempsale interfecto miserat, praecepit, omnis mortalis pecunia aggrediantur. **2.** Qui postquam Romam adventabant senatus a Bestia consultus est, placeretne legatos Iugurthae recipi moenibus: iique decrevere, nisi regnum ipsumque deditum venissent, uti in diebus proximis decem Italia decederent. **3.** Consul Numidis ex senati decreto nuntiari iubet: ita infectis rebus illi domum discedunt.

4. Interim Calpurnius, parato exercitu, legat sibi homines nobilis, factiosos, quorum auctoritate quae deliquisset munita fore sperabat; in quis fuit Scaurus, cuius de natura et habitu supra memoravimus. **5.** Nam in consule nostro multae bonaeque artes animi et corporis erant, quas omnes avaritia praepediebat; patiens laborum, acri ingenio, satis providens, belli haud ignarus, firmissumus contra pericula et insidias. **6.** Sed legiones per Italiam Rhegium atque inde Siciliam, porro ex Sicilia in Africam transvectae. **7.** Igitur Calpurnius initio paratis commeatibus acriter Numidiam ingressus est, multosque mortalis et urbis aliquot pugnando capit.

XXIX. Sed ubi Iugurtha per legatos pecunia tentare, bellique, quod administrabat, asperitatem ostendere coepit, animus aeger avaritia facile convorsus est. **2.** Ceterum socius et administer omnium consiliorum assumitur Scaurus; qui tametsi a principio, plerisque ex factione eius corruptis, acerrume regem impugnaverat, tamen magnitudine pecuniae a bono honestoque in pravom abstractus est. **3.** Sed Iugurtha primum tantummodo belli moram redimebat, existumans sese aliquid interim Romae pretio aut gratia effecturum: postea vero quam participem negotii Scaurum accepit, in maxumam spem adductus recuperandae pacis statuit cum iis de omnibus pactionibus praesens agere. **4.** Ceterum interea fidei causa mittitur a consule Sextius quaestor in oppidum Iugurthae Vagam, cuius rei species erat acceptio frumenti, quod Calpurnius palam legatis imperaverat, quoniam deditionis mora indutiae agitabantur. **5.** Igitur rex, uti constituerat, in castra venit, ac pauca praesenti consilio locutus de invidia facti sui, atque in deditionem uti acciperetur, reliqua cum Bestia et Scauro secreta transigit; dein postero die, quasi per saturam exqui-

sitis sententiis, in deditionem accipitur. **6.** Sed, uti pro
consilio imperatum erat, elephanti triginta, pecus atque
equi multi cum argenti parvo pondere, quaestori traduntur.
7. Calpurnius Romam ad magistratus rogandos proficiscitur. In Numidia et exercitu nostro pax agitabatur.

XXX–XXXI. *At Rome the settlement was hotly debated. The tribune Memmius spoke against it: 'Will you, citizens of Rome, born to power, endure slavery?
But there shall be no violence; the nobles shall be put on trial, and Jugurtha brought
from Africa to give evidence.'*

XXX. Postquam res in Africa gestas, quoque modo
actae forent, fama divolgavit, Romae per omnis locos et
conventus de facto consulis agitari. Apud plebem gravis
invidia; patres solliciti erant; probarentne tantum flagitium, an decretum consulis subvorterent, parum constabat.
2. Ac maxume eos potentia Scauri, quod is auctor et
socius Bestiae ferebatur, a vero bonoque impediebat. **3.** At
C. Memmius, cuius de libertate ingenii et odio potentiae
nobilitatis supra diximus, inter dubitationem et moras
senati, contionibus populum ad vindicandum hortari;
monere, ne rempublicam, ne libertatem suam desererent;
multa superba et crudelia facinora nobilitatis ostendere;
prorsus intentus omni modo plebis animum accendebat.
4. Sed quoniam ea tempestate Romae Memmii facundia
clara pollensque fuit, decere existumavi, unam ex tam
multis orationem perscribere: ac potissumum ea dicam,
quae in contione post reditum Bestiae huiuscemodi verbis
disseruit.

XXXI. 'Multa me dehortantur a vobis, Quirites, ni
studium reipublicae omnia superet; opes factionis, vostra
patientia, ius nullum, ac maxume, quod innocentiae plus

periculi quam honoris est. **2.** Nam illa quidem piget dicere, his annis xv, quam ludibrio fueritis superbiae paucorum; quam foede, quamque inulti perierint vostri defensores; ut vobis animus ab ignavia atque socordia corruptus sit, **3.** qui ne nunc quidem, obnoxiis inimicis, exsurgitis, atque etiam nunc timetis eos, quibus decet terrori esse. **4.** Sed quamquam haec talia sunt, tamen obviam ire factionis potentiae animus subigit: **5.** certe ego libertatem, quae mihi a parente tradita est, experiar: verum id frustra an ob rem faciam, in vestra manu situm, Quirites. **6.** Neque ego hortor, quod saepe maiores vostri fecere, uti contra iniurias armati eatis. Nihil vi, nihil secessione opus est: necesse est suomet ipsi more praecipites eant.

7. Occiso Tiberio Graccho, quem regnum parare aiebant, in plebem Romanam quaestiones habitae sunt: post C. Gracchi et M. Fulvii caedem item vostri ordinis multi mortales in carcere necati sunt: utriusque cladis non lex, verum lubido eorum finem fecit. **8.** Sed sane fuerit regni paratio plebi sua restituere: quidquid sine sanguine civium ulcisci nequitur, iure factum sit. **9.** Superioribus annis taciti indignabamini aerarium expilari; reges et populos liberos paucis nobilibus vectigal pendere; penes eosdem et summam gloriam et maxumas divitias esse: tamen haec talia facinora impune suscepisse parum habuere: itaque postremo leges, maiestas vostra, divina et humana omnia hostibus tradita sunt. **10.** Neque eos qui ea fecere, pudet aut poenitet; sed incedunt per ora vostra magnifice, sacerdotia et consulatus, pars triumphos suos ostentantes, perinde quasi ea honori, non praedae habeant.

11. Servi aere parati imperia iniusta dominorum non perferunt: vos, Quirites, imperio nati, aequo animo servitutem toleratis? **12.** At qui sunt hi, qui rempublicam occupa-

vere? homines sceleratissumi, cruentis manibus, immani
avaritia, nocentissumi idemque superbissumi; quis fides,
decus, pietas, postremo honesta atque inhonesta omnia quae-
stui sunt. **13.** Pars eorum occidisse tribunos plebis, alii quaestiones iniustas, plerique caedem in vos fecisse pro munimento habent. **14.** Ita quam quisque pessume fecit, tam
maxume tutus est; metum a scelere suo ad ignaviam vostram transtulere; quos omnis eadem cupere, eadem odisse,
eadem metuere in unum coëgit. **15.** Sed haec inter bonos
amicitia, inter malos factio est. **16.** Quod si tam vos liber-
tatis curam haberetis, quam illi ad dominationem accensi
sunt, profecto neque res publica, sicuti nunc, vastaretur,
et beneficia vostra penes optumos, non audacissumos forent. **17.** Maiores vostri parandi iuris et maiestatis con-
stituendae gratia bis per secessionem armati Aventinum
occupavere: vos pro libertate, quam ab illis acepistis,
non summa ope nitemini? atque eo vehementius, quod
maius dedecus est parta amittere quam omnino non
paravisse?

18. Dicet aliquis: Quid igitur censes? Vindicandum in
eos, qui hosti prodidere rempublicam? Non manu, neque
vi, quod magis vos fecisse quam illis accidisse indignum
est, verum quaestionibus et indicio ipsius Iugurthae; **19.**
qui si dediticius est, profecto iussis vostris obediens erit;
sin ea contemnit, scilicet existimabitis qualis illa pax aut
deditio sit, ex qua ad Iugurtham scelerum impunitas, ad
paucos potentes maxumae divitiae, in rempublicam damna
atque dedecora pervenerint. **20.** Nisi forte nondum etiam
vos dominationis eorum satietas tenet, et illa, quam haec
tempora, magis placent, cum regna, provinciae, leges,
iura, iudicia, bella atque paces, postremo divina et humana
omnia penes paucos erant; vos autem, hoc est populus

Romanus, invicti ab hostibus, imperatores omnium gentium, satis habebatis animam retinere; nam servitutem quidem quis vostrum recusare audebat? **21.** Atque ego tametsi viro flagitiosissumum existumo impune iniuriam accepisse, tamen vos hominibus sceleratissumis ignoscere, quoniam cives sunt, aequo animo paterer, nisi misericordia in perniciem casura esset. **22.** Nam et illis, quantum importunitatis habent, parum est impune male fecisse, nisi deinde faciundi licentia eripitur; et vobis aeterna sollicitudo remanebit, cum intellegetis, aut serviundum esse, aut per manus libertatem retinendam. **23.** Nam fidei quidem aut concordiae quae spes est? Dominari illi volunt, vos liberi esse; facere illi iniurias, vos prohibere: postremo sociis vostris veluti hostibus, hostibus pro sociis utuntur. **24.** Potestne in tam divorsis mentibus pax aut amicitia esse? **25.** Quare moneo hortorque vos ne tantum scelus impunitum omittatis. Non peculatus aerarii factus est, neque per vim sociis ereptae pecuniae; quae, quamquam gravia, tamen consuetudine iam pro nihilo habentur. Hosti acerrumo prodita senati auctoritas, proditum imperium vostrum; **26.** domi militiaeque respublica venalis fuit. Quae nisi quaesita erunt, ni vindicatum in noxios, quid reliquom, nisi ut illis, qui ea fecere, obedientes vivamus? nam impune quae lubet facere id est regem esse. **27.** Neque ego vos, Quirites, hortor, ut malitis cives vostros perperam quam recte fecisse, sed ne ignoscundo malis bonos perditum eatis. **28.** Ad hoc in republica multo praestat beneficii quam maleficii immemorem esse: bonus tantummodo segnior fit ubi neglegas, at malus improbior. **29.** Ad hoc si iniuriae non sint, haud saepe auxilii egeas.'

[XXXII–XXXV. Memmius' proposal was passed, and Jugurtha came to Rome, but when Memmius called on him to speak another tribune stopped the proceedings by his veto.

Another grandson of Masinissa, Massiva, was persuaded to claim the throne of Numidia at Rome. Jugurtha had him murdered and enabled the murderer to escape. The senate ordered Jugurtha to leave Rome.

XXXVI–XXXVIII. The new consul Spurius Albinus, renewed the war, but when he returned to Rome to hold elections his brother Aulus Albinus, left in charge of the army, was outmanœuvred and compelled to surrender. Jugurtha made a treaty on condition that the whole Roman army should pass under the yoke, and evacuate Numidia.]

XXXIX – XLI.   *The Mamilian Commission and the state of parties at Rome.*

XXXIX. Sed ubi ea Romae comperta sunt, metus atque maeror civitatem invasere: pars dolere pro gloria imperii; pars, insolita rerum bellicarum, timere libertati: Aulo omnes infesti, ac maxume qui bello saepe praeclari fuerant, quod armatus dedecore potius quam manu salutem quaesiverat.   **2.** Ob ea consul Albinus ex delicto fratris invidiam ac deinde periculum timens, senatum de foedere consulebat; et tamen interim exercitu supplementum scribere; ab sociis et nomine Latino auxilia arcessere; denique modis omnibus festinare.   **3.** Senatus ita, uti par fuerat, decernit, suo atque populi iniussu nullum potuisse foedus fieri.   **4.** Consul impeditus a tribunis plebis, ne quas paraverat copias secum portaret, paucis diebus in Africam proficiscitur; nam omnis exercitus, uti convenerat, Numidia deductus, in provincia hiemabat.   **5.** Postquam eo venit, quamquam persequi Iugurtham et mederi fraternae invidiae animus ardebat, cognitis militibus, quos

praeter fugam soluto imperio licentia atque lascivia cor-
ruperat, ex copia rerum statuit sibi nihil agitandum.
XL. Interea Romae C. Mamilius Limetanus tribunus
plebis rogationem ad populum promulgat 'uti quaereretur
in eos, quorum consilio Iugurtha senati decreta neglegisset; quique ab eo in legationibus, aut imperiis pecunias
accepissent; qui elephantos, quique perfugas tradidissent;
item qui de pace aut bello cum hostibus pactiones fecissent.'
2. Huic rogationi partim conscii sibi, alii ex partium invidia
pericula metuentes, quoniam aperte resistere non poterant, quin illa et alia talia placere sibi faterentur, occulte
per amicos, ac maxume per homines nominis Latini et
socios Italicos impedimenta parabant. 3. Sed plebes
incredibile memoratu est quam intenta fuerit, quantaque
vi rogationem iusserit, decreverit, voluerit; magis odio
nobilitatis, cui mala illa parabantur, quam cura reipublicae: tanta lubido in partibus erat. 4. Igitur ceteris metu
perculsis M. Scaurus, quem legatum Bestiae fuisse supra
docuimus, inter laetitiam plebis et suorum fugam, trepida
etiam tum civitate, cum ex Mamilia rogatione tres quaesitores rogarentur, effecerat, uti ipse in eo numero crearetur.
5. Sed quaestio exercita aspere violenterque, ex rumore et
lubidine plebis: ut saepe nobilitatem, sic ea tempestate
plebem ex secundis rebus insolentia ceperat.
XLI. Ceterum mos partium et factionum, ac deinde
omnium malarum artium paucis ante annis Romae ortus
est, otio et abundantia earum rerum, quae prima mortales ducunt. 2. Nam ante Carthaginem deletam populus
et senatus Romanus placide modesteque inter se rempublicam tractabant; neque gloriae, neque dominationis certamen inter civis erat; metus hostilis in bonis artibus
civitatem retinebat. 3. Sed ubi illa formido mentibus

decessit, scilicet ea, quae secundae res amant, lascivia atque superbia, incessere. **4.** Ita quod in advorsis rebus optaverant otium, postquam adepti sunt, asperius acerbiusque fuit. **5.** Namque coepere nobilitas dignitatem, populus libertatem in lubidinem vortere; sibi quisque ducere, trahere, rapere. Ita omnia in duas partis abstracta sunt; respublica, quae media fuerat, dilacerata. **6.** Ceterum nobilitas factione magis pollebat; plebis vis soluta atque dispersa in multitudine minus poterat; **7.** paucorum arbitrio belli domique agitabatur; penes eosdem aerarium, provinciae, magistratus, gloriae triumphique erant; populus militia atque inopia urgebatur; praedas bellicas imperatores cum paucis diripiebant. **8.** Interea parentes aut parvi liberi militum, ut quisque potentiori confinis erat, sedibus pellebantur. **9.** Ita cum potentia avaritia sine modo modestiaque invadere, polluere et vastare omnia; nihil pensi neque sancti habere, quoad semet ipsa praecipitavit. **10.** Nam ubi primum ex nobilitate reperti sunt, qui veram gloriam iniustae potentiae anteponerent, moveri civitas, et dissensio civilis quasi permixtio terrae oriri coepit.

[XLII. The nobility, having killed first Tiberius Gracchus, then Gaius Gracchus, and also M. Fulvius Flaccus, strengthened their hold on the state by the death or exile of many of the opposition. But in fact they made themselves feared rather than powerful.]

III OUTRIGHT WAR

1 *Metellus and the turning of the tide*

XLIII – LV. *Q. Caecilius Metellus, consul of 109, takes command in Africa, and the war enters a new phase. He restores the morale of the Roman army and invades Numidia. The battle of the Muthul. The difficulties of an army fighting against guerrillas.*

XLIII. Post Auli foedus exercitusque nostri foedam fugam Q. Metellus et M. Silanus, consules designati, provincias inter se partiverant, Metelloque Numidia evenerat, acri viro et quamquam advorso populi partium fama tamen aequabili et inviolata. **2.** Is ubi primum magistratum ingressus est, alia omnia sibi cum collega ratus, ad bellum, quod gesturus erat, animum intendit. **3.** Igitur diffidens veteri exercitui, milites scribere, praesidia undique arcessere, arma, tela, equos, et cetera instrumenta militiae parare, ad hoc commeatum affatim; denique omnia, quae bello vario et multarum rerum egenti usui esse solent. **4.** Ceterum ad ea patranda senati auctoritate socii nomenque Latinum, et reges ultro auxilia mittere; postremo omnis civitas summo studio adnitebatur. **5.** Itaque ex sententia omnibus rebus paratis compositisque, in Numidiam proficiscitur magna spe civium, cum propter bonas artis, tum maxume, quod advorsum divitias invictum animum gerebat, et avaritia magistratuum ante id tempus in Numidia nostrae opes contusae, hostiumque auctae erant.

XLIV. Sed ubi in Africam venit, exercitus ei traditur Sp. Albini proconsulis iners, imbellis, neque periculi neque laboris patiens, lingua quam manu promptior, praedator ex sociis et ipse praeda hostium, sine imperio et modestia habitus. **2.** Ita imperatori novo plus ex malis moribus sollicitudinis quam ex copia militum auxilii aut spei bonae accedebat. **3.** Statuit tamen Metellus, quamquam et aestivorum tempus comitiorum mora imminuerat, et exspectatione eventus civium animos intentos putabat, non prius bellum attingere, quam maiorum disciplina milites laborare coëgisset. **4.** Nam Albinus, Auli fratris exercitusque clade perculsus, postquam decreverat non egredi provincia, quantum temporis aestivorum in imperio fuit plerumque milites stativis castris habebat, nisi cum odos aut pabuli egestas locum mutare subegerat. **5.** Sed neque muniebantur ea, neque more militari vigiliae deducebantur; uti cuique lubebat ab signis aberat. Lixae permixti cum militibus die noctuque vagabantur, et palantes agros vastare, villas expugnare, pecoris et mancipiorum praedas certantes agere; eaque mutare cum mercatoribus vino advecticio et aliis talibus; praeterea frumentum publice datum vendere, panem in dies mercari; postremo, quaecumque dici aut fingi queunt ignaviae luxuriaeque probra, in illo exercitu cuncta fuere, et alia amplius.

XLV. Sed in ea difficultate Metellum non minus quam in rebus hostilibus magnum et sapientem virum fuisse comperior, tanta temperantia inter ambitionem saevitiamque moderatum. **2.** namque edicto primum adiumenta ignaviae sustulisse, ne quisquam in castris panem, aut quem alium coctum cibum venderet; ne lixae exercitum sequerentur; ne miles gregarius in castris neve in agmine servum aut iumentum haberet: ceteris arte modum statuisse: praeterea transvorsis itineribus cotidie castra movere; iuxta ac si hostes adessent, vallo atque fossa munire, vigilias crebras ponere, et ipse cum legatis circumire: item in agmine in primis modo, modo in postremis, saepe in medio adesse, ne quisquam ordine egrederetur, uti cum signis frequentes incederent, miles cibum et arma portaret. **3.** Ita prohibendo a delictis, magis quam vindicando exercitum brevi confirmavit.

XLVI. Interea Iugurtha, ubi, quae Metellus agebat ex nuntiis accepit simul de innocentia eius certior Roma factus, diffidere suis rebus, ac tum demum veram deditionem facere conatus est. **2.** Igitur legatos ad consulem cum suppliciis mittit, qui tantummodo ipsi liberisque vitam peterent, alia omnia dederent populo Romano. **3.** Sed Metello iam antea experimentis cognitum erat genus Numidarum infidum, ingenio mobili, novarum rerum avidum esse. **4.** Itaque legatos alium ab alio divorsos adgreditur; ac, paulatim tentando, postquam opportunos cognovit, multa pollicendo, persuadet uti Iugurtham, maxume vivom, sin id parum procedat, necatum sibi traderent: ceterum palam, quae ex voluntate forent, regi nuntiari iubet. **5.** Deinde ipse paucis diebus intento atque infesto exercitu in Numidiam procedit; ubi, contra belli faciem, tuguria plena hominum, pecora cultoresque in agris erant: ex oppidis et mapalibus praefecti regis obvii procedebant, parati frumentum dare, commeatum portare, postremo omnia, quae imperarentur, facere. **6.** Neque Metellus idcirco minus, sed pariter ac si hostes adessent, munito agmine incedere, late explorare omnia, illa deditionis signa ostentui credere, et insidiis locum tentari. **7.** Itaque ipse cum expeditis cohortibus, item funditorum et sagittariorum delecta manu apud primos erat; in postremo C. Marius legatus cum equitibus curabat; in utrumque latus auxiliarios equites tribunis legionum et praefectis cohortium dispertiverat, uti cum his permixti velites, quacumque accederent equitatus hostium, propulsarent. **8.** Nam in Iugurtha tantus dolus, tantaque peritia locorum et militiae erat, uti, absens an praesens pacem an bellum gerens perniciosior esset in incerto haberetur.

XLVII. Erat haud longe ab eo itinere, quo Metellus pergebat, oppidum Numidarum, nomine Vaga, forum rerum venalium totius regni maxume celebratum; ubi et incolere et mercari consueverant Italici generis multi mortales. **2.** Huc consul, simul tentandi gratia si paterentur, et ob opportunitates loci praesidium imposuit; praeterea imperavit frumentum et alia, quae bello usui forent, comportare; ratus, id quod res monebat, frequentiam negotiatorum et commeatu iuvaturam exercitum, et iam paratis rebus munimento fore. **3.** Inter haec negotia Iugurtha impensius modo legatos supplices mittere, pacem orare, praeter suam liberorumque vitam, omnia Metello dedere. Quos item, uti priores, consul illectos ad proditionem domum dimittebat: regi pacem, quam postulabat, neque abnuere neque polliceri, et inter eas moras promissa legatorum exspectare.

XLVIII. Iugurtha ubi Metelli dicta cum factis composuit, ac se suis artibus tentari animadvertit, quippe cui verbis pax nuntiabatur, ceterum re bellum asperrumum erat, urbs maxuma alienata, ager hostibus cognitus, animi popularium tentati; coactus rerum necessitudine statuit armis certare. **2.** Igitur explorato hostium itinere in spem victoriae adductus ex opportunitate loci quam maxumas copias potest omnium generum parat, ac per tramites occultos exercitum Metelli antevenit. **3.** Erat in ea parte Numidiae, quam Adherbal in divisione possederat, flumen oriens a meridie, nomine Muthul; a quo aberat mons ferme milia passuum xx., tractu pari, vastus ab natura et humano cultu: sed ex eo medio quasi collis oriebatur, in immensum pertingens, vestitus oleastro ac myrtetis aliisque generibus arborum, quae humi arido atque arenoso gignuntur. **4.** Media autem planities deserta penuria aquae, praeter flumini propinqua loca: ea consita arbustis, pecore atque cultoribus frequentabantur.

XLIX. Igitur in eo colle, quem transvorso itinere porrectum docuimus, Iugurtha extenuata suorum acie consedit; elephantis et parti copiarum pedestrium Bomilcarem praefecit, eumque edocet quae ageret; ipse propior montem cum omni equitatu et peditibus delectis suos collocat. **2.** Dein singulas turmas atque manipulos circumiens monet atque obtestatur, uti memores pristinae virtutis et victoriae sese regnumque suum ab Romanorum avaritia defendant: cum his certamen fore, quos antea victos sub iugum miserint: ducem illis, non animum, mutatum: quae ab imperatore decuerint, omnia suis provisa; locum superiorem, uti prudentes cum imperitis, ne pauciores cum pluribus, aut rudes cum bello melioribus manum consererent; proinde parati intentique essent signo dato Romanos invadere; **3.** illum diem aut omnis labores et victorias confirmaturum, aut maxumarum aerumnarum initium fore. **4.** Ad hoc viritim, uti quemque ob militare facinus pecunia aut honore extulerat, commonefacere beneficii sui, et eum ipsum aliis ostentare; postremo pro cuiusque ingenio, pollicendo, minitando, obtestando alium alio modo excitare; cum interim Metellus, ignarus hostium monte degrediens cum exercitu conspicatur; primo dubius, quidnam insolita facies ostenderet (nam inter virgulta equi Numidaeque consederant, **5.** neque plane occultati humilitate arborum, et tamen incerti, quidnam esset, cum natura loci tum dolo ipsi atque signa militaria obscurati), dein, brevi

cognitis insidiis, paulisper agmen constituit. **6.** Ibi commutatis ordinibus in dextero latere, quod proxumum hostis
erat, triplicibus subsidiis aciem instruxit: inter manipulos
funditores et sagittarios dispertit; equitatum omnem in
cornibus locat, ac pauca pro tempore milites hortatus
aciem, sicuti instruxerat, transvorsis principiis, in planum
deducit.

L. Sed, ubi Numidas quietos neque colle degredi ani-
madvortit, veritus ex anni tempore et inopia aquae, ne siti
conficeretur exercitus, Rutilium legatum cum expeditis
cohortibus et parte equitum praemisit ad flumen, uti
locum castris antecaperet, existumans, hostis crebro impetu
et transvorsis proeliis iter suum remoraturos, et quoniam
armis diffiderent, lassitudinem et sitim militum tentaturos.
2. Dein ipse pro re atque loco, sicuti monte descenderat,
paulatim procedere; Marium post principia habere; ipse
cum sinistrae alae equitibus esse, qui in agmine principes
facti erant. **3.** At Iugurtha, ubi extremum agmen Metelli
primos suos praetergressum videt praesidio quasi duum
milium peditum montem occupat, qua Metellus descenderat, ne forte cedentibus adversariis receptui ac post
munimento foret: dein repente signo dato hostis invadit.
Numidae alii postremos caedere, pars a sinistra ac dextra
tentare, infensi adesse atque instare, omnibus locis Romanorum ordines conturbare; quorum etiam qui firmioribus
animis obvii hostibus fuerant ludificati incerto proelio ipsi
modo eminus sauciabantur, neque contra feriundi aut
manum conserundi copia erat. **5.** Ante iam docti ab Iugurtha equites, ubicumque Romanorum turba insequi
coeperat, non confertim, neque in unum sese recipiebant,
sed alius alio quam maxume divorsi. **6.** Ita numero priores
si ab persequendo hostis deterrere nequiverant, disiectos

ab tergo, aut lateribus circumveniebant; sin opportunior fugae collis quam campi fuerant, ea vero consueti Numidarum equi facile inter virgulta evadere; nostros asperitas et insolentia loci retinebant.

LI. Ceterum facies totius negotii varia, incerta, foeda, atque miserabilis; dispersi a suis pars cedere, alii insequi; neque signa neque ordines observare; ubi quemque periculum ceperat, ibi resistere ac propulsare; arma, tela, equi, viri, hostes, cives permixti; nihil consilio neque imperio agi; fors omnia regere. 2. Itaque multum diei processerat, cum etiam tum eventus in incerto erat. 3. Denique omnibus labore et aestu languidis, Metellus, ubi videt Numidas minus instare, paulatim milites in unum conducit, ordines restituit, et cohortis legionarias quattuor advorsum pedites hostium collocat. Eorum magna pars superioribus locis fessa consederat. 4. Simul orare, hortari milites ne deficerent, neu paterentur hostes fugientes vincere; neque illis castra esse, neque munimentum ullum quo cedentes tenderent: in armis omnia sita. 5. Sed ne Iugurtha quidem interea quietus; circumire, hortari, renovare proelium, et ipse cum delectis tentare omnia; subvenire suis, hostibus dubiis instare, quos firmos cognoverat, eminus pugnando retinere.

LII. Eo modo inter se duo imperatores, summi viri, certabant; ipsi pares, ceterum opibus disparibus. 2. Nam Metello virtus militum erat, locus advorsus; 3. Iugurthae alia omnia praeter milites opportuna. Denique Romani, ubi intellegunt neque sibi perfugium esse, neque ab hoste copiam pugnandi fieri, et iam die vesper erat; advorso colle, sicuti praeceptum fuerat, evadunt. 4. Amisso loco Numidae fusi fugatique: pauci interiere; plerosque velocitas et regio hostibus ignara tutata sunt. 5. Interea Bomilcar,

quem elephantis et parti copiarum pedestrium prae-
fectum ab Iugurtha supra diximus, ubi eum Rutilius prae-
tergressus est, paulatim suos in aequom locum deducit;
ac, dum legatus ad flumen, quo praemissus erat, festinans
pergit, quietus, uti res postulabat, aciem exornat, neque
remittit, quid ubique hostis ageret, explorare. **6.** Postquam Rutilium consedisse iam et animo vacuom accepit,
simulque ex Iugurthae proelio clamorem augeri, veritus
ne legatus cognita re laborantibus suis auxilio foret, aciem,
quam diffidens virtuti militum arte statuerat, quo hostium
itineri officeret, latius porrigit, eoque modo ad Rutilii
castra procedit.

LIII. Romani ex improviso pulveris vim magnam ani-
madvortunt, nam prospectum ager arbustis consitus pro-
hibebat; et primo rati humum aridam vento agitari, post
ubi aequabilem manere, et sicuti acies movebatur magis
magisque adpropinquare vident, cognita re properantes
arma capiunt, ac pro castris, sicuti imperabatur, consis-
tunt. **2.** Deinde, ubi propius ventum est, utrimque magno
clamore concurritur. **3.** Numidae tantummodo remorati,
dum in elephantis auxilium putant, postquam eos impedi-
tos ramis arborum atque ita disiectos circumveniri vident,
fugam faciunt, ac plerique, abiectis armis collis aut noctis,
quae iam aderat, auxilio integri abeunt. **4.** Elephanti
quattuor capti, reliqui omnes, numero quadraginta, interfecti. **5.** At Romani quamquam itinere atque opere cast-
rorum et proelio fessi lassique erant, tamen, quod Metellus
amplius opinione morabatur, instructi intentique obviam
procedunt; nam dolus Numidarum nihil languidi neque
remissi patiebatur. **7.** Ac primo obscura nocte, postquam haud procul inter se erant, strepitu velut hostes
adventare, alteri apud alteros formidinem simul et tumul-

tum facere; et paene imprudentia admissum facinus miserabile, ni utrimque praemissi equites rem exploravissent. Igitur pro metu repente gaudium exortum; **8.** milites alius alium laeti appellant, acta edocent atque audiunt; sua quisque fortia facta ad caelum ferre. Quippe res humanae ita sese habent: in victoria vel ignavis gloriari licet; advorsae res etiam bonos detractant.

LIV. Metellus in isdem castris quatriduo moratus saucios cum cura reficit, meritos in proeliis more militiae donat, univorsos in contione laudat atque agit gratias; hortatur ad cetera, quae levia sunt, parem animum gerant; pro victoria satis iam pugnatum, reliquos labores pro praeda fore. **2.** Tamen interim transfugas et alios opportunos, Iugurtha ubi gentium aut quid agitaret, cum paucisne esset, an exercitum haberet uti sese victus gereret, exploratum misit. **3.** At ille sese in loca saltuosa et natura munita receperat; ibique cogebat exercitum numero hominum ampliorem, sed hebetem infirmumque, agri ac pecoris magis quam belli cultorem. **4.** Id ea gratia eveniebat, quod praeter regios equites nemo omnium Numidarum ex fuga regem sequitur; quo cuiusque animus fert, eo discedunt; neque id flagitium militiae ducitur; ita se mores habent. **5.** Igitur Metellus ubi videt regis etiam tum animum ferocem esse; bellum renovari, quod nisi ex illius lubidine geri non posset; praeterea iniquom certamen sibi cum hostibus, minore detrimento illos vinci, quam suos vincere; statuit non proeliis neque acie, sed alio more bellum gerundum. **6.** Itaque in Numidiae loca opulentissuma pergit, agros vastat, multa castella et oppida temere munita aut sine praesidio capit incenditque; puberes interfici iubet, alia omnia militum praedam esse. Ea formidine multi mortales Romanis dediti obsides; frumentum et alia, quae usui

forent, adfatim praebita; ubicumque res postulabat, praesidium impositum. **7.** Quae negotia multo magis quam
proelium male pugnatum ab suis regem terrebant; **8.**
quippe, cui spes omnis in fuga sita erat, sequi cogebatur,
et qui sua loca defendere nequiverat, in alienis bellum
gerere. **9.** Tamen ex copia quod optumum videbatur consilium capit; exercitum plerumque in iisdem locis opperiri
iubet, ipse cum delectis equitibus Metellum sequitur; noc-
turnis et aviis itineribus ignoratus Romanos palantis repente adgreditur. **10.** Eorum plerique inermes cadunt,
multi capiuntur, nemo omnium intactus profugit, et Numidae prius quam ex castris subveniretur, sicuti iussi erant,
in proximos collis discedunt.

LV. Interim Romae gaudium ingens ortum cognitis
Metelli rebus; ut seque et exercitum more maiorum gereret, in advorso loco, victor tamen virtute fuisset, hostium
agro potiretur, Iugurtham, magnificum ex Auli socordia
spem salutis in solitudine aut fuga coëgisset habere. **2.** Itaque senatus ob ea feliciter acta dis immortalibus supplicia
decernere, civitas trepida antea et sollicita de belli eventu
laeta agere, de Metello fama praeclara esse. **3.** Igitur eo
intentior ad victoriam niti, omnibus modis festinare;
cavere tamen, necubi hosti opportunus fieret, meminisse
post gloriam invidiam sequi. **4.** Ita quo clarior eo magis
animi anxius erat, neque post insidias Iugurthae effuso
exercitu praedari; ubi frumento aut pabulo opus erat, cohortes cum omni equitatu praesidium agitabant; exercitus
partem ipse, reliquos Marius ducebat. **5.** Sed igni magis
quam praeda ager vastabatur. **6.** Duobus locis haud longe
inter se castra faciebant; **7.** ubi vi opus erat, cuncti aderant; ceterum, quo fuga atque formido latius cresceret,
divorsi agebant. **8.** Eo tempore Iugurtha per collis sequi,

tempus aut locum pugnae quaerere, qua venturum hostem audierat, pabulum et aquarum fontis, quorum penuria erat, corrumpere, modo se Metello, interdum Mario ostendere, postremos in agmine tentare, ac statim in collis regredi; rursus aliis, post aliis minitari, neque proelium facere, neque otium pati, tantummodo hostem ab incepto retinere.

[LVI–LX. The siege of Zama: Metellus lays siege to Zama, thinking that Jugurtha must fight for it. He encamps near the town, and makes a series of violent attacks on it, while from time to time Jugurtha raids the Roman camp and attacks the besieging army. After much fighting Metellus abandons the siege.

LXI–LXII. Winter: Metellus places garrisons in the most defensible towns of Numidia, and quarters his army in the western part of the province of Africa. He tries to bribe Bomilcar, the Numidian general, to betray Jugurtha to him; Jugurtha pays an indemnity and agrees to surrender to Metellus, but at the last minute changes his mind.]

2 *Marius and Reinforcements*

LXIII–LXIV. *Marius plans to become consul.*

LXIII. Per idem tempus Uticae forte C. Mario per hostias dis supplicanti magna atque mirabilia portendi haruspex dixerat: proinde quae animo agitabat, fretus dis ageret, fortunam quam saepissume experiretur; cuncta prospera eventura. 2. At illum iam antea consulatus ingens cupido exagitabat; ad quem capiundum praeter vetustatem familiae alia omnia abunde erant; industria, probitas, militiae magna scientia; animus belli ingens, domi modicus, lubidinis et divitiarum victor, tantummodo gloriae avidus. 3. Sed is natus et omnem pueritiam Arpini altus, ubi primum aetas militiae patiens fuit, stipendiis

faciundis, non Graeca facundia neque urbanis munditiis
sese exercuit: ita inter artis bonas integrum ingenium
brevi adolevit. **4.** Ergo ubi primum tribunatum militarem
a populo petit, plerisque faciem eius ignorantibus, factis
notus per omnis tribus declaratur. **5.** Deinde ab eo magis-
tratu alium post alium sibi peperit; semperque in potestatibus eo modo agitabat, uti ampliore quam gerebat dig-
nus haberetur. **6.** Tamen is ad id locorum talis vir (nam
postea ambitione praeceps datus est), petere non audebat:
etiam tum alios magistratus plebes, consulatum nobilitas
inter se per manus tradebat: **7.** novus nemo tam clarus
neque tam egregiis factis erat, quin indignus illo honore,
et is quasi pollutus, haberetur.

LXIV. Igitur ubi Marius haruspicis dicta eodem inten-
dere videt, quo cupido animi hortabatur, ab Metello
petundi gratia missionem rogat: cui quamquam virtus,
gloria, atque alia optanda bonis superabant, tamen inerat
contemptor animus et superbia, commune nobilitatis
malum. **2.** Itaque primum commotus insolita re mirari
eius consilium, et quasi per amicitiam monere ne tam prava
inciperet, neu super fortunam animum gereret; non omnia
omnibus cupiunda esse; debere illi res suas satis placere;
postremo caveret id petere a populo Romano, quod illi
iure negaretur. **3.** Postquam haec atque alia talia dixit,
neque animus Marii flectitur, respondit ubi primum pot-
uisset per negotia publica, facturum sese quae peteret. **4**
Ac postea saepius eadem postulanti fertur dixisse ne fes-
tinaret abire: satis mature illum cum filio suo consulatum
petiturum. Is eo tempore contubernio patris ibidem mili-
tabat, annos natus circiter xx. Quae res Marium cum pro
honore quem adfectabat tum contra Metellum vehementer
accenderat. **5.** Ita cupidine atque ira, pessumis consul-

toribus, grassari; neque facto ullo neque dicto abstinere, quod modo ambitiosum foret; milites, quibus in hibernis praeerat, laxiore imperio quam antea habere; apud negotiatores, quorum magna multitudo Uticae erat, criminose simul et magnifice de bello loqui: dimidia pars exercitus sibi permitteretur, paucis diebus Iugurtham in catenis habiturum; ab imperatore consulto trahi, quod homo inanis et regiae superbiae imperio nimis gauderet. **6.** Quae omnia illis eo firmiora videbantur, quod diuturnitate belli res familiaris corruperant, et animo cupienti nihil satis festinatur.

[LXV–LXXII. Marius persuaded the businessmen and other equestrians in Africa to write to their friends in Rome criticising Metellus and saying that Marius would make a better general; thus supporting his claim to the consulship.

Fighting was renewed with the new year (108); Bomilcar again plotted to capture Jugurtha, and was put to death by him.]

LXXIII. *Marius is elected consul and appointed to the command in Africa.*

LXXIII. Igitur Metellus, ubi de casu Bomilcaris et indicio patefacto ex perfugis cognovit, rursus tamquam ad integrum bellum cuncta parat festinatque. **2.** Marium, fatigantem de profectione, simul et invitum et offensum sibi parum idoneum ratus, domum dimittit. **3.** Et Romae plebes, litteris, quae de Metello ac Mario missae erant, cognitis, volenti animo de ambobus acceperant. **4.** Imperatori nobilitas, quae antea decori, invidiae esse: at illi alteri generis humilitas favorem addiderat: ceterum in utroque magis studia partium quam bona aut mala sua moderata sunt. **5.** Praeterea seditiosi magistratus volgum exagitare, Metellum omnibus contionibus capitis arcessere, Marii virtutem in maius celebrare. **6.** Denique plebes sic accensa, uti opifices agrestesque omnes, quorum res fidesque in manibus sitae erant, relictis operibus frequentarent Marium, et sua necessaria post illius honorem ducerent. **7.** Ita perculsa nobilitate post multas tempestates novo homini consulatus mandatur; et postea populus a tribuno plebis Manlio Mancino rogatus quem vellet cum Iugurtha bellum gerere, frequens Marium iussit. Sed senatus paulo ante Metello Numidiam decreverat: ea res frustra fuit.

[LXXIV–LXXIX. Metellus captured the town of Thala. Digression on the early history of Carthage and Cyrene.]

LXXX–LXXXIII. *Jugurtha, driven out of Numidia, appeals for help to Bocchus, king of Mauretania.*

LXXX. Iugurtha postquam amissa Thala nihil satis firmum contra Metellum putat, per magnas solitudines cum paucis profectus pervenit ad Gaetulos, genus hominum ferum incultumque et eo tempore ignarum nominis Romani. **2.** Eorum multitudinem in unum cogit, ac paulatim consuefacit ordines habere, signa sequi, imperium observare, item alia militaria facere. **3.** Praeterea regis Bocchi proxumos magnis muneribus et maioribus promissis ad studium sui perducit; quis adiutoribus regem aggressus impellit uti advorsum Romanos bellum suscipiat. **4.** Id ea gratia facilius proniusque fuit, quod Bocchus initio huiusce belli legatos Romam miserat, foedus et amicitiam petitum; **5.** quam rem opportunissumam incepto bello pauci impediverant, caeci avaritia, 'quis omnia, honesta atque inhonesta, vendere mos erat. Etiam antea Iugurthae filia

Bocchi nupserat. **6.** Verum ea necessitudo apud Numidas Maurosque levis ducitur; quod singuli, pro opibus quisque quam plurumas uxores, denas alii, alii pluris habent; sed reges eo amplius. **7.** Ita animus multitudine distrahitur; nulla pro socia obtinet; pariter omnes viles sunt.

LXXXI. Igitur in locum ambobus placitum exercitus conveniunt; ibi, fide data et accepta, Iugurtha Bocchi animum oratione accendit: Romanos iniustos, profunda avaritia, communis omnium hostis esse: eandem illos causam belli cum Boccho habere, quam secum et cum aliis gentibus, lubidinem imperitandi, quis omnia regna advorsa sint: tum sese, paulo ante Carthaginienses, item regem Persen, post uti quisque opulentissumus videatur, ita Romanis hostem fore. **2.** His atque aliis talibus dictis ad Cirtam oppidum iter constituunt, quod ibi Metellus praedam captivosque et impedimenta locaverat. **3.** Ita Iugurtha ratus aut capta urbe operae pretium fore aut si Romanus auxilio suis venisset, proelio sese certaturos. **4.** Nam callidus id modo festinabat, Bocchi pacem imminuere, ne moras agitando aliud quam bellum mallet.

LXXXII. Imperator postquam de regum societate cognovit, non temere neque, uti saepe iam victo Iugurtha consueverat, omnibus locis pugnandi copiam facit; ceterum haud procul ab Cirta castris munitis reges opperitur; melius ratus cognitis Mauris, quoniam is novos hostis accesserat, ex commodo pugnam facere. **2.** Interim Roma per litteras certior fit provinciam Numidiam Mario datam: nam consulem factum ante acceperat. Quis rebus supra bonum atque honestum perculsus, neque lacrimas tenere, neque moderari linguam: vir egregius in aliis artibus nimis molliter aegritudinem pati. **3.** Quam rem alii in superbiam vortebant, alii bonum ingenium contumelia accensum esse, multi, quod iam parta victoria ex manibus eriperetur; nobis satis cognitum est, illum magis honore Marii quam iniuria sua excruciatum, neque tam anxie laturum fuisse, si adempta provincia alii quam Mario traderetur.

LXXXIII. Igitur eo dolore impeditus, et quia stultitiae videbatur alienam rem periculo suo curare, legatos ad Bocchum mittit postulatum ne sine causa hostis populo Romano fieret; habere tum magnam copiam societatis amicitiaeque coniungendae, quae potior bello esset; quamquam opibus confideret, non debere incerta pro certis mutare; omne bellum sumi facile, ceterum aegerrume desinere; non in eiusdem potestate initium eius et finem esse: incipere cuivis, etiam ignavo, licere; deponi, cum victores velint: proinde sibi regnoque consuleret, neu florentis res suas cum Iugurthae perditis misceret. 2. Ad ea rex satis placide verba facit: sese pacem cupere, sed Iugurthae fortunarum misereri; si eadem illi copia fieret, omnia conventura. 3. Rursus imperator contra postulata Bocchi nuntios mittit: ille probare, partim abnuere. Eo modo saepe ab utroque missis remissisque nuntiis tempus procedere, et ex Metelli voluntate, bellum intactum trahi.

LXXXIV–LXXXVI. *Marius, consul in Rome, enlists his reinforcements. Speech of Marius to the people.*

LXXXIV. At Marius, ut supra diximus, cupientissuma plebe consul factus, postquam ei provinciam Numidiam populus iussit, ante iam infestus nobilitati, tum vero multus atque ferox instare; singulos modo, modo univorsos laedere; dictitare sese consulatum ex victis illis spolia cepisse; alia praeterea magnifica pro se, et illis dolentia. 2. Interim, quae bello opus erant, prima habere; postulare legionibus supplementum, auxilia a populis et regibus sociisque arcessere; praeterea ex Latio fortissumum quemque, plerosque militiae, paucos fama cognitos accire, et ambiundo cogere homines emeritis stipendiis secum proficisci. 3. Neque illi senatus, quamquam advorsus erat, de ullo negotio abnuere audebat; ceterum supplementum etiam laetus decreverat, quia neque plebi militia volenti putabatur, et Marius aut belli usum aut studia volgi amissurus. Sed ea res frustra sperata; tanta lubido cum Mario eundi plerosque invaserat. 4. Sese quisque praeda locupletem fore, victorem domum rediturum, alia huiuscemodi, animis trahebant: et eos non paulum oratione sua Marius arrexerat. 5. Nam postquam, omnibus quae postulaverat decretis, milites scribere vult, hortandi causa, simul et nobilitatem, uti consueverat, exagitandi, contionem populi advocavit. Deinde hoc modo disseruit.

LXXXV. 'Scio ego, Quirites, plerosque non isdem artibus imperium a vobis petere et, postquam adepti sunt, gerere; primo industrios, supplices, modicos esse; deinde per ignaviam et superbiam aetatem agere. Sed mihi contra ea videtur; 2. nam quo universa respublica pluris est quam consulatus aut praetura, eo maiore cura illam administrari quam haec peti debere. 3. Neque me fallit, quantum cum maxumo beneficio vostro negotii sustineam. Bellum parare simul et aerario parcere; cogere ad militiam eos quos nolis offendere; domi forisque omnia curare; et ea agere inter invidos, occursantis, factiosos, opinione, Quirites, asperius est. 4. Ad hoc alii si deliquere, vetus nobilitas, maiorum fortia facta, cognatorum et adfinium opes, multae clientelae, omnia haec praesidio adsunt: mihi spes omnes in memet sitae, quas necesse est et virtute et innocentia tutari: nam alia infirma sunt. **5.** Et illud intellego, Quirites, omnium ora in me convorsa esse; aequos bonosque favere: quippe bene facta mea reipublicae procedunt: nobilitatem locum invadundi quaerere. **6.** Quo mihi acrius adnitundum est, ut neque vos capiamini, et illi frustra sint. **7.** Ita ad hoc aetatis a pueritia fui, ut omnis labores, pericula consueta habeam. **8.** Quae ante vostra beneficia gratuito faciebam, ea uti accepta mercede deseram, non est consilium, Quirites. **9.** Illis difficile est in potestatibus temperare, qui per ambitionem sese probos simulavere; mihi, qui omnem aetatem in optumis artibus egi, bene facere iam ex consuetudine in naturam vortit. **10.** Bellum me gerere cum Iugurtha iussistis; quam rem nobilitas aegerrume tulit. Quaeso, reputate cum animis vostris, num id mutare melius sit, si quem ex illo globo nobilitatis ad hoc aut aliud tale negotium mittatis, hominem veteris prosapiae ac multarum imaginum et nullius stipendii: scilicet, ut in tanta re ignarus omnium trepidet, festinet, sumat aliquem ex populo monitorem officii sui. **1.** Ita plerumque evenit, ut quem vos imperare iussistis, is sibi imperatorem alium quaerat. **12.** Atque ego scio, Quirites, qui, postquam consules facti sunt, acta maiorum, et Graecorum militaria praecepta legere coeperint; homines praeposteri. Nam gerere quam fieri tempore posterius, re atque usu prius est. **13.** Comparate nunc, Quirites, cum illorum superbia me hominem novum. Quae illi audire et legere solent, eorum partem vidi, alia egomet gessi; quae illi litteris, ego militando didici. **14.** Nunc vos existimate, facta an dicta pluris sint. Contemnunt novitatem meam; ego illorum ignaviam: mihi fortuna, illis probra obiectantur; quamquam ego naturam unam et communem omnium

existumo, sed fortissumum quemque generosissumum.
16. Ac si iam ex patribus Albini aut Bestiae quaeri posset
mene an illos ex se gigni maluerint, quid responsuros credi-
tis, nisi sese liberos quam optumos voluisse? **17.** Quod si iure
me despiciunt, faciant idem maioribus suis, quibus, uti
mihi, ex virtute nobilitas coepit. Invident honori meo;
18. ergo invideant labori, innocentiae, periculis etiam meis,
quoniam per haec illum cepi. **19.** Verum homines cor-
rupti superbia ita aetatem agunt, quasi vostros honores
contemnant; ita hos petunt, quasi honeste vixerint. **20.**
Ne illi falsi sunt, qui diversissumas res pariter exspec-
tant, ignaviae voluptatem et praemia virtutis. **21.** Atque
etiam cum apud vos aut in senatu verba faciunt, pleraque
oratione maiores suos extollunt; eorum fortia facta memo-
rando clariores sese putant. **22.** Quod contra est: nam quanto vita illorum praeclarior, tanto horum socordia flagitiosior.
Et profecto ita se res habet; **23.** maiorum gloria pos-
teris lumen est, neque bona neque mala in occulto patitur.
24. Huiusce rei ego inopiam patior, Quirites; verum, id
quod multo praeclarius est, meamet facta mihi dicere
licet. **25.** Nunc videte, quam iniqui sint. Quod ex aliena
virtute sibi arrogant, id mihi ex mea non concedunt: scilicet, quia imagines non habeo, et quia mihi nova nobilitas
est; quam certe peperisse melius est, quam acceptam corru-
pisse. **26.** Equidem ego non ignoro, si iam respondere
velint, abunde illis facundam et compositam orationem
fore. Sed in maxumo vostro beneficio cum omnibus locis
me vosque maledictis lacerent, non placuit reticere, ne quis
modestiam in conscientiam duceret. **27.** Nam me quidem,
ex animi mei sententia nulla oratio laedere potest: quippe
vera necesse est bene praedicet; **28.** falsam vita mores-
que mei superant. Sed quoniam vostra consilia accusan-

tur, qui mihi summum honorem et maxumum negotium imposuistis, etiam atque etiam reputate, num eorum paenitendum sit. **29.** Non possum fidei causa imagines neque triumphos aut consulatus maiorum meorum ostentare; at, si res postulet, hastas, vexillum, phaleras, alia militaria dona; praeterea, cicatrices advorso corpore. **30.** Hae sunt meae imagines, haec nobilitas, non hereditate relicta, ut illa illis, sed quae ego plurumis laboribus et periculis quaesivi. **31.** Non sunt composita verba mea; parvi id facio; ipsa se virtus satis ostendit: illis artificio opus est, uti turpia facta oratione tegant. **32.** Neque litteras Graecas didici: parum placebat eas discere, quippe quae ad virtutem doctoribus nihil profuerunt. **33.** At illa multo optuma reipublicae doctus sum: hostem ferire, praesidia agitare; nihil metuere, nisi turpem famam; hiemem et aestatem iuxta pati; humi requiescere; eodem tempore inopiam et laborem tolerare. **34.** His ego praeceptis milites hortabor: neque illos arte colam, me opulenter; neque gloriam meam, laborem illorum faciam. Hoc est utile, hoc civile imperium. **35.** Namque, cum tute per mollitiem agas, exercitum supplicio cogere, id est dominum, non imperatorem, esse. **36.** Haec atque talia maiores vostri faciundo seque remque publicam celebravere: **37.** quis nobilitas freta, ipsa dissimilis moribus, nos illorum aemulos contemnit; et omnis honores non ex merito, sed quasi debitos a vobis repetit. Ceterum homines superbissumi procul errant. **38.** Maiores eorum omnia quae licebat illis reliquere, divitias, imagines, memoriam sui praeclaram; virtutem non reliquere, neque poterant; ea sola neque datur dono, neque accipitur. **39.** Sordidum me et incultis moribus aiunt, quia parum scite convivium exorno, neque histrionem ullum, neque pluris pretii cocum quam villicum habeo; quae mihi lubet confiteri. **40.** Nam ex parente meo et ex aliis sanctis viris ita accepi, munditias mulieribus, viris laborem convenire, omnibusque bonis oportere plus gloriae, quam divitiarum esse; arma, non supellectilem decori esse. **41.** Quin ergo quod iuvat, quod carum aestimant, id semper faciant; ament, potent; ubi adulescentiam habuere, ibi senectutem agant, in conviviis, dediti ventri et turpissumae parti corporis; sudorem, pulverem, et alia talia, relinquant nobis, quibus illa epulis iucundiora sunt. **42.** Verum non est ita. Nam ubi se flagitiis dedecoravere turpissumi viri, bonorum praemia ereptum eunt. **43.** Ita iniustissume luxuria et ignavia, pessumae artes, illis, qui coluere eas, nihil officiunt; reipublicae innoxiae cladi sunt. **44.** Nunc, quoniam illis, quantum mores mei, non illorum flagitia poscebant, respondi, pauca de republica loquar. **45.** Primum omnium de Numidia bonum habetote animum, Quirites. Nam quae ad hoc tempus Iugurtham tutata sunt, omnia removistis, avaritiam, imperitiam, superbiam. Deinde exercitus ibi est locorum sciens; sed mehercule magis strenuos quam felix. **46.** Nam magna pars eius avaritia aut temeritate ducum attrita est. **47.** Quamobrem vos, quibus militaris est aetas, adnitimini mecum et capessite rempublicam; neque quemquam ex calamitate aliorum aut imperatorum superbia metus ceperit. Egomet in agmine, in proelio, consultor idem et socius periculi vobiscum adero; meque vosque in omnibus rebus iuxta geram. **48.** Et profecto dis iuvantibus omnia matura sunt, victoria, praeda, laus; quae si dubia aut procul essent, tamen omnis bonos reipublicae subvenire decebat. **49.** Etenim ignavia nemo immortalis factus, neque quisquam parens liberis uti aeterni forent optavit; magis, uti boni honestique vitam exigerent **50.** Plura dicerem, Quirites, si timidis virtutem verba adderent; nam strenuis abunde dictum puto.'

LXXXVI. Huiuscemodi oratione habita Marius postquam plebis animos arrectos videt, propere commeatu, stipendio, armis, aliis utilibus navis onerat: cum his A. Manlium legatum proficisci iubet. Ipse interea milites scribere, non more maiorum, neque ex classibus, sed uti cuiusque lubido erat, capite censos plerosque. **3.** Id factum alii inopia bonorum, alii per ambitionem consulis memorabant, quod ab eo genere celebratus auctusque erat; et homini potentiam quaerenti egentissumus quisque opportunissumus, cui neque sua curae, quippe quae nulla sunt, et omnia cum pretio honesta videntur. **4.** Igitur Marius cum maiore aliquanto numero, quam decretum erat, in Africam profectus diebus paucis Uticam advehitur. **5.** Exercitus ei traditur a P. Rutilio legato; nam Metellus conspectum Marii fugerat, ne videret ea quae audita animus tolerare nequiverat.

LXXXVII – XCII 4. *Marius' campaigns in Africa; capture of Capsa.*

LXXXVII. Sed consul, expletis legionibus cohortibusque auxiliariis, in agrum fertilem et praeda onustum proficiscitur: omnia ibi capta militibus donat; dein castella et oppida natura et viris parum munita aggreditur: proelia multa, ceterum levia, alia aliis locis facere. **2.** Interim novi milites sine metu pugnae adesse; videre fugientis capi, occidi; fortissumum quemque tutissumum; armis libertatem, patriam, parentesque et alia omnia tegi; gloriam atque divitias quaeri. **3.** Sic brevi spatio novi veteresque coaluere, et virtus omnium aequalis facta. **4.** At reges, ubi de adventu Marii cognoverunt, divorsi in locos difficilis abeunt. Ita Iugurthae placuerat, speranti mox effusos hostis invadi posse; Romanos, sicuti plerosque, remoto metu laxius licentiusque futuros. LXXXVIII. Metellus interea Romam profectus contra spem suam laetissumis animis excipitur; plebi patribusque, postquam invidia decesserat, iuxta carus. **2.** Sed Marius impigre prudenterque suorum et hostium res pariter attendere; cognoscere quid boni utrisque aut contra esset; explorare itinera regum, consilia et insidias antevenire; nihil apud se remissum, neque apud illos tutum pati. **3.** Itaque et Gaetulos et Iugurtham ex sociis nostris praedam agentis saepe aggressus in itinere fuderat, ipsumque regem haud procul ab oppido Cirta armis exuerat. **4.** Quae postquam gloriosa modo, neque belli patrandi, cognovit, statuit urbis, quae viris aut loco pro hostibus et advorsum se opportunissumae erant, singulas circumvenire: ita Iugurtham aut praesidiis nudatum, si ea pateretur, aut proelio certaturum. **5.** Nam Bocchus nuntios ad eum saepe miserat, velle populi Romani amicitiam, ne quid ab se hostile timeret. **6.** Id simulaveritne, quo improvisus gravior accideret, an mobilitate ingenii pacem atque bellum mutare solitus, parum exploratum est.

LXXXIX. Sed consul, uti statuerat, oppida castellaque munita adire; partim vi, alia metu aut praemia ostentando avortere ab hostibus. **2.** Ac primo mediocria gerebat, existumans Iugurtham ob suos tutandos in manus venturum. **3.** Sed ubi illum procul abesse et aliis negotiis intentum accepit, maiora et magis aspera aggredi tempus visum est. **4.** Erat inter ingentis solitudines oppidum magnum atque valens, nomine Capsa, cuius conditor Hercules Libys memorabatur. Eius cives apud Iugurtham immunes, levi imperio, et ob ea fidelissumi habebantur, muniti advorsum hostes non moenibus modo et armis atque viris, verum etiam multo magis locorum asperitate. **5.** Nam praeter oppido propinqua alia omnia vasta, inculta, egentia aquae, infesta serpentibus; quarum vis, sicuti omnium ferarum, inopia cibi acrior; ad hoc natura serpentium, ipsa perniciosa, siti magis quam alia re accenditur. **6.** Eius potiundi Marium maxima cupido invaserat, cum propter usum belli, tum quia res aspera videbatur; et Metellus oppidum Thalam magna gloria ceperat, haud dissimiliter situm munitumque, nisi quod apud Thalam haud longe a moenibus aliquot fontes erant, Capsenses una modo, atque ea intra oppidum, iugi aqua, cetera pluvia utebantur. **7.** Id ibique et in omni Africa, quae procul a mari incultius agebat, eo facilius tolerabatur, quia Numidae plerumque lacte et ferina carne vescebantur, neque salem neque alia irritamenta gulae quaerebant; cibus illis advorsum famem atque sitim, non lubidini neque luxuriae erat.

XC. Igitur consul, omnibus exploratis, credo dis fretus (nam contra tantas difficultates satis providere consilio non poterat; quippe etiam frumenti inopia tentabatur, quod Numidae pabulo pecoris magis quam arvo student, et, quodcumque natum fuerat iussu regis in loca munita contulerant, ager autem aridus et frugum vacuos ea tempestate, nam aestatis extremum erat); tamen pro rei copia satis providenter exornat;[2] pecus omne, quod superioribus diebus praedae fuerat, equitibus auxiliariis agundum attribuit, A. Manlium legatum cum cohortibus expeditis ad oppidum Laris, ubi stipendium et commeatum locaverat, ire iubet; se praedabundum post paucos dies eodem venturum. **3.** Sic incepto suo occultato pergit ad flumen Tanain.

XCI. Ceterum in itinere cotidie pecus exercitui per centurias, item turmas aequaliter distribuerat, et ex coriis utres uti fierent curabat; simul et inopiam frumenti lenire, et ignaris omnibus parare, quae mox usui forent. Denique sexto die, cum ad flumen ventum est, maxuma vis utrium effecta. 2 Ibi castris levi munimento positis, milites cibum capere, atque uti simul cum occasu solis egrederentur, paratos esse iubet omnibus sarcinis abiectis, aqua modo seque et iumenta onerare. 3. Dein, postquam tempus visum, castris egreditur, noctemque totam itinere facto consedit: idem proxuma facit: dein tertia multo ante lucis adventum pervenit in locum tumulosum, ab Capsa non amplius duum milium intervallo; ibique quam occultissume potest cum omnibus copiis opperitur. 4. Sed ubi dies coepit, et Numidae, nihil hostile metuentes, multi oppido egressi, repente omnem equitatum, et cum his velocissumos pedites cursu tendere ad Capsam et portas obsidere, iubet; deinde ipse intentus propere sequi, neque milites praedari sinere. 5. Quae postquam oppidani cognovere, res trepidae, metus ingens, malum improvisum, ad hoc pars civium extra moenia in hostium potestate, coegere, uti deditionem facerent. 6. Ceterum oppidum incensum; Numidae puberes interfecti; alii omnes venum dati; praeda militibus divisa. 7. Id facinus contra ius belli non avaritia neque scelere consulis admissum; sed quia locus Iugurthae opportunus, nobis aditu difficilis, genus hominum mobile, infidum, neque beneficio neque metu coërcitum.

XCII. Postquam tantam rem Marius sine ullo suorum incommodo patravit, magnus et clarus antea, maior et clarior haberi coepit. 2. Omnia, non bene consulta modo, verum etiam casu data in virtutem trahebantur; milites, modesto imperio habiti simul et locupletes, ad caelum ferre; Numidae magis quam mortalem timere; postremo omnes, socii atque hostes, credere illi aut mentem divinam esse, aut deorum nutu cuncta portendi. **3.** Sed consul, ubi ea res bene evenit, ad alia oppida pergit, pauca repugnantibus Numidis capit, plura, deserta propter Capsensium miserias, igni corrumpit: luctu atque caede omnia complentur. **4.** Denique multis locis potitus, ac plerisque exercitu incruento, aliam rem aggreditur, non eadem asperitate qua Capsensium, ceterum haud secus difficilem.

3 *Sulla and the End of the War*

[XCII5–XCIV. The attacks on the fort fail; Marius is frustrated 'for many days'. At length a Ligurian soldier finds an unexpected way up the back and the fort is taken.]

XCV–CII4. *The arrival of Sulla. Attacks by the joint forces of Jugurtha and Bocchus are defeated.*

XCV. Ceterum dum ea res geritur, L. Sulla quaestor cum magno equitatu in castra venit; quos uti ex Latio et a sociis cogeret Romae relictus erat. Sed quoniam tanti viri res admonuit, idoneum visum est de natura cultuque eius paucis dicere; neque enim alio loco de Sullae rebus dicturi sumus; et L. Sisenna, optume et diligentissume omnium qui eas dixere persecutus, parum mihi libero ore locutus videtur. **3.** Igitur Sulla gentis patriciae nobilis fuit, familia prope iam exstincta maiorum ignavia; **3.** litteris Graecis atque Latinis iuxta atque doctissume eruditus, animo ingenti, cupidus voluptatum, sed gloriae cupidior; otio luxurioso esse; tamen ab negotiis numquam voluptas remorata, nisi quod de uxore potuit honestius consuli; facundus, callidus, et amicitia facilis; ad simulanda negotia altitudo ingenii incredibilis; multarum rerum ac maxume pecuniae largitor. **4.** Atque illi, felicissumo omnium ante civilem victoriam, numquam super industriam fortuna fuit; multique dubitavere, fortior an felicior esset: nam postea quae fecerit incertum habeo pudeat magis an pigeat disserere.

XCVI. Igitur Sulla, uti supra dictum est, postquam in Africam atque in castra Marii cum equitatu venit, rudis antea et ignarus belli, sollertissumus omnium in paucis tempestatibus factus est. **2.** Ad hoc milites benigne appellare; multis rogantibus, aliis per se ipse dare beneficia, invitus accipere, sed ea properantius quam aes mutuom reddere; ipse ab nullo repetere, magis id laborare ut illi quam plurumi deberent; ioca atque seria cum humillumis agere; **3.** in operibus, in agmine, atque ad vigilias multus adesse, neque interim, quod prava ambitio solet, consulis, aut cuiusquam boni, famam laedere; tantummodo neque consilio neque manu priorem alium pati, plerosque antevenire. **4.** Quibus rebus et artibus brevi Mario militibusque carissumus factus.

XCVII. At Iugurtha, postquam oppidum Capsam aliosque locos munitos et sibi utilis, simul et magnam pecuniam amiserat, ad Bocchum nuntios mittit: quam primum in Numidiam copias adduceret; proelii faciundi tempus adesse. **2.** Quem ubi cunctari accepit et dubium belli atque pacis rationes trahere, rursus, uti antea, proxumos eius donis corrumpit, ipsique Mauro pollicetur Numidiae partem tertiam, si aut Romani Africa expulsi, aut integris suis finibus bellum compositum foret. **3.** Eo praemio illectus Bocchus cum magna multitudine Iugurtham accedit. Ita amborum exercitu coniuncto Marium, iam in hiberna proficiscentem, vix decima parte die reliqua, invadunt, rati noctem, quae iam aderat, et victis sibi munimento fore, et si vicissent nullo impedimento, quia locorum scientes erant; contra Romanis utrumque casum in tenebris difficiliorem fore. **4.** Igitur simul consul ex multis de hostium adventu cognovit, et ipsi hostes aderant; et, priusquam exercitus aut instrui, aut sarcinas colligere, denique antequam signum aut imperium ullum accipere quivit, equites Mauri atque Gaetuli, non acie neque ullo more proelii, sed catervatim, uti quosque fors conglobaverat, in nostros concurrunt; **5.** qui omnes trepidi improviso metu, ac tamen virtutis memores, aut arma capiebant, aut capientis alios ab hostibus defensabant; pars equos escendere, obviam ire hostibus; pugna latrocinio magis quam proelio similis fieri; sine signis, sine ordinibus, equites pedites permixti caedere alios, alios obtruncare, multos, contra advorsos acerrume pugnantes, ab tergo circumvenire; neque virtus neque arma satis tegere, quod hostes numero plures et undique circumfusi; denique Romani novi veteresque et ob ea scientes belli, si quos locus aut casus coniunxerat, orbis facere; atque ita ab omnibus partibus simul tecti et instructi hostium vim sustentabant.

XCVIII. Neque in eo tam aspero negotio territus, Marius aut magis, quam antea, demisso animo fuit, sed cum turma sua, quam ex fortissumis magis quam familiarissumis paraverat, vagari passim, ac modo laborantibus suis succurrere, modo hostis, ubi confertissumi obstiterant, invadere; manu consulere militibus, quoniam imperare conturbatis omnibus non poterat. **2.** Iamque dies consumptus erat, cum tamen barbari nihil remittere, atque, uti reges praeceperant, noctem pro se rati, acrius instare. **3.** Tum Marius ex copia rerum consilium trahit, atque, uti suis receptui locus esset, collis duos propinquos inter se occupat; quorum in uno, castris parum amplo, fons aquae magnus erat, alter usui opportunus, quia magna parte editus et praeceps pauca munimenta quaerebat. **4.** Ceterum apud aquam Sullam cum equitibus noctem agitare iubet; ipse paulatim dispersos milites, neque minus hostibus conturbatis, in unum contrahit; dein cunctos pleno gradu in collem subducit. **5.** Ita reges loci difficultate coacti, proelio deterrentur; neque tamen suos longius abire sinunt, sed utroque colle multitudine circumdato effusi consedere. **6.** Dein crebris ignibus factis plerumque noctis barbari suo more laetari, exsultare, strepere vocibus, et ipsi duces feroces, quia non fugerant, pro victoribus agere. **7.** Sed ea cuncta Romanis ex tenebris et editioribus locis facilia visu magnoque hortamento erant.

XCIX. Plurumum vero Marius imperitia hostium confirmatus quam maxumum silentium haberi iubet; ne signa quidem, uti per vigilias solebant, canere. Deinde, ubi lux adventabat, defessis iam hostibus et paulo ante somno captis, de improviso vigiles, item cohortium, turmarum, legionum tubicines simul omnes signa canere, milites clamorem tollere atque portis erumpere. **2.** Mauri atque Gaetuli, ignoto et horribili sonitu repente exciti, neque fugere neque arma capere neque omnino facere aut providere quidquam poterant; **3.** ita cunctos strepitu, clamore, nullo subveniente, nostris instantibus, tumultu, terrore formido quasi vecordia ceperat. Denique omnes fusi fugatique, arma et signa militaria pleraque capta, pluresque eo proelio quam omnibus superioribus interempti; nam somno et metu insolito impedita fuga.

C. Dein Marius, uti coeperat, in hiberna proficiscitur; quae propter commeatum in oppidis maritumis agere decreverat; neque tamen victoria socors aut insolens factus; sed pariter atque in conspectu hostium quadrato agmine incedere. **2.** Sulla cum equitatu apud dextumos, in sinistra A. Manlius cum funditoribus et sagittariis, praeterea cohortis Ligurum curabat; primos et extremos cum expeditis manipulis tribunos locaverat. **3.** Perfugae, minume cari et regionum scientissumi, hostium iter explorabant; simul consul, quasi nullo imposito, omnia providere; apud omnis adesse; laudare, increpare merentis. **4.** Ipse armatus intentusque, item milites cogebat; neque secus atque iter facere, castra munire, excubitum in portas cohortis ex legionibus, pro castris equites auxiliarios mittere; praeterea alios super vallum in munimentis locare, vigilias ipse circumire, non tam diffidentia futurum, quae imperavisset, quam uti militibus exaequatus cum imperatore labos volentibus esset. **5.** Et sane Marius illo et aliis temporibus Iugurthini belli pudore magis quam malo exercitum coercebat; quod multi per ambitionem fieri aiebant, pars, quod a pueritia consuetam duritiam et alia, quae ceteri miserias vocant, voluptati habuisset: nisi tamen res publica, pariter ac saevissumo imperio, bene atque decore gesta.

CI. Igitur quarto denique die haud longe ab oppido Cirta undique simul speculatores citi sese ostendunt, qua re hostis adesse intellegitur. **2.** Sed quia divorsi redeuntes, alius ab alia parte atque omnes idem significabant, consul incertus, quonam modo aciem instrueret, nullo ordine commutato, advorsum omnia paratus ibidem opperitur. **3.** Ita Iugurtham spes frustrata, qui copias in quattuor partis distribuerat, ratus ex omnibus aeque aliquos ab tergo hostibus venturos. **4.** Interim Sulla, quem primum hostes attigerant, cohortatus suos, turmatim et quam maxume confertis equis ipse aliique Mauros invadunt, ceteri in loco

manentes ab iaculis eminus emissis corpora tegere, et si
qui in manus venerant obtruncare. **5.** Dum eo modo
equites proeliantur, Bocchus cum peditibus, quos Volux
filius eius adduxerat, neque in priore pugna, in itinere
morati, affuerant, postremam Romanorum aciem invadunt.
6. Tum Marius apud primos agebat, quod ibi Iugurtha
cum plurimis erat. Dein Numida, cognito Bocchi adventu,
clam cum paucis ad pedites convortit; ibi Latine (nam
apud Numantiam loqui didicerat) exclamat nostros frustra
pugnare; paulo ante Marium sua manu interfectum;
simul gladium sanguine oblitum ostendere, quem in pugna
satis impigre occiso pedite nostro cruentaverat. **7.** Quod
ubi milites accepere, magis atrocitate rei quam fide nuntii
terrentur: simulque barbari animos tollere, et in perculsos
Romanos acrius incedere. **8.** Iamque paulum ab fuga
aberant, cum Sulla, profligatis iis quos advorsum ierat,
Mauris ab latere incurrit. Bocchus statim avortitur. **9.** At
Iugurtha, dum sustentare suos et prope iam adeptam victoriam retinere cupit, circumventus ab equitibus dextra, sinistra
omnibus occisis, solus inter tela hostium vitabundus erum-
pit. **10.** Atque interim Marius fugatis equitibus occurrit
auxilio suis, quos pelli iam acceperat. **11.** Denique hostes
undique fusi. Tum spectaculum horribile in campis paten-
tibus: sequi, fugere, occidi, capi; equi, viri afflicti, ac multi
vulneribus acceptis neque fugere posse, neque quietem pati;
niti modo, ac statim concidere; postremo omnia, qua visus
erat, constrata telis, armis, cadaveribus, et inter ea humus
infecta sanguine.

    CII. Postea loci consul haud dubie iam victor pervenit
in oppidum Cirtam, quo initio profectus intenderat. **2.** Eo
post diem quintum quam iterum barbari male pugnaverant,
legati a Boccho veniunt, qui regis verbis ab Mario peti-

vere, duo quam fidissumos ad eum mitteret: velle de suo
et de populi Romani commodo cum iis disserere.   **3** Ille
statim L. Sullam et A. Manlium ire iubet. Qui quamquam acciti ibant, tamen placuit verba apud regem facere,
uti ingenium aut avorsum flecterent, aut cupidum pacis
vehementius accenderent. **4.** Itaque Sulla, cuius facundiae,
non aetati, a Manlio concessum, pauca verba huiuscemodi
locutus.

[CII 5–CX. Diplomacy then took over. An embassy was sent to
Rome, where the senate agreed to make a treaty with Bocchus 'when
he had earned it'. Sulla again went to Bocchus, who promised to cease
helping Jugurtha and to retire behind his frontier.]

CXI–CXIV. *Bocchus eventually agrees to surrender Jugurtha to the Romans,
and after much hesitation he keeps his word to Sulla. The war over, Marius is elected consul for the second time, and returns to defend Italy from invasion from the
north.*

CXI. Ad ea Sulla pro se breviter et modice, de pace et
de communibus multis disseruit. Denique regi patefecit,
quod polliceatur, senatum et populum Romanum, quoniam amplius armis valuissent, non in gratiam habituros:
faciundum aliquid, quod illorum magis quam sua retulisse videretur; id adeo in promptu esse, quoniam Iugurthae copiam haberet; quem si Romanis tradidisset, fore
uti illi plurumum deberetur; amicitiam, foedus, Numidiae
partem quam nunc peteret, tunc ultro adventuram. **2.** Rex
primo negitare: adfinitatem, cognationem, praeterea foedus intervenisse; ad hoc metuere, ne fluxa fide usus, popularium animos avorteret, quis et Iugurtha carus, et Romani invisi erant. **3.** Denique saepius fatigatus lenitur, et ex
voluntate Sullae omnia se facturum promittit. **4.** Ceterum

ad simulandam pacem, cuius Numida defessus bello avidis-
sumus erat quae utilia visa constituunt. Ita composito
dolo digrediuntur.

CXII. At rex postero die Asparem, Iugurthae legatum,
appellat, dicitque sibi per Dabarem ex Sulla cognitum
posse condicionibus bellum poni; quamobrem regis sui
sententiam exquireret. 2. Ille laetus in castra Iugurthae
venit. Deinde, ab illo cuncta edoctus, properato itinere
post diem octavom redit ad Bocchum, et ei nuntiat Iugurtham cupere omnia quae imperarentur facere; sed Mario
parum fidere: saepe antea cum imperatoribus Romanis
pacem conventam frustra fuisse. 3. Ceterum si ambobus
consultum et ratam pacem vellet, daret operam ut una ab
omnibus quasi de pace in colloquium veniretur, ibique
sibi Sullam traderet; cum talem virum in potestate haberet, tum fore uti iussu senatus atque populi Romani foedus fieret: neque hominem nobilem, non sua ignavia sed
ob rempublicam, in hostium potestate relictum iri.

CXIII. Haec Maurus secum ipse diu volvens tandem
promisit; ceterum dolo an vere cunctatus, parum comperimus. Sed plerumque regiae voluntates, ut vehementes, sic
mobiles, saepe ipsae sibi adversae. 2. Postea tempore et
loco constituto, in colloquium uti de pace veniretur, Bocchus Sullam modo, modo Iugurthae legatum appellare,
benigne habere, idem ambobus polliceri. Illi pariter laeti,
ac spei bonae pleni. 3. Sed nocte ea, quae proxuma fuit
ante diem colloquio decretum, Maurus adhibitis amicis, ac
statim inmutata voluntate remotis, dicitur secum ipse multa
agitavisse, vultu pariter atque animo varius; quae scilicet,
tacente ipso, occulta pectoris patefecisse. 4. Tamen postremo
Sullam accersiri iubet, et ex eius sententia Numidae
insidias tendit. Deinde, ubi dies advenit, et ei nuntiatum

est Iugurtham haud procul abesse, cum paucis amicis et quaestore nostro, quasi obvius honoris causa procedit in tumulum facillumum visu insidiantibus. **6.** Eodem Numida cum plerisque necessariis suis inermis, uti dictum erat, accedit; ac statim signo dato undique simul ex insidiis invaditur. **7.** Ceteri obtruncati: Iugurtha Sullae vinctus traditur, et ab eo ad Marium deductus est.

CXIV. Per idem tempus advorsum Gallos ab ducibus nostris Q. Caepione et Cn. Manlio male pugnatum; quo metu Italia omnis contremuerat. **2.** Illique et inde ad nostram memoriam Romani sic habuere, alia omnia virtuti suae prona esse; cum Gallis pro salute, non pro gloria certare. **3.** Sed postquam bellum in Numidia confectum et Iugurtham vinctum adduci Romam nuntiatum est, Marius consul absens factus, et ei decreta provincia Gallia; isque Kalendis Ianuariis magna gloria consul triumphavit. **4.** Ea tempestate spes atque opes civitatis in illo sitae.

Notes

Bellum scripturus: this is the real beginning of the *Jugurtha*; this opening statement recalls the beginning of Thucydides' *History of the Peloponnesian War*.

Numidarum: the Latin for a Numidian is first declension.

primum: of the two reasons given, the second is to Sallust the more important.

victoria: ablative.

tum primum: not really true; Gaius Gracchus had a strong bias against the nobility. But he did not have any of them condemned to death, and they appeared in 120 to have survived his attack.

nobilitatis: among politicians the word *nobilis* has an exact meaning, that among a man's ancestors was one who had held the consulship (the praetorship gave a kind of second-class nobility); this meaning was beginning to be accepted at the time of the Jugurthine War, and was normal in Sallust's time.

2. **cuncta:** all things, whether sacred or profane. Sallust is well equipped with words describing violence and confusion.

   eo: adverb: 'to such a state of . . .'.

   bellum atque vastitas Italiae: this could be that the dissensions of Jugurtha's lifetime ended in the Social War and the victory of Sulla, or, on a longer view, that the struggle began which culminated in the Civil Wars of 49–45, and of the triumviral period in which Sallust is writing.

3. **repetam:** the usual verb for going back to the beginning of a story; often *altius repetere*.

   ad cognoscundum: 'for our understanding'; the old spelling of the gerund regularly used by Sallust (see p. xxxiv).

4. **post magnitudinem . . . maxume:** 'the greatest disaster since Rome achieved greatness'.

   in amicitiam: this is the *amicitia populi Romani*, the honourable diplomatic relationship which in fact gradually transformed independent rulers into clients of Rome (see Introduction, p. xiii).

a P. Scipione: it was common for a foreign people, when dealing with the Roman senate, to rely on an influential senator to look after their interests and present their case. This personal element in Roman foreign policy has been described by Badian (*Foreign Clientelae*, ch. VII).

Africano: dative, in apposition with *cui*. This is the victor of Zama. It was his grandson, the younger Africanus, who advanced Masinissa's grandson Jugurtha.

facinora: this word is mostly used of crimes, but sometimes of distinguished acts which are not criminal; as a man who loved action Sallust uses it frequently.

Syphace: the king of Numidia who aided Carthage against the invasion of Scipio. His capture by Masinissa and the Romans is described in Livy XXX.

magnum atque late: adjective and adverb; Sallust's love of variety sometimes borders on the perverse.

dono: this predicative dative is frequently used with *dare*. The gift is described by Livy (XXX 44). The subject of *ceperat* is probably *populus Romanus*.

5. **finis idem:** a fine-sounding phrase, but all it seems to mean is that Masinissa did not abdicate. For the family tree see p. xv.

7. **dereliquerat:** this compound has the notion of abandoning.

VI

1. **pollens ... facie ... validus:** a typical variety of construction. Character-sketches were a recognised feature of Roman historical writing; see Introduction, p. xlvi.

luxu: the old dative of the fourth declension. Some MSS. have *luxui*, but, as usual, the more difficult reading is likely to be right: if Sallust had written *luxui*, no copyist would have been likely to change it to *luxu*.

equitare: this is the traditional education of the 'noble savage', intended as a contrast to that of the sophisticated and degenerate Romans. Sallust may be thinking of the education of a Persian noble, as described by Herodotus (I 136) – 'to ride, to shoot, to speak the truth'.

Three or more main verbs close together, without conjunctions, in the historic infinitive is a literary device frequent in Sallust. A succession of indicatives would be tedious and prosaic, and a succession of clauses would give the Ciceronian style which he is avoiding. An effective use of these infinitives is that which describes the violence of Chapter XII.

omnis: accusative plural.

ad hoc: 'in addition'.

2. **parvis liberis:** continues the ablative absolute.

3. **transvorsos:** 'astray'.

  interfecisset: he said to himself 'there may be a revolution *si interfecero*.

XII

1. **supra:** in Chapter XI.

2. **alio:** the adverb; they went in different directions.

  concessere: *cedo* is first of all a verb of motion.

3. **lictor:** Sallust naturally uses the Roman word for a magistrate's attendant.

  visens: *visere* means to go and see; its frequentative *visitare* is the origin of our word 'visit'.

  referebantur: 'used to be taken back' – every evening.

  postularet: a subordinate clause in indirect speech; Jugurtha said *postulabit*.

4. **brevi:** frequently used for *brevi tempore*.

5. **quaerere:** this sentence is a good example of the use of historic infinitives.

  dormientis alios, alios occursantis: this inversion of the order of words (sometimes called *chiasmus*, from the Greek letter χ) is one of Sallust's rhetorical tricks. It is normally used only when the sentence is short, and is not as common in other writers as is sometimes supposed.

  miscere: again this verb to indicate general chaos.

  reperitur: *cum* is in effect a relative starting a new sentence; the indicative therefore.

XIII

1. **Ceterum:** this word is frequently used by Sallust and Livy when a new paragraph or chapter continues the narrative; literally 'as for the rest'.

   facinoris: this word in its more usual sense of 'crime'.

   bello meliores: notably the tibesmen of the western part of the kingdom, which was eventually allotted to Jugurtha (see XVI 5 below).

2. **partim:** the combination of *partim* and *alius* is used also by Cicero. It will be found again in XL 2 below.

4. **provinciam:** the Roman province of Africa; it had been formed in 146 out of the territory of the defeated Carthage; not the province which Sallust later governed, which was Africa Nova, formed by Julius Caesar in 46.

5. **patratis:** one of Sallust's archaic words (Syme, p. 261). So also *tempestate*, below, in the sense of *time*.

   Numidiae: the genitive following *potior* is less common than the ablative and for perhaps that reason preferred by Sallust.

   avaritia ... pecunia: the real subject of the book makes its appearance.

6. **mittit:** the object is contained in the clause which follows.

   parare: this depends on *cunctentur*.

7. **auctoritas:** this word is especially used of the influence of the senator. Derived from *auctor* (which can be followed by an indirect command – *auctor est ut adsim*), it is a practical Roman word for prestige in action, and a favourite of Cicero.

   ex maxuma invidia: 'far from being very upopopular'.

8. **spe:** also dependent on *inducti*.

   ambiundo: a transitive verb, to go round asking favours of individuals; candidates for office at Rome were expected to canvass personally in the forum, and the noun *ambitus* became the regular word for electoral bribery.

   consuleretur: besides meaning to consult (i.e. to ask advice) *consulere* is used of the senate passing decrees (in theory, giving advice to magistrates); the decree is known as a *senatus consultum*.

9. **utrisque:** *uterque* in the singular for two individuals, in the plural for two groups; here Adherbal speaks for himself, but Jugurtha is represented by several envoys.

accepimus: 'we have heard', as often in Sallust, especially when not vouching for the exact truth.

XV

interfectum: for *interfectum esse*.

ultro: this word is used of doing something beyond what is required or expected. They are saying that Adherbal was the aggressor.

alium . . . ac: 'other than'. *alium* is for *se alium esse*.

Numantiae: when he had served with Scipio in Spain (see Introduction, p. xvii); the war had been ended by the capture of Numantia, and was sometimes called the *bellum Numantinum*.

2. **consulitur:** presumably by one of the consuls.

fautores: from the root of *faveo*.

praeterea: 'and following them'; the majority were corrupted by their influence.

3. **pauci:** here a word of approval; usually in Sallust it expresses hostility.

bonum et aequom: this use of the neuter adjective as an abstract noun is common in Thucydides, whom Sallust admired (when the vowel *u* followed the consonant *u* in the last syllable of a word it was spelt, and perhaps pronounced, *o*, at least in Republican times.).

4. **Aemilius Scaurus:** a short but somewhat contradictory character sketch. Scaurus had been consul in 115, and was now *princeps senatus* (i.e. in voting, his opinion was asked first). He was a pillar of the establishment and was often mentioned by Cicero as one of the heroes of the Republic (e.g. *pro Sestio* 101); Sallust gives a very different picture of the man, but one which is not easy to believe in; here Scaurus is on the right side, but his motives had to be bad; in the negotiations with Jugurtha Sallust believes the worst of him (Ch. XXIX), so that his appointment to the Mamilian commission (Ch. XL) comes to us a great surprise. It has been suggested (by Hands, in *JRS* XLIX 56) that Scaurus was a subtle and cautious politician, and that by temperament Cicero approved of him and that Sallust, a more forthright person, did not. His heroes were the men of action, Metellus Numidicus in the *Jugurtha*, Cato and Caesar in the *Catiline*. Sallust's portrayal of Scaurus is criticised by Earl (*JRS* LV 236). In Cicero's list of orators of this time (*Brutus*,

136) Scaurus is praised for his style: *Scaurus non saepe dicebat sed polite. Latine vero in primis est eleganter locutus.*

factiosus: a party man; Sallust uses **factio,** like *factio paucorum,* of the nobles (for his political vocabulary see Introduction, p. xxviii).

5. **polluta:** a strong word; some have suspected that our text is wrong, but in Ch. XLI Sallust has *avatitia . . . polluere . . . omnia.*

XVI

vero: dative.

2. **decem legati:** it was by this time the practice that, when a major piece of provincial organisation was to be done, a commission of ten senators should be sent out to make the detailed arrangements on the spot. This had been done for the provinces of Sicily in 131 and Asia in 129, and the charters of those provinces were named after the presidents of the commission, the *lex Rupilia* and *lex Aquilia* respectively. If Numidia had been made a province, the work of this commission would have been issued in a *lex Opimia*.

obtinuerat: a compound of *teneo,* 'to hold', not 'to get'.

consul: this was early in 121, when Gracchus was tribune. Opimius led the attack on the Aventine, in which the Gracchan party was massacred. In the following year he was prosecuted in the courts for putting Roman citizens to death, and pleaded that there was a state of emergency. His acquittal seemed to show that the nobles had recovered control. He was eventually condemned by the Mamilian commission (Ch. XL).

M. Fulvio Flacco: consul in 125; some consider him to have been the real leader of the Gracchan party.

exercuerat: the nobles followed up their victory on the Aventine by outlawing many Gracchan sympathisers.

3. **in inimicis:** another noble who had resisted Jugurtha's bribes, after all; and he had been made chairman of the commission. That *inimicis* is the right reading (the MSS. have *amicis*) is proved by *tametsi . . . tamen.* First, a copyist, confronted with *ininimicis,* writes *inimicis* (for another haplography see note on XXXI 23); later, when it is being copied again, this is divided into *in imicis,* and then naturally 'corrected' to *in amicis.* But the reading *in amicis* has been defended. We can assume that the Scipios and their

friends were friends of Jugurtha; beyond that it is not easy to pick sides.

accuratissume: 'with great formality'.

multa: as usual when the object is a neuter adjective; if you write *dandis multis* the gender is not clear.

fama: ablative because *anteferret* implies comparison.

5. **In divisione:** Sallust is determined to say that the commission favoured Jugurtha; in fact it can be taken as certain that East Numidia, which included the Bagradas valley and most of the towns, was richer than the west; *specie quam usu* is an attempt to disguise the facts. Subsequent events give the impression that even Cirta was in Adherbal's portion, in which case he has nearly all the agricultural wealth, as well as most of the towns. In fact it is difficult to see what is left for Jugurtha. This division is discussed in the Note on the Boundaries of Numidia on p. liv.

XX

contra timorem: contrary to what he had feared.

venalia: in Ch. VIII (not in this selection) Roman nobles in Spain had told Jugurtha *Romae omnia venalia esse.* The thought is repeated in Ch. XXVIII below, and again in the famous remark of Jugurtha when he leaves Rome after his visit *o urbem venalem et mature perituram si emptorem invenerit!*

2. **petebat:** *petere* often means to attack.

quietus: the opposite of *acer*; the comparison favours Jugurtha.

4. **convortit:** intransitive, an unusual use.

5. **neque:** this is *et non, et* meaning 'both' and making a pair with the following *et.*

amicitia: since the senatorial commission had established him in his kingdom. His father and grandfather had been *amici populi Romani* (see Introduction, p. xvi). Sallust does not see that if Adherbal had so litttle support in his own country he was an unreliable ally for the Romans.

secus: differently (from his expectations). The subject is *bellum.*

6. **eo:** as a result of this.

quippe: shows that *qui* is causal; by the time of Sallust, usually followed by the subjunctive.

animo: in his mind's eye.

XXI

eo . . . uti: 'so far that'.

2. **Interim:** 'for a while'.

Cirtam: see map on p. lxiv. This must be near the western end of Adherbal's kingdom. See also note on p. liv.

obscuro . . . lumine: ablative absolute.

fugant funduntque: these words are so frequently used together that even Sallust pairs them, though he does not often use two words where one would do.

profugit: this compound is used of taking refuge.

togatorum: a *togatus* may be a civilian (as opposed to a soldier), or an Italian (as opposed to a foreigner); here they are the local community of Italian – including Roman – businessmen. Roman writers tell us little about these people, and it comes as a surprise to find that they had so much influence in Cirta, but their activities in the Mediterranean world were beginning to be important. Their part in the election of Marius is described in Ch. LXIV 5.

3. **vineis:** *vineae* were shelters – wooden roofs covered with hides supported by posts – which were pushed up to the walls on rollers to protect the attackers who were battering at the wall or mining under it. *turres* enabled archers and javelin throwers to make the defenders take cover, and were either built on mounds or pushed up on rollers.

expugnare: infinitive after *aggreditur*.

tempus: the time needed for Adherbal's emissaries to reach Rome and the senate to take some action.

ante proelium factum: before the beginning of the battle; *ab Adherbale* with *missos*.

4. **tres adulescentes:** for the understanding of the next few chapters it is essential to know something of the Roman procedure for declaring (or avoiding) war. Without this, the narrative, though mostly accurate in fact, is highly misleading.

In spite of Sallust's implications, it is clear that the Romans have now decided that Jugurtha is the aggressor; a resolution has been passed to this effect by both senate and people (*Velle et censere*). The next stages which may lead to war, and which by Roman priestly law must not be omitted, are as follows: (1) *rerum repetitio*: since all Roman wars were in theory defensive wars (as some modern governments call their war department a Ministry of Defence), it is assumed that the enemy has done them some wrong, and a deputation is sent to demand restitution or satisfaction; these men *res repetunt*, and if satisfaction is given the matter is closed. (2) *denuntiatio*: if satisfaction is not given, the enemy has to be given what amounts to a second warning, a deputation which comes with explicit threats of what will happen if he does not comply; these men *bellum denuntiant*, which carries with it some such proviso as *nisi parueris*. It is still possible for the enemy to avoid war by doing what he is told. (3) *belli indictio*: this is now a purely formal act and Rome is at war.

Originally the ambassadors were the *fetiales*; priests who made wars and treaties, and when they *bellum indicunt* they used to throw a spear from Roman to enemy territory. But by the second century, when most wars were overseas, the ambassadors were senators, and the spear-throwing was done at Rome, where the *Columna Bellica*, near the temple of Bellona, marked a spot which was in theory hostile soil.

It is now possible to read Sallust's narrative with understanding: the *adulescentes* are the first embassy (there are precedents for sending young senators on this kind of mission); they *res repetunt*; they bring with them the resolution of the Roman government (*Velle et censere*; *velle* of the assembly, *censere* of the senate, this is formula); they are not mediators, mediation having failed (*ambo* is Sallust's only factual mistake), but they take back Jugurtha's reply, which is that he is loyal and will send envoys to Rome to explain.

The *maiores natu nobiles* (XXV 4) are the second embassy; they *bellum denuntiant* (XXV 11 *minae graves nuntiabantur*); Adherbal's letter has shown that the *repetitio* has failed. Jugurtha now has his last chance, which he throws away by the murder of Adherbal.

The senate having decided on war, the *indictio* is a formality, which Sallust does not bother to record; it has even been doubted whether the Romans bothered to do it. Certainly they soon abandoned the whole fetial procedure − it has no place in Caesar's ultimatum to the Helvetii or Ariovistus.

The compressed summary which is all we have of Livy's account of these years uses the technical terms correctly (Livy, *Ep*. LXIV); 'Adherbal . . . contra *denuntiationem* senatus ab eo occisus est. ob hoc ipsi Jugurthae bellum *indictum*.'

Two main conclusions follow from this: (1) Once the people have voted, the senate is in control; they decide whether to accept the enemy's explanations or to go to war. (2) The embassies of this year have a formal purpose; if the senate had already decided on war they could no doubt have shortened the process, and instructed one embassy to deliver both messages, but if they still hoped that Jugurtha would draw back there was reason to allow the full procedure to take its course. We could also add that since the army for the invasion of Numidia had to be enrolled in Italy, organised, and transported to Africa, a more speedy decision would not have saved Cirta. See Oost, *AJP* (1954) 147.

verbis: 'in the name of'; *eos* is the subject of *discedere*.

de controversiis . . . disceptare: this phrase is omitted in some MSS., but it has the look of a diplomatic formula.

XXII

eo magis: 'all the more'.

oppugnatione Cirtae: to balance *proelio facto* we should expect *oppugnata Cirta*; but Sallust would think this dull.

clemens: less violent than the reality.

2. **senati:** this early genitive of *senatus* is common in Sallust.

optumo quoque: a phrase often used by the Roman nobles about themselves; their party is often called the *boni* (Introduction, p. xxviii).

ita: this shows that *ut . . . probaretur* is consecutive, not final; he had succeeded in winning their approval.

malitia: usually this word is confined to one particular vice, maliciousness; here Sallust is using it as the general word for vice, the noun of *malus*, as *virtus* is the noun corresponding to *bonus*.

P. Scipioni: at Numantia. He had been Jugurtha's patron, and, though now dead, his name would still carry weight at Rome.

4. **insidiatum:** deponent verb; understand *esse*; the subject of *obviam isse* is Jugurtha.

pro bono: 'for their own advantage'.

iure gentium: we could translate 'international law' the *ius gentium* was one of the ideas which contributed to the development of Roman classical law, especially in the two generations before Sallust; from the necessity of adjudicating between men who be-

longed to different states where no statute law could apply, there
arose the idea that there must be some principles which would be
valid between human beings whatever their nationality. The
result was to stimulate the search for what was naturally right,
rather than what was in accordance with the letter of the law.

missurum: typical delaying tactics.

5. **Adherbalis:** this last sentence has the sort of finality which Tacitus
copied. In fact there was no reason why they should see Adherbal.

XXIII

loci naturam: If Cirta is, as is always assumed, the modern Constantine (but see Note on the Boundaries of Numidia, p. liv), it is
indeed difficult to take by storm. But as it is almost surrounded
by the river Ampsaga it can hardly be true that the besiegers
built a rampart round it. Sallust knows that they besieged it, and
has added the conventional *vallum* and *fossa* – not having been to
the place himself.

vallo atque fossa: the earth dug from the ditch is piled up to make
the rampart.

circumdat: you could say *circumdo fossam urbi*, or *circumdo urbem
fossa*. The first of these is found in ch. XXIII 9, *exercitu circumdato*.

praesidiis: avoid the word 'garrison', of course.

per vim . . . dolis: the usual variation in construction.

prorsus: a contraction of *proversus*, facing straight ahead; hence
completely, without distraction; used by Sallust to simplify the
story after some distracting details.

2. **multa pollicendo:** for the grammer see note on XVI 3, *multa*.

XXIV

2. **invasit:** often used by Sallust when fear or greed possesses a man;
quem is its object.

3. **quintum iam mensem:** with a verb in the present, 'I have been
confined'.

socius et amicus: a title the client kings were proud of (Introduction, p. xiv); Adherbal thought it gave him a claim to Roman
protection, as indeed it did.

ferro an fame: the preliminary *utrum* ('which of two') is not essential to the alternative question.

5. **nisi tamen**: 'except that'.
   supra quam ego sum: 'a target higher than me', as if *supra* were a comparative adjective.
   gravius: 'more important'.
7. **vostrum**: true in a sense; anyway a good argument.
   quanti fecerit: 'what price he puts upon'.
8. **possit**: the subject is Jugurtha.
9. **illa**: his previous letter; its reception is described in Ch. XV above.
   forent: this means no more than *essent*, and is directly attached to *vellem*; this is midway between an independent wish (*forent* 'would that they were') and a subordinate clause (*vellum ut forent*). This kind of subjunctive (*velim facias*) was normal in conversation and occurs frequently in Cicero's letters.
10. **eo**: 'for the purpose that'.
    manibus: dative, as usual with verbs of giving and taking away.
    per maiestatem imperii: when Saturninus, tribune in 103, established a lawcourt to try magistrates who had failed in their duties, the phrase used was *maiestatem populi Romani minuere* (to diminish the majesty of the Roman people); it was for this reason that *maiestas* became the Latin for 'treason'. *per amicitiae fidem* is the appeal of client to patron.

XXV

uti consuleretur: also depends on *censerent*, 'that there should be a debate'; the result of the debate would be a *consultum*, for which *decretum* is often a synonym.
4. **maiores natu**: contrasted with the *adulescentes* of Ch. XXI. See note on XXI 4.
   amplis: this (or rather *amplissimus*) is Cicero's favourite word for describing the distinction of senators. Sallust is sparing in the use of superlatives.
   in senatu princeps: Sallust takes a perverse delight in altering words in conventional phrases. The *princeps senatus* was the first senator on the censors' list, and from Livy, XXVII 11, we learn that he should by tradition be the senior living ex-censor. Scaurus had been consul in 115 but had not yet been censor. (He held that office in 109.)

5. **triduo:** the *adulescentes* in XXII 1 went *maturantes*; the senate decided to go through the full formal procedure, but apart from that there was no delay.

   navim: a few *i*-stem nouns sometimes keep the *i* even in the accusative singular.

   Uticam: see map; since the destruction of Carthage this had been the chief town of the Roman province of Africa.

   accedat: the ambassadors were summoning Jugurtha, not visiting him.

6. **metu atque lubidine:** to be taken with *agitabatur* rather than with *commotus*.

   divorsus: 'in different directions'; the compounds of *versus* are worth collecting (for one of the less obvious see note on Ch. XXIII *prorsus*)' The verb *agitare* (frequentative of *agere*) is a favourite of Sallust.

7. **ni paruisset:** he said to himself 'the senate will be angry *nisi paruero*'; this is in effect an indirect statement in historic time, and *paruero* must become a historic subjunctive.

   porro: 'on the other hand'; this is his second motive, the *lubido*; *Timebat iram* was the first. *Vicit* tells us which was the winner. Syme writes of Sallust's 'keen interest in the psychology of ambition' (*Sallust*, p. 269).

9. **diducta:** *di* 'in different directions', as in *divorsus*; the enemy would have to guard the whole perimeter, and therefore disperse his forces. Some MSS. have *deducta*, which misses the point.

   casum: 'a chance', derived from *cado*, with the meaning found in *accidit*.

10. **secus:** differently from his hopes.

   intenderat: more often this is used with an object, such as *animum*.

   conveniret: *priusquam* is followed by a subjunctive when the idea is that of forestalling (a kind of *negative* purpose).

11. **senati:** this form of the genitive may be an old-fashioned affectation.

   desisteret: subjunctive because it is part of the *nuntius*.

   frustra: they have in fact delivered the *denuntiatio*.

XXVI

Italici: these are the *togati* of Ch. XXI. Most Italians at this time were not Roman citizens.

deditione facta: they said to themselves *si deditio facta erit.*

tantum: 'only'.

fore: statement now, not command; since Jugurtha and Adherbal had both appealed to Rome, the Italians assumed that the senate would arbitrate.

2. **si advorsaretur:** his thought was *si advorsabor.*

uti quisque: *quisque* has the effect of splitting up a plural noun (*omnis*) into individuals.

XXVII

coepta: *coepi* is used in the passive if the infinitive is passive.

ministri: this word is often used contemptuously, here of Roman senators – keeping alive Sallust's accusations against the nobility.

leniebant: the imperfect can have the meaning 'try to . . .'.

2. **designatus:** Memmius had been elected in the summer of 112 to be tribune in 111 (to be exact, tribunes, unlike magistrates, came into office on 10 December). He continued a senatorial career, was a candidate for the consulship in 100 when he was murdered. *acer* is a word of approval, *potentia* of disapproval, and Sallust sides with Memmius; it seems, however, that Memmius is using Jugurtha as a stick to beat the nobles with, and that a compromise peace would have been better for Numidia as well as Rome.

paucos factiosos: two propaganda words; see Introduction, p. xxviii.

3. **lege Sempronia:** this law of C. Gracchus applied to the allotment of consular provinces (it did not apply to praetorian provinces); the senate had to select which two provinces the two consuls would eventually administer, before those consuls were elected. When elected, the consuls divided those provinces between them by agreement or by casting lots. The intention was to prevent the majority in the senate from rewarding its supporters with good provinces and punishing its opponents with bad ones.

Gracchus' full name was Gaius Sempronius Gracchus, and a law is named after the *gens*-name of the magistrate who proposes it; the full name of this law is *lex Sempronia de provinciis consularibus.*

4. **Calpurnio:** L. Calpurnius Bestia; *obvenit* suggests that they cast lots. They are all consuls of 111; at this time it was quite usual for a consul to be sent to a foreign command during his year of office. (After Sulla's reforms the consul stayed at Rome for his year of

office before going abroad as proconsul; but even then there were exceptions.)

5. **decernuntur:** money would only be paid out of the treasury on a decree of the senate.

XXVIII

venum ire: *venum eo* (*veneo*) is used as the passive of *venum do* (*vendo*). See note on XCI 6.

ut: 'as'; the previous embassy is described in Ch. XIII.

2. **placeretne:** *placet* is the usual word for the decision of a committee. The consul is presiding, as usual, and we are now in the year 111. **deditum:** supine.

3. **ex . . . decreto:** 'in accordance with the decree'.

4. **legat:** a Roman commander took with him a staff of *legati*, normally about three, of senatorial rank; they were appointed by the senate, but usually at the recommendation of the commander, who in effect chose his own *legati*. It was not unknown for a consul to choose an ex-consul older than himself (Scaevola, consul 95, took with him to Asia Rutilius Rufus, consul 105).

But it is normally up to the consul to ask a man to go with him as his *legatus*, and he would need some special reason for approaching a man who was usually senior to himself. The position of such a *legatus* was bound to be in some way special. Bestia and Scaurus have been identified as political *amici*, and Sallust is probably right in assuming that the legate was as much responsible for what happened as the consul.

factiosos: from the heart of the *factio*.

deliquisset: stands for a future perfect, he is already contemplating crime, according to Sallust.

supra: in Ch. XV.

5. **bonae . . . artes:** this is, for Sallust, high praise (see Introduction, p. lii); and indeed, but for the agitation of Memmius, Bestia would have settled the Numidian question without a full-scale war.

patiens laborum: the present participle is treated as an adjective, taking an objective genitive, where the verb would require an accusative. The style of the character-sketch is noticeable in this description.

6. **ex Sicilia**: to shorten the sea crossing, as usual when an army was going to Africa (Scipio in 204, Pompey in 81, Caesar in 46).

7. **Numidiam**: a vigorous attack to bring Jugurtha to his senses.

XXIX

administrabat: the subject is the consul, who is also to be understood as the object of *tentare*.

2. **socius et administer**: conspiratorial words (see *ministri* in Ch. XXVII).

abstractus: if this is true, the appointment of Scaurus as a member of the Mamilian commission (Ch. XL) is very remarkable.

3. **pactionibus**: 'conditions'.

4. **quaestor**: the governor's financial administrator; usually of senatorial family but not yet a senator; they were elected by the people and appointed to their various posts by lot, or by the governor's choice.

quod . . . legatis: dative of the person to whom the order is given, accusative of the thing ordered. If Jugurtha wanted time to negotiate, he must feed the Roman army.

agitabantur: 'was being observed'. *mora* 'because of the delay'.

5. **consilio**: the Roman magistrate sitting with his advisers was like the *iudex* with his *consilium* in Roman law; the proceedings are formal. The magistrate could choose his advisers, but usually included at least one of his *legati* if they were available. Since this interview was held in camp, the *tribuni militum* would be likely to be included.

de invidia: to explain away the unpopularity of his behaviour; *locutus* is then followed by the indirect command *uti acciperetur*.

cum Bestia et Scauro: after the *consilium* had been adjourned.

per saturam: originally a mixed fruit salad, the word is used when a number of different proposals are put together and all decided by a single vote. In the Roman assemblies it was illegal to tack together proposals on different subjects, and Sallust is implying that it should not have been done here; his real objection is that this is a bargain, not an unconditional surrender.

sententiis: the consilium has assembled again; the magistrate is not bound to take their advice, but he would be reluctant to act against it.

in deditionem: it is important to be clear about the meaning of this. A Roman general was not empowered to make a peace, and any arrangement he may make can be cancelled by the senate. He can however promise that if the enemy surrenders he will use his influence with the senate to secure reasonable terms.

Since Jugurtha was by no means defeated, and could easily prolong the war, Bestia has to offer him something substantial to persuade him to surrender; the offer obviously was that he should continue to be king. On this compromise both sides gain, and the war might have ended here.

The senate's opponents at Rome complain that the surrender is not genuine; that Bestia has made a treaty with a free enemy – which he cannot legally do. The irregularities in the collection of the indemnity (XXXII 3) help them to whip up feeling against the agreement.

In fact the test of the surrender was whether Jugurtha could be brought to Rome (see Ch. XXXI 19), and in Ch.XXXIII he comes. We should remember that these generals did secure, at comparatively small cost, the person of Jugurtha, which it took Metellus and Marius four hard years of war to achieve.

This surrender has been fully discussed by von Fritz in *TAPA* LXXIV 134 (see Bibliography).

6. **quaestori:** he would have to account to the senate for what passed through his hands.

7. **ad magistratus rogandos:** 'to hold the elections'; *rogare* is used of a magistrate who proposes a law in the assemblies, and when the law is passed it is a *lex rogata*; the same verb is used of elections, since they are held in the assemblies.

pax: a state of peacefulness, not a treaty.

agitabatur: 'was the subject of constant discussion'; the use of the frequentative *agitare* is here effective, but Sallust diminishes its force by using it so frequently – e.g. twice in Ch. XXIX 4 *indutiae agitabantur* and XXXIX 7 *pax agitabatur*.

XXX

flagitium: this partisan word begs the real question. So does the use of *potentia* and *vero bonoque* below.

parum: this is often very nearly equivalent to *non*.

2. **auctor:** this is more than *socius*, and suggests that Scaurus was the senior partner.

3. **supra:** Ch. XXVII.

    contionibus: 'by holding public meetings'; a *contio* was a public meeting called by a magistrate and addressed by him. No resolution was passed, but it was official to the extent that no one was allowed to interfere or to speak at it without the magistrate's permission. The same word *contio* is also used of the magistrate's speech, and it is not always possible to tell which meaning is intended.

    multa superba: this is Roman party politics, and the speech which Sallust records bears out the impression that Memmius was not interested in the welfare of the Numidians – or in the safety of the Roman troops who would be involved.

    intentus: 'he strained every nerve to'; the first meaning of *intendere* is to stretch.

4. **Memmii facundia:** in one of his works on oratory (*Brutus*, 136) Cicero gives a list of orators of the generation before his own; Scaurus is praised for his style, but Memmius and his brother are described as *oratores mediocres, accusatores acres et acerbi*; just the sort of people who would appeal to Sallust. Unlike most senators, they preferred to prosecute rather than defend.

    ea: acc. pl. neuter; some MSS. have *eam . . . quam.*

XXXI

    dehortantur: a fact, and therefore indicative; before *ni . . . superet* we must understand 'or would do if'. *a vobis* 'from addressing you'.

    factionis: this speech is full of the propaganda words of the *populares*. They are discussed in the Introduction, p. xxviii.

    nullum: 'the absence of'.

    innocentiae: dative.

2. **XV:** a round number which includes the tribunate of Gaius Gracchus and the repressive measures which followed it.

    quam: 'how'; so also *ut* below.

    inulti: we think of the failure to condemn Opimius.

3. **obnoxiis:** 'at your mercy'.

4. **subigit:** a compound of *agere* to drive.

5. **frustra an ob rem:** the preliminary *utrum* (the neuter of *uter*) is never essential to an alternative question; *ob rem*, 'to some effect'.

6. **quod . . . fecere:** this belongs to *eatis*, not to *hortor*.
   secessione: see below, § 17.
   praecipites: 'to destruction'.
   suo . . . more: that is to say by conviction in the courts; this is
   made clear by § 18 below; *quaestiones* (special law-courts), not *vis*,
   are to be the people's weapons. *suo* because the nobles had themselves used such courts in its resistance to the Gracchi.
   After the death of Tiberius Gracchus in 132, the senate appointed
   a special *quaestio* which condemned many of his supporters,
   who were then put to death without being allowed to appeal to
   the people. In 123 Gaius reaffirmed that it was illegal to execute a
   citizen without appeal; after his death, the consul Opimius was
   even more summary, and had his friends killed with no trial of any
   kind.

7. **regnum parare:** the usual accusation levelled at anyone who
   seemed to be becoming too powerful. It had been used against
   Spurius Maelius in 439, and was to be used against Sulla
   (*Sullanum regnum*) and Caesar. That such propaganda could still
   be effective is a tribute to the power of words.
   M. Fulvii: see XVI 2.

8. **fuerit:** 'Let it be': *plebi sua restituere* is the subject, *paratio* the com-
   plement. i.e. 'Let us assume that Ti. Gracchus was in the wrong';
   Memmius now turns to other crimes of the nobles.

9. **taciti:** an emphatic word; they had done nothing about it.
   expilari: a vague and general accusation, but it cannot be denied
   that some nobles had enriched themselves at the state's expense.
   paucis nobilibus; politics at Rome were largely a matter of personalities, so that foreign peoples found it more effective to direct
   their requests to individual senators than to the senate collec-
   tively, and whole districts came to look upon a particular noble as
   their patron. The Sicilians, for instance, expected the Claudius
   Marcellus family to look after their interests, ever since a member
   of it had recaptured Syracuse from the Carthaginians in 211. In
   the same way, after Zama and Carthage, the people of Africa and
   Numidia looked to the Scipios. Such requests were often accom-
   panied by presents, though *vectigal* is an exaggerated word.
   parum habuere: 'they thought little of '.
   maiestas: a topical word in Memmius' time. Its technical use is
   noted on XXIV 10.

hostibus: the nobles, of course.

10. **incedunt:** this compound is used of moving solemnly, as in a procession. Vergil uses it of the first appearance of Queen Dido in the *Aeneid* (I 497).

sacerdotia: the Romans used priesthoods much as we use life peerages; Caesar was a pontifex, Pompey and Cicero were both augurs. Under the empire the height of nobility was to acquire three priesthoods (*triplex sacerdotium*).

triumphos: the greatest honour of them all; Augustus had statues of the great *triumphatores* set up in his new forum at Rome.

quasi: they were of course (in Memmius' eyes), *praedae. honori habeo* is an easy extension of the predicative dative *honori est*.

11. **vos:** emphatically placed, to contrast with *Servi*.

Quirites: the most solemn and formal way of addressing the Roman people in their capacity as civilians. Their full title was *populus Romanus Quiritium*. A Sabine word, it goes back to the time when the Romans and Sabines became one people.

12. **occupavere:** this is a derivative of *capio*, and means to seize, not to hold.

idemque: a strong way of saying 'also'; the same men who are guilty are also proud. Superlatives are commoner in the speeches of Sallust than in the narrative (see Introduction, p. xxxiii).

13. **occidisse:** Gracchan history again. *habent* has three objects – two infinitives and a noun; violence is their defence.

14. **quisque pessume:** *quisque* with superlative is close in meaning to *quo* with comparative.

a scelere: they have made you afraid, instead of themselves.

omnis: agrees with *quos*; the infinitives *cupere, odisse, metuere* are the subjects of *in unum coëgit*.

15. **haec:** unity, the result of *in unum coëgit*; here is propaganda admitted.

16. **profecto:** this is from *pro* and *facto* and is a favourite of Cicero.

penes optumos: 'would be granted to the best men'; these *beneficia* are elections to magistracies.

17. **Aventinum:** until the time of the Emperor Claudius the Aventine was outside the city boundary; but only just outside, less than half a mile from the Palatine. To go and camp outside the city was the traditional plebeian form of civil disobedience, but it is not clear how often they actually did it. Nor was it always to the Aventine. In the tradition, the first secession was in 494, the last in 287.

omnino: frequently with negatives – 'not at all'.

18. **censes:** this verb is used for proposing a course of action.
    quaestionibus: this was foretold in § 7.

19. **dediticius:** this is the technical language of a military surrender; if the enemy *se dedit,* that is a *deditio* and he is *dediticius;* the conqueror should observe the normal laws of war (not to plunder, etc.), and any particular assurance he may have given (his own *fides* is involved), but apart from that the surrendered enemy is in his power.

    The fact that the people did actually have Jugurtha brought to Rome (XXXII, not printed here) is an indication that the surrender was genuine.

20. **Nisi forte:** the rhetorical absurdity which clinches the argument.
    illa, quam haec: *illa* are the times *cum regna . . . erant,* imagined as already past, which they are accused of preferring to *haec,* the times which can now come to pass if they assert themselves. When *cum* has an antecedent (here *tempora*) it is an ordinary relative (originally spelt *quom*), and is naturally followed by an indicative.
    nam: this is a reason for believing that they really did prefer the bad old days.

21. **viro:** sometimes we remember that this word is connected with *virtus* and *virilis.*

22. **quantum:** 'such is . . .'; a short parenthesis and not really a relative.
    parum est: 'it is not enough'.
    eripitur: 'is extracted from you'; take *deinde* with *faciundi.*

23. **Dominari:** a partisan word, like *dominationem* in XXXI 16 above.
    hostibus, hostibus: as we might have expected, some of the MSS. have the word only once; this is a common mistake in MSS. – haplography ('writing once').

25. **domi militiaeque:** the regular phrase for at home and on active service; the case is locative.

26. **Quae nisi quaesita:** 'unless these things are enquired into'.
    quae lubet: we are more used to seeing these written as one word.

27. **perperam:** like the other adverbs in -*am,* this is in origin an accusative singular; not very common, mostly as an opposite of *recte.*
    perditum: supine.

28. **ad hoc:** used as a kind of conjunction, 'in addition'.
    neglegas: this subjunctive appears to be due to the fact that the second person is the general, impersonal, 'you'.

29. **iniuriae**: it must be less important to encourage the *bonus*, since all you do is forfeit some *beneficia*; and if you have dealt properly with the *malus*, you will not need the *beneficia*.

XXXIX

insolita: nominative, followed, as *peritus* usually is, by an objective genitive. *libertati*, *'for* their liberty'.

2. **scribere**: for the more usual *conscribere*; common in Sallust but also used by Cicero and Livy. A magistrate with *imperium* had the right of recruiting troops, though it was normally only done with senatorial approval.

sociis: in Metellus' time these were predominantly but not exclusively Italian. See the next two notes, and XL 2 below, where only Italians are meant.

nomine Latino: cities which had Latin rights were more closely associated with Rome than the other Italian allies (e.g. intermarriage and commercial contracts with Romans were recognised by Roman Law; the details can be found in the *Oxford Classical Dictionary* under *Ius Latii* and *Commercium*). As early as a senatorial decree of 188 (*de Bacchanalibus*), and again in the *lex Acilia* of 122, *nomen Latinum* appears as an intermediate grade between *cives Romani* and *socii*. Like the other allies, they had an obligation to supply troops for the Roman armies.

auxilia: cohorts supplied by the allies of Rome, who served under Roman officers, alongside the Roman legions, often totalling half of the army. After 89 B.C., when all Italians up to the river Po became Roman citizens (and eligible to serve in the legions), the *auxilia* were recruited in the provinces.

3. **par**: 'right and proper'.

suo atque populi: the senate in fact took most decisions on foreign policy, though constitutionally the decision to go to war had to be taken, or at least ratified, in the assembly. A general in the field could accept a surrender, but could not make peace. Jugurtha was not the first foreigner to take the word of a Roman general and find out too late that it was not valid. It had happened twice in Spain, to Viriathus the Lusitanian in 141 and to the Numantians in 137, when even the word of Tiberius Gracchus was not enough.

4. **impeditus**: the Roman foreign wars of the second century were made more difficult by the extreme unpopularity of recruiting in

Italy. On this subject see Introduction, p. xxii and Chs LXIV and LXVI below. It was the solution of this problem which enabled Marius to win the war. In this instance the popular leaders are trying to have it both ways – compelling the senate, for idealistic, or partisan reasons, to fight a war and then obstructing the unpopular measures necessary for its success.

5. **imperio**: 'discipline'.

ex copia rerum: 'judging by his resources'.

XL

Mamilius: tribune in 110.

rogationem: see note XXIX 7 above, *ad magistratus rogandos*; a bill before it is passed is a *rogatio*. *Promulgare* is the formal announcement by a magistrate of a bill which he intends to propose; by the *lex trium nundinarum* ('law of the three marke-days') at least seventeen days must elapse between promulgation and proposal.

quaereretur: the court was called a *quaestio*, and its members are *quaesitores* below (§ 4).

senati: the old genitive of *senatus* again.

neglegisset: the perfect is normally *neglexi*, very occasionally *neglegi*.

tradidissent: in Ch. XXXII (omitted in this edition) Sallust says that when Calpurnius Bestia had returned to Rome after his agreement with Jugurtha, Roman officers in Africa had allowed Jugurtha to buy back his elephants, and also handed back some Numidian deserters.

pactiones fecissent: this is aimed at Bestia and Scaurus; for the truth of the accusation see note on XXIX 5, *in deditionem*.

2. **nominis Latini**: see note on Ch. XXXIX 2 above; many of the nobles had large estates in Italy, and kept on good terms with the local aristocracy; they could therefore hope for their support against the Roman plebs. The Latins probably had the right of voting if they were at Rome, but how the other Italians could help is not clear. The relationship of Roman nobles and the Italian aristocracy is discussed by Badian in *Foreign Clientelae*, ch. VIII

3. **plebes . . . iusserit**: Sallust is mixing his words; the correct terminology is *populus iussit* (in the *comitia*), and *plebes scivit* (in the *concilium plebis*, whose decisions are therefore not *leges* but *plebiscita*). *plebes* is an old-fashioned nominative singular.

magis odio: Sallust has no more faith in the plebs than he has in the nobles.

4. **supra:** Ch. XXVIII, the first mention of Scaurus was in Ch. XV.

etiam tum: before the confusion had died down.

quaesitores: the verb used in XL 1 above was *quaero*. For *rogarentur* see Ch. XXIX 7, *ad magistratus rogandos*.

5. **aspere:** Opimius, Sp. Albinus (the Consul of 110, not his brother) and Bestia were among those condemned. Sallust sees the Mamilian Commission as part of the immediate short-term political battle; rightly, of course; but it did also, like the treason law of Saturninus' first tribunate, state a principle which needed stating – that the Roman nobles should not conduct the affairs of the empire to suit their own convenience or profit. Though both Mamilius and Saturninus claimed victims, it was a lesson that the nobles never learnt.

XLI

partium et factionum: I have followed Rolfe's text here; most MSS. have *partium popularium et senatus factionum*: but not only does one of them omit *popularium* and *senatus*, but some others have the ungrammatical *senatores* in place of *senatus*. It seems likely therefore, that Sallust wrote *partium et factionum*, and a copyist, knowing that *factio* was regularly used of the nobility (see 6 below) inserted by way of explanation, *populares* and *senatores*; later copyists incorporated the words, with varying success, into the text. The incorporation of marginal comments is a frequent source of errors in MSS.

paucis ante annis: a criticism of this naïve view of Roman history will be found in the Introduction, p. xxv.

ducunt: 'value'; the gender of *quae* is determined by *prima*, though its antecedent is *rerum*.

2. **deletam:** this is 146, and the use of this verb is a reminder of Cato's constant agitation *delenda est Carthago*.

populus et senatus: the usual order of these words, *senatus populusque Romanus*, will not do here; by constant use it had come to mean the constitutional government of Rome, and assumed the unity of senate and people; Sallust needs a phrase which implies that they are separate, and need not have combined.

certamen inter civis: H. H. Scullard, *Roman Politics 220–150* (1951) demolishes this idyllic picture.

metus hostilis: an echo of the views attributed to Scipio Nasica, who was said to have opposed the conquest of Carthage in the Third Punic War on the ground that the fear of Carthage was good for Rome.

bonis artibus: Sallust's usual phrase for practical virtue; see Introduction, p. lii.

3. **amant:** 'usually produce'.

5. **in lubidinem vortere:** either corrupted them to suit their passions or actually changed them into selfishness.

6. **factione:** 'by their party strength'.

7. **belli domique:** locatives, with the impersonal *agitabatur*.

   aerarium: the treasury; the money was kept in the temple of Saturn beside the forum. When writing his *Histories* shortly after the *Jugurtha*, Sallust reported (or composed, see Introduction, p. xliii) a speech by the Tribune Macer in 73, in words very similar to these. There (*Or. Macr.* 6) the *paucorum dominatio* includes *aerarium, exercitus, regna, provincias*, and the grievances about war booty and triumphs are also mentioned.

   praedas: war booty belonged of course to the Roman state, and was handled by the quaestor, but it was an accepted principle that the general should first take a share for himself and for his troops, and this privilege was sometimes abused.

8. **pellebantur:** the Roman army was mainly recruited from the farming community, and the continuous foreign wars of the second century, especially the Spanish wars, had a disastrous effect on Italian agriculture. The unpopularity of military service before the reform of Marius is constantly stressed. There may well be a reference in these words also to the injustices of the years after Philippi, when Sallust was writing the *Jugurtha*. Octavian was then settling his demobilised troops on farming land in Italy, and the injustices of this are the background of Vergil's *Eclogues*.

9. **nihil pensi:** nothing weighty – their greed had no respect for anything.

10. **ex nobilitate:** though the subjunctive *anteponerent* is generic – 'the sort of men who preferred' – the next chapter shows that Sallust is thinking of the Gracchi. Their father had been consul and

censor, the elder Africanus was their grandfather and the younger Africanus their brother-in-law; it was usually under aristocratic leaders that the popular party could challenge the supremacy of the senate.

permixtio terrae: earthquake.

XLIII

foedam: the pun with *foedus* is no doubt intentional: Roman ideas of etymology were sometimes very amateur, and Sallust may have assumed that the words had a common derivation – which in fact they have not.

consules designati: one way or another Sallust has made a mistake in his dates. In Ch. XXXVII (not printed in this edition) he says that Aulus' expedition set out in January (obviously January 109); by that time Metellus and Silanus would be already consuls, not *consules designati*. Ironically the date in Ch. XXXVII *mense ianuario*, is the only exact date in the book, and either it is wrong, or, more probably, the word *designati* is wrong here: Sallust is forgetting that the news of Aulus' disaster did not arrive in Rome until at least the end of January. In any case Metellus would not be likely to go out to Africa until the Spring, so no great harm is done. In January, though at Rome he was already consul, he could in Africa be considered as governor designate.

evenerat: this word could be used if they had cast lots, but in view of the importance now of the war it is more likely to have been arranged.

acri: this word in Sallust is high praise; it sometimes seems to be the adjective corresponding to the noun *virtus*.

aequabili: 'without exception'.

2. **sibi cum collega:** 'that he shared'.

3. **scribere:** not dependent on *diffidens*. Now that the senate has decided on war to a finish, they realise that an altogether larger and more efficient army will be needed. Further comments on recruitment will be found in the notes to Ch. LXXXIV.

vario: they recognise that it will not be a traditional Italian war.

4. **reges:** for the use of client kings see Introduction, p. xiii; who these would be is not clear – perhaps African tribes to the east of the province, or chieftains in Spain and Gaul. For the *socii* and *nomen . . . Latinum* see note on Ch. XXXIX 2.

ultro: this implies doing something beyond what is necessary.

5. bonas artis: this is high praise from Sallust (see Ch. XLI 2).

XLIV

Sp. Albini: he had returned to his province after his brother's defeat.

praedator . . . praeda: one of Sallust's effective contrasts.

modestia: 'discipline'.

2. sollicitudinis: depends on plus.

3. comitiorum mora: this is part of the problem of dating discussed in the note on Ch. XXXVII 3. One unknown is the length of time between the start of Aulus' expedition (mense ianuario) and his defeat. It seems likely that Metellus' late arrival was due to the preparations described in Ch. XLIII rather than to his late election. The whole scale of the war was altered by Aulus' defeat, and it would take time to mount the new offensive. aestiva is the campaigning season.

maiorum disciplina: like the more common mos maiorum, these words remind us of the Roman habit of idealising the past.

coëgisset: the pluperfect subjunctive representing an original future perfect should be familiar by now, and will not be noted again.

4. decreverat: decrevit would be the more usual tense.

non egredi provincia: i.e. not to invade Numidia again.

in imperio: by the usual Roman practice he would retain his command until his successor arrived.

odos: in an African summer, ill-health could be as dangerous as the enemy.

5. ea: the camps; the verb is rightly in the imperfect. In enemy country the Roman army dug protective ramparts wherever they halted.

aberat: the subject is quisque, understood from cuique.

certantes: in competition with each other.

advecticio: presumably they did not like the local African wine.

frumentum . . . panem: Roman soldiers were expected to bake their own bread, and the remains of their circular ovens have been found at many camp sites.

in dies: 'by the day'; this is usually in diem.

XLV

magnum . . . comperior: Tacitus read this sentence and remembered it: he writes of the M'. Lepidus who was consul in A.D. 11, *gravem et sapientem virum fuisse comperior* (*Ann. IV 20*).

ambitionem: this is derived from the verb *ambire*, which means to go round canvassing for votes: the noun is also used of 'courting popularity', which in the case of an officer usually means relaxing discipline.

2. **sustulisse:** indirect statement; the historic infinitives have all been present tense.

ne quisquam: *quisquam* is used after most negatives, but *ne* usually has *quis* – to which it reverts in *quem alium*.

ceteris: 'other practices'; *arte* is adverb, not an ablative.

movere: back to the historic infinitive; hence *ipse* in the nominative.

frequentes: 'in close order'; *frequentia* is often used of a crowd.

XLVI

innocentia: the information that he could not be bribed was important to Jugurtha.

Roma: the MSS. have *Romae*, but that cannot be right.

veram: different from the pretended surrender of Ch. XXIX.

2. **suppliciis:** olive branches, the equivalent of the white flag.

3. **experimentis:** presumably the events of the previous years.

4. **postquam . . . cognovit:** this belongs to *pollicendo*, not to *tentando*.

maxume: 'preferably'.

procedat . . . traderent: the historic present may be followed by primary or historic subjunctives; not usually by both.

ex voluntate: 'in accordance with his (the king's) wishes'; this is the *official* reply.

5. **intento atque infesto:** the result of its training by Metellus.

contra belli faciem: he expected the Numidians also to be prepared for war.

6. **ostentui:** understand *esse*, the normal verb for a predicative dative.

7. **expeditis cohortibus:** heavy infantry who are travelling light, in battle order, are called *expediti* (with their packs on their backs they would be *impediti*). Light-armed troops are *velites* or *levis armatura*. Of these, the *velites* are Roman citizens, drawn from those

who were too poor to join the legions. They were very lightly armed – a small shield and throwing spears. In fire power they were no match for slingers or archers, either in range or quantity of ammunition, and for use with infantry they were by now obsolete. But they could move fast, and can still be used to thicken up the cavalry (cavalry horses were inferior by modern standards, and their riders had neither stirrups nor saddles), since they could keep up with them over short distances.

The *levis armatura* include the slingers and archers; they are not Romans, but recruited abroad, most of them probably from Spain. They are now becoming the standard light-armed troops of the Roman army, and within twenty years of the end of the Jugurthine War the *velites* disappear. As the empire grew, foreign specialised troops are increasingly used to supply what had always been the weaknesses of the Roman army.

cum equitibus: if Sallust is intending a contrast with *auxiliarios equites* below, then these *equites* must be Romans. The legion did traditionally have its cavalry contingent, but, as happened with light-armed troops, their place was being taken by allied *auxilia*; in the next thirty years the word *equites* at Rome came to be used of a social class, whose connection with the army was largely theoretical.

curabat: 'was in command'.

tribunis legionum: usually called *tribuni militum*; these are the subalterns of the legions, mostly young senators. *praefecti cohortium* are the officers of the *auxilia*, who had no unit larger than a cohort; by the time of the early empire these *praefecti* were usually equestrians.

dispertiverat: the middle of this word is derived from *pars*.

velites: see above; one of the difficulties of the *velites* when used like this was that if the cavalry were beaten and ran away they could not escape.

8. **in incerto:** that some MSS. should have *incerto* (omitting *in*) was almost inevitable. For another 'haplography' see XXXI 23 and note.

XLVII

Vaga: see map on p. lxiv. The Bagradas valley is the obvious route into Numidia.

celebratum: 'frequented', not 'celebrated'.

Italici: we have already met an Italian business community at Cirta (Ch. XXVI).

2. **si:** for *si forte*, 'in the hope that' they would submit. Metellus has taken the town. If the text is correct, Sallust is varying his construction, balancing *ob opportunitates* against *tentandi gratia*.

comportare: *imperavit frumentum* would have been normal; *impero* with an infinitive, especially an active infinitive, is rare.

res: the facts of the situation.

iuvaturam: the MSS. have *iuvaturum*, a copyist having assumed that it agreed with *exercitum*.

rebus: dative, for the supplies he had already collected.

3. **impensius modo:** 'even more urgently'.

ad proditionem: with *illectos*.

promissa: he waited for them to carry out their promises.

XLVIII

se suis artibus tentari: Livy copied this phrase, when he wrote (*XXII 16*) that Hannibal realised *suis se artibus peti*; Hannibal was being frustrated by the cautious manoeuvres of Q. Fabius Maximus.

ceterum: 'but'; *verbis* and *re* give the contrast between word and deed which is so common in Sallust's model, Thucydides; a contrast which would be clearer without *ceterum*.

popularium: 'of his subjects'.

2. **explorato . . . itinere:** he picked a place on Metellus' route.

ex opportunitate loci: the story of the battle shows thus the nature of the country favoured Jugurtha's tactics, not least LIV 3 *in loca saltuosa*.

3. **Adherbal:** for the division of Numidia see Ch. XVI.

Muthul: there are two possibilities; the first is that after the capture of Vaga, Metellus marched down to the coastal plain and then westwards, intending eventually to threaten Cirta from the north; in that case the Muthul will be a river flowing directly into the sea (marked on the map but not named). The more usual view is that he rejoined the Bagradas and continued up along its southern bank; the Muthul will then be one of the tributaries which flow into it from the south, and the most likely one is named on the map.

In either case, Metellus is marching towards the Muthul, not along it, and comes down from the mountain ridge about twenty Roman miles from it; the open space between the ridge and the Muthul was broken by the *collis* on which Jugurtha's troops were drawn up; this lay either parallel with Metellus' march or diagonally across it, so that at the point of attack the Romans were on the plain and the Numidians could charge down from the hill.

tractu pari: this must mean that the ridge was parallel to the river.

vastus: the root of *vastare*; here used of desolation, not of size.

ex eo medio: it has been suggested that the order of words affects the meaning, that *medius mons* means 'the middle of the mountain', but that *mons medius* is 'the middle mountain'; this is certainly not true here.

quasi: the natural order would link this with *collis*, 'a kind of hill'; but probably Sallust means us to take it with *medio*, 'about the middle'.

humi: genitive, *arido* and *arenoso* being treated as nouns.

4. **Media:** 'which lies in the middle'.

XLIX

transvorso: a *versus* compound; either crosswise to the lines of mountain and river, and therefore parallel to Metellus' march, or crosswise to Metellus' march and therefore, since it starts from the middle of the mountain, stretching diagonally towards the river. In either case, it is clear from the sequel that Jugurtha chose a spot where he would be on the *collis* and Metellus below in the *planities*.

quae ageret: a kind of indirect command.

suos: this does not seem to include more than the *omnis equitatus* and the *pedites delecti*.

2. **manipulos:** it is possible that Jugurtha, having served with the Roman army in Spain, had adopted Roman formations in his army; but Sallust's use of the Roman word here does not prove it.

memores pristinae virtutis: the regular harangue of the general before battle; Sallust could find no lack of models in Thucydides, such as the Spartan king Archidamus before the first invasion of Attica (*Thucydides*, II 11), or the Spartan admirals in the Corinthian Gulf (II 87).

sese: grammatically this could be either the soldiers or Jugurtha.

avaritia: the kingdom of Numidia had benefited in the past from

Roman protection, but patrons cannot expect continual gratitude from their clients.

sub iugum: the story is told in Ch. XXXVIII (not included in this edition); this was the humiliation which finally compelled the Romans to fight it out. Two spears were stuck in the ground, a third was used to make a crossbar, and the defeated soldiers marched through.

omnia: these are then enumerated as the noun *locum* and the clause *uti . . . consererent*.

prudentes: this is the opposite of being taken by surprise; *imperitis*, beside the contrast with it, also contains the notion of not knowing the country.

3. **proinde:** 'and so'; *essent* is indirect command.
4. **Ad hoc:** 'in addition'.

uti quemque: 'anyone whom . . .'.

pro: 'according to'.

conspicatur: *conspicor* is usually deponent, and the MSS. have the ordinary *conspicitur*; but the fifth-century grammarians Donatus and Priscus both quote Sallust as having written *conspicatur*, which they would not have invented; no doubt our MSS. are derived from a copy which was 'corrected'. Sallust was either choosing a more striking word or aiming at a more rhetorical rhythm: the end rhythm of this sentence, $- \cup --\cup - \cup$, was a favourite in Cicero's speeches.

5. **incerti:** in passive sense, 'obscure'.

obscurati: not completely out of sight, but difficult to recognise.
6. **commutatis ordinibus:** Metellus has been marching in column (*agmen*) towards the river. He now deploys facing right towards the enemy, in a *triplex acies* (see next note). Then, to continue the advance to the river, each man turns to his left, and the march is resumed in three columns, the right-hand column, nearest the enemy, being the front section of the *acies*.

triplicibus subsidiis: we have here not four lines but three – the *triplex acies*, which is the normal battle formation of the Roman army. *acies* can be used both of the whole army when deployed and also of each line, but Sallust obviously could not write *acies triplicibus aciebus*.

In the traditional formation the troops were formed up in maniples (pairs of centuries), with a gap between each and the maniples of the second line covering the gaps in the first. At some time in the second century (or a few years earlier, even) it was decided that the maniple was not strong enough to stand on its own, and the larger unit – the cohort of three maniples – was used, still in a *triplex acies*, with four of the ten cohorts in the front line.

Here Metellus has his army drawn up in the old style, by maniples. When the battle had been going on for some time, and he decides that greater solidity is needed, he causes the maniples to draw together, and face the enemy as cohorts (LI 3). The troops must of course have been familiar with both formations. Twice after this Sallust uses the word *cohortes* in describing an army of Metellus.

The adoption of the cohort has sometimes been attributed to Marius, but here it is in Metellus' army – and for this battle Sallust has the evidence of one of the participants, Rutilius Rufus. Besides this, the word 'cohort' does occur in Polybius, who died about 122. Bell (*Historia*, XIV 404) argues that it was evolved in Spain, to meet the ferocious charges of the Spanish infantry. After this war the maniple formation is not heard of again.

funditores: see note on XLVI 7.

transvorsis principiis: a difficult phrase; the *principia* are the front ranks (not to be confused with the *principes*); the words should mean 'with the front ranks moving sideways', instead of advancing against the enemy, but then *all* the ranks were doing this. Perhaps 'with the front ranks on one side' (so that they could face to the flank if attacked).

L

Rutilium: like Marius, Rutilius Rufus was a *novus homo* and a distinguished soldier. He is now a *legatus* of Metellus; he went on to be consul in 105, and did much of the work of training the army which Marius then used in his North Italian campaign. The result was an enmity between him and Marius which eventually proved disastrous. Rufus went out to Asia as legatus of Scaevola, to set the finances of the province to rights, and on his return was condemned in the extortion court by an equestrian jury. He wrote his memoirs, which were used by later historians but which have not survived. Sallust had no doubt read them, and derived from them his detailed account of this battle.

2. **pro re atque loco**: as suited the situation and the ground.

post principia: Sallust really means that Marius was so placed that if the army had to turn right to face Jugurtha he would be behind the front lines and in the centre of the battle. This is the normal place for the commander. In this case Metellus judges that his own place is with the cavalry who lead the march, and he delegates the command of the infantry to one of his *legati*, having sent another on with the advance party.

3. **primos suos**: in fact his left wing.

quasi: 'about', with the numeral.

qua: 'at the place from which' (*mons* is masculine).

foret: the subject is *mons*; *post* is an adverb.

4. **a sinistra**: if Sallust is thinking of the Romans as still facing the river, some Numidians have ridden right round them. But this battle is confused, and so, perhaps, is the author.

adesse: a more purposeful word than it looks.

fuerant ... sauciabantur: these are the 'whenever' tenses in Latin, and show that this kept on happening.

modo: 'only'; with *eminus*.

5. **alio**: the adverb, the same formation as *quo* and *eo*.

6. **numero priores**: 'thanks to their superiority in numbers'.

fugae: dative; *fuerant* is plural because of *campi*, though its real subject is *collis*.

ea vero: 'there also'.

LI

arma, tela: shields and spears.

2. **erat**: indicative in the 'inverted *cum*' clause; the grammatical main verb comes first, and sets the time, the *cum* clause then tells what happens.

3. **aestu**: Roman soldiers are fighting in Africa.

cohortis: See note on XLIX 6 *triplicibus subsidiis*.

4. **illis**: the Romans.

LII

1. **ceterum**: 'but'.

3. **die**: a shortened form of the genitive.

advorso colle: only as a last resort did an army charge up hill.

5. **explorare**: to keep watch on, depending on *neque remittit*.

6. **vacuom**: without fear of danger.
   accepit: realised.
   arte: adverb, 'in close formation'.
   latius: Bomilcar has decided to take a risk.

LIII

1. **vim**: this word is often used of a large mass.
   prospectum: a noun; *arbustis consitus*, 'covered with bushes'.
   manere: the subject is *vim pulveris*.
4. **Elephanti**: against determined Roman infantry, elephants were rarely successful. Regulus had been defeated by them in 255, but his tactics were wrong. Scipio Africanus had got the better of them at Zama in 202, and so later did Julius Caesar at Thapsus in 46. The tactical problems of the handling of elephants are well set out by R. F. Glover in *Greece and Rome*, xvii (Jan. 1948).
5. **opere**: when a Roman army halted in hostile country it always surrounded itself with a trench and rampart.
   lassique: the best MSS. have *laetique*, but this does not suit the sense of *quamquam . . . tamen*, though *fessi laetique* would be a more interesting pair of words. Some editors omit the word.
7. **velut hostes**: like enemies.
   admissum: this compound is regularly used for committing a crime; understand *est*; the subjunctive condition *ni . . . exploravissent* follows quite easily.

LIV

1. **more militiae**: decorations for valour were given to individual soldiers by the commander, in the presence of the army; such a parade is described by Livy (XXX 15). For the Roman military decorations see note on Ch. LXXXV 27.
   gerant: *ut* is really never necessary to an indirect command.
2. **ubi gentium**: 'where on earth'; the indirect questions depend on *exploratum*; *uti* 'how'.
4. **gratia**: equivalent to *causa*.
   sequitur: not a historic present, this is the usual Numidian custom. Jugurtha's following depended on his success.
   militiae: either genitive, 'a crime of military service', or dative, *militia* being used for *milites*.
5. **ex . . . lubidine**: 'as he chose'.

6. **agros vastat:** having failed to capture Jugurtha, which was now the Roman's war aim, Metellus turns to terrorism. He calculates that if Jugurtha does not protect his people he will lose their support, and that therefore he must come back and fight.

praesidium: another new departure. Marius is able to do this more effectively later because he has a larger army; but Metellus has begun it. Military occupation is now the aim.

8. **quippe:** goes closely with *cogebatur. cui,* 'he whose'.

9. **in iisdem locis:** 'where it was'.

ignoratus: 'unperceived'.

LV

tamen: in spite of the *advorsus locus.*

ex . . . socordia: this goes closely with *magnificum.*

2. **supplicia:** the usual word is *supplicatio,* which is used e.g. for the thanksgiving for Caesar's successes in Gaul (Caes. *B.G.* II 35, VII 90); it was for the senate to decide whether to have one and for how long it should last (Caesar's in 52 B.C. lasted for twenty days).

3. **niti:** the subject is Metellus.

opportunus: 'exposed to'.

post gloriam: Metellus, for Sallust, is nearly faultless.

4. **insidias:** the one described in the previous chapter.

7. **ubi vi:** following the military maxim 'March separately, fight together'.

8. **interdum:** a variant for *modo*; similarly *rursus* and *post* are an unequal pair.

LXIII

Per idem tempus: during the winter of 109–8.

haruspex: a soothsayer, who foretold the future from the inspection of the entrails of animals; both this art and augury (which used mainly the flight of birds) came to Rome originally from Etruria, but were now a recognised part of the religion of the Roman state.

ageret: indirect command; *eventura* is indirect statement.

2. **alia omnia:** we have here a character-sketch of the kind which was traditional in Roman historians (see Introduction, p. xliv). There is the catalogue *industria, probitas,* etc., and the conventional anti-

theses *belli ingens, domi modicus* and *stipendiis . . . non . . . munditiis.*
In this, and in the summary of his early career which follows,
Sallust is building up Marius as a typical *novus homo*, excluding
any reference to his wealth and aristocratic friends. (In fact he
had early won the approbation of Scipio Aemilianus, and enjoyed
the patronage of the Metellus family – and was now a legate of a
Metellus.) This role is the essential background for the great
speech on the nobility which Sallust puts into the mouth of
Marius (Ch. LXXXV); though he has no illusions about the *novi*,
the nobility are Sallust's main target.

belli . . . domi: locatives, as in the phrase *domi et militiae.*

victor: these active nouns are useful for compressed epigrammatic
expression – Cato in Livy (XXXIX 40) is *contemptor gratiae.*

3. **altus:** from *alo.*

faciundis . . . facundia: the similarity cannot be accidental. (See
also *faciem . . . factis* below. This is not artless writing.)

Graeca: to study oratory, the young Roman normally went to
Greece; Cicero went to Rhodes to study under Molon, and Caesar
was on his way there when he was captured by pirates.

munditiis: Horace has since made this word famous (*Odes,* I 5,
simplex munditiis).

artis bonas . . . ingenium: see Introduction, p. li. These words
are important in Sallust's doctrine of virtue.

4. **a populo:** *tribuni militum* were the subalterns of the Roman legions;
the *tribuni* of the first four legions were elected by the people (the
'consular' legions, since it was once the presumption that each
consul would command an army of two legions).

5. **alium post alium:** even more than the character-sketch above,
this short account is misleading, and Sallust must have known it.
Marius' tribunate in 119 (*tribunis plebis,* that is) was not plain sail-
ing at all, and when he stood for the praetorship of 115 he was
elected, but of those elected he had the fewest votes, and was then
almost unseated by a prosecution for bribery. After that, a praetor
of 115 who was in full flood of success would be consul in 112 or
111; this is 108, and Marius' plan to stand for the consulship
comes as a surprise to Metellus.

6. **ad id locorum:** 'up to this time'; *postea* probably means from about
the year 100, when Marius' struggle for power could no longer be
excused by military necessity.

ambitione: ablative, as if *praeceps datus* was one word (*pessum dare* is sometimes written as one word).

alios . . . consulatum: a typical rhetorical antithesis; the second limb of the sentence dictates the choice of the verb *tradebat*. Of course the plebs elected the consuls as much as they did praetors and aediles, but it is true that the noble families kept a much tighter hold on the consulship; since there were only two consuls each year, the nobles usually had enough candidates of their own to fill both places, and they marshalled the full force of their patronage to ensure their election.

7. **is:** the consulship, which was considered polluted if held by a *novus*. The MSS. place *is* before *indignus*, in which case *is* must be the *novus*, and *pollutus* must mean 'unclean'.

LXIV

1. **eodem:** adverb.

   virtus: Metellus is the only Roman in this book to whom Sallust attributes *virtus*. *superbia* is a traditional characteristic of the nobles. For the use of active nouns in *-tor* see note on Ch. LXIII 2, *victor*.

2. **prava:** 'improper', *fortunam* is his station in life.

   petere: after *caveret*, *ne peteret* would be more usual.

   per negotia publica: 'as soon as the exigencies of the service should permit'.

4. **cum filio suo:** to stand at the same time as Metellus' son would mean waiting over twenty years, since the earliest age at which a plebian could be elected consul was 42.

   contubernio: the young Roman noble's first experience of military service was usually on the staff of a relation or friend of the family. The word really means sharing the same tent.

   cum . . . tum: 'both . . . and'.

5. **grassari:** deponent; the word is normally used of rioting or murder, and here has a sinister ring about it.

   modo: as in *dummodo*, 'provided that'.

   ambitiosum: *ambire* is to canvass for support, and *ambitio* often has the bad meaning of courting popularity.

   negotiatores: we hear sometimes in this book of Italian trading communities in Africa; at Cirta, Jugurtha had had them massacred (Ch. XXVI above). Since they came from the same class as himself, Marius could hope for their support.

criminose simul et magnifice: i.e. finding fault with Metellus and praising himself.

trahi: understand *bellum* as the subject.

homo: the word is slightly contemptuous; *inanis* agrees with it, and *superbiae* depends on it.

6. **firmiora**: 'more credible'.

corruperant: 'they had lost'.

festinatur: the contrast with the tense of *corruperant* shows that this is a general statement.

LXXIII

1. **indicio**: information about Bomilcar's plot.

integrum: from the root of *in – tango*, untouched, unspoilt, new; if a magistrate passes a case on to his successor undecided, so that his successor will have to start again, he *rem integram remittit*.

2. **parum idoneum**: Metellus had every right to be angry.

3. **litteris**: see the summary of Chapters LXV–LXXII, p. 33.

4. **humilitas**: by the standards expected of the higher magistrates; we must not think of Marius as being low-born in the ordinary sense of the word.

moderata sunt: 'were the determining factors'.

5. **seditiosi**: Sallust uses this word especially of tribunes; the popular agitators do not escape his criticism (see Introduction, p. xxviii).

capitis: genitive of the type of charge on which they accused him; capital punishment included exile as well as physical death.

in maius: to make it seem greater.

6. **plebes**: this was an old-fashioned form of the nominative singular.

res fidesque: property and credit; these were men who could not really afford to take time off.

ducerent: let their own needs take second place to Marius' consulship.

7. **tempestates**: this does not really mean more than *tempus*; a long time since the last election of a *novus*.

rogatus, iussit: these are technical terms applicable to magistrate and assembly. Decisions of the whole people in the *comitia centuriata* or *comitia tributa* are described by the words *populus . . . iussit*, and the decision is a *lex rogata*.

frequens: this word is often used of a crowded meeting.

decreverat: the words between *paulo* and *decreverat* are not in the MSS., but they must be approximately right. According to the *lex Sempronia de provinciis consularibus* (which had been passed in 122 by Gaius Sempronius Gracchus), the senate had to nominate, before the consular elections, the provinces which the new consuls should eventually govern. Presumably, therefore, they had already decided which provinces Marius and his colleague would hold, and allotted them two other provinces, and confirmed Metellus in his command in Africa. *paulo . . . decreverat* refers to this, and either, as in our text, states that they gave Africa to Metellus again, or tells us which provinces they had chosen for the new consuls.

ea res: the senate's decree has been overruled. Of course in the Roman state the people were sovereign, in the sense that any law which they passed was immediately valid, even against a decree of the senate. But this sovereignty had in practice been limited in two ways: first, they could only vote on the proposal of a magistrate, and magistrates normally consulted the senate beforehand; secondly, they did not interfere in certain expert matters, including foreign policy and the appointment of governors. The first of these limits had been broken before (notably by the Gracchi, who had both died for it), but was at this time still usually respected; on the second count this is an entirely new precedent – the people asserting their sovereignty in the appointment of a commander. This was a precedent more dangerous for the Republic than any which the Gracchi had set, since it was by this means that Pompey and Caesar, and, later, Octavian and Antony gained command of the armies which enabled them to dominate and eventually destroy the civilian government. A government which loses control of its generals may find itself at their mercy.

LXXX

Thala: recently captured by Metellus.

ad Gaetulos: Metellus has driven Jugurtha out of his own country, and compelled him, if he is to continue the struggle, to seek allies abroad: first the mountain tribes of the Gaetulians and then the powerful king of Mauretania to the west. From now on, Bocchus dominates the Numidian War, since only with his help can Jugurtha continue the struggle.

2. **ordines, signa, imperium:** Roman military terms.
3. **proxumos:** the closest friends.
   quis: ablative; in LXXX 5 below *quis* is dative.
4. **ea gratia:** the antecedent of *quod*.
5. **bello:** dative, depending on *opportunissumam*. Sallust is saying that the Romans, in view of the coming war with Jugurtha, should have seized their opportunity of ensuring the friendship of Bocchus.
   vendere: an obscure, and more than usually unsubstantiated charge.
   Iugurthae: dative; Jugurtha was Bocchus' son-in-law (so Plutarch, *Marius* 10). The best MSS. of Sallust here have *Boccho* (not *Bocchi*), and if that were right *Iugurthae* would be genitive, and the relationship would be reversed.
6. **Verum:** as usual, 'but'.
   ducitur: 'is considered'.
   singuli: each individual; this meaning is strengthened by the singular *quisque*, though the verb remains plural.
   pro: 'in proportion to'.
   eo: either 'than that number' (i.e. more than ten or so), or 'for that reason' (because they are wealthier.)
7. **obtinet:** 'holds her place'. What we know of the Numidian royal family does not agree with this account of their marriages; at least Micipsa appears to have had only two sons of his own.

LXXXI

data et accepta: *dare et accipere* is the usual Latin phrase for exchanging. In Vergil (*Aen.* VIII 150) Aeneas says to Evander 'Accipe daque fidem'.

Romanos iniustos: this hostile description of the Roman Empire through the eyes of a native prince was carried further by Tacitus, in the speech he put into the mouth of the Scottish chieftain Calgacus (*Agr.* 30, where the Romans are described as *raptores orbis*).

tum: at this time; contrasted with *paulo ante* and *post*. Understand first *esse*, then *fuisse*, leading up to *fore*.

Persen: Perses (or Perseus) was king of Macedonia, defeated by the Romans after a four-year war (usually called the Third Macedonian War) in 168. Roman relations with Macedon were never straightforward, and charges of bad faith, on both sides, could easily be made. *Persen* is accusative, a Greek termination.

uti quisque: *ut quisque* with a superlative is a common way of saying 'in proportion to'.

2. **ad Cirtam:** *ad* with the name of a town means 'towards'.

locaverat: Sallust has already recorded (Ch. LXI, not included in this edition) that Metellus had established Roman garrisons in the most important and defensible towns of Numidia. This makes it more difficult for Jugurtha to return as the Roman army moves on. Cirta had been the scene of Adherbal's defeat and death (see Ch. XXI).

sese: Jugurtha and Bocchus, against Metellus.

4. **id:** this anticipates *imminuere*.

LXXXII

cognitis Mauris: before fighting he must get to know the new enemy.

2. **supra bonum:** 'beyond what was right and proper'.

egregius: this adjective is equivalent to an 'although' clause; *pati*, like the others, is historic infinitive.

3. **vortebant:** 'attributed to'; then *accensum esse* depends on it as if it was a verb of saying, and *quod . . . eriperetur* as if it was a verb of complaining.

iam: goes closely with *parta* (from *pario*); a common use of this participle (e.g. Augustus recorded that he closed the temple of Janus *cum esset parta victoriis pax* – *Mon Anc.* XIII 2 42).

nobis: strongly placed, contrasting with the three *alii*.

laturum fuisse: the past unfulfilled condition in indirect speech.

LXXXIII

stultitiae: that it was a mark of folly.

alienam rem: any danger he incurred in fighting would only benefit Marius.

habere: the subject is Bocchus.

mutare: to receive in exchange.

sumi facile: *aegerrume* shows that *facile* is an adverb, and *sumi* is infinitive of indirect speech. Thucydides (I 82 6) makes their king Archidamus give the Spartans the same warning when they were debating whether to declare war on Athens in 432: once you have

embarked on a war it is not easy to stop – οὐ ῥᾴδιον εὐπρεπῶς
θέσθαι; a passage no doubt known to Sallust.

non eiusdem: certainly true of Roman generals, and now true
of Jugurtha; a warning to Bocchus.

deponi: passive; indirect statement therefore – 'war was stopped' –
not dependent on *licere*.

proinde: 'and so'; *consuleret* is indirect command.

2. **copia**: opportunity of making peace.

LXXXIV

multus: this adjective is used where we should use an adverb; the
Greek equivalent, πολύς, is used in exactly this sense by Greek
authors, e.g. Hdt. VII 158; this use seems to originate with the
description of a river in full flood.

dolentia: *dolere to cause* pain, followed by a dative is rarely found
after the time of Plautus. In Sallust's day it must have been old-
fashioned, though the impersonal *mihi dolet* was occasionally used
by Cicero.

2. **prima habere**: he made them his first consideration.

supplementum: it was normal for a general going out to a province to take reinforcements for the army. There are three main
elements in the Roman army: the legions, composed of Roman
citizens, the core of the Roman army; the *auxilia*, allied soldiers,
at this time mostly Italians, serving under Roman officers and
brigaded in cohorts – often as numerous as the legions, and an
essential part of the army; contingents supplied by foreign tribes
or nations, serving under their own officers, but obeying, with
more or less regularity, the orders of the Roman commander-in-
chief. *a populis et regibus* is the third of these, also loosely called
auxilia; *ex Latio* is the second.

Some editors put *sociisque* after *Latio* instead of after *regibus*;
this is in line with the use of the words in Marius' day – the Latins
were the inner ring of allies with close ties with Rome, and *socii*
meant the other Italians. In Ch. XXXIX 2 Sallust has correctly
joined them *ab sociis et nomine Latino auxilia arcessere*. It is tempting
therefore to improve the text here; but our text should be what
Sallust wrote, not what he ought to have written, and it is possible
that he was confused, since in his day the *socii* were non-Italian,
all Italians south of the river Po being *cives Romani*.

militiae: locative; depends, like *fama*, on *cognitos*.

ambiundo: by personal request.

homines emeritis stipendiis: when a man had served for twenty years (not necessarily consecutively), he could not be called up again, but he could be persuaded to serve voluntarily; those who did so were called *evocati* and had special privileges. *emeritis* passive, from *emereo*; usually it is deponent, from *emereor*, and is used of the ex-soldier himself.

3. **laetus:** in fact they looked forward to the prospective recruiting drive with some glee. It was the rule at Rome that the *imperator* held his own levy (with senatorial approval), and since this entailed taking men compulsorily off the land to serve overseas for several years at a time, it was intensely unpopular. Owing to the depopulation of the Italian countryside (well explained in *CAH* IX ch. 1) men were becoming harder to find, and once found were being kept longer in the army. The farmers naturally blamed the commanders for this, and the nobles had long been the objects of a bitterness which was not their fault. They were now hoping to sit back and watch Marius, the people's choice, struggling with the same problem.

volenti: agreeing with *plebi*, 'to the people's liking'; this again is a Greek idiom translated into Latin, and was also copied by Tacitus (e.g. *Agricola*, XVIII, *quibus bellum volentibus erat*).

4. **praeda:** there had been some occasions in the past when Roman soldiers had returned enriched by war, notably the scandalous campaign of Manlius Vulso in Asia Minor in 189, but the great days of plunder were still in the future.

animis trahebant: this has three objects, two of them accusative and infinitive; the third is *alia*.

5. **exagitandi:** gerund with direct object, preferred to the gerundive because it balances *hortandi*.

contionem: see note on Ch. XXX 3.

hoc modo: Plutarch has a chapter (*Marius*, IX) on Marius' post-election speeches, and his account coincides closely with Sallust's: 'then he would ask the people whether they did not think that the ancestors of those men would have wished rather to leave a posterity like him; since they themselves did not rise to glory by their high birth but by their virtue and great actions.' No doubt Plutarch had read his Sallust, but in general he does not seem unduly dependent on him, and it is likely that the text of Marius' oratory was preserved. This speech has a sarcastic tone which may well have been his own. Plutarch speaks of speeches in the plural; it would be in keeping with Sallust's dramatic method that he should compress them into one.

This speech has been analysed by Skard and Carney (see Bibliography). It has four main elements:

The Roman idea that nobility comes from ancestors is held up to ridicule, the ancestors of the present nobility being made to disown their progeny and prefer Marius.

The Greek philosophical notion that virtue is the only nobility is made to exalt Marius, whose character and achievements made him the most noble of them all.

The abstract thought is enlivened by the wit and coarseness of the real Marius; popular Italian as well as philosophical Greek; and the philosophy itself deriving mostly from the humble, down-to-earth Cynics; the hero is the old Roman type of earnestness and courage.

The speech is a political manifesto, an attempt to take over the leadership of the *populares*; as Plutarch says, he 'had seen that the people took pleasure in seeing the senate insulted'; Marius is echoing the other great *novus*, Cato the Censor.

The nobles were infuriated by Marius' oratory – in ridiculing the appeal to ancestors he was striking at the roots of their privilege. His successes in the next seven years did not endear him to them. However, in the year 100 they had their revenge – he found the leadership of the *populares* incompatible with his new nobility.

LXXXV

Quirites: see note on XXVI 27.

petere: the usual Latin for standing for office. The noun *petitio* is also used.

supplices: it was necessary for the candidate to go round the forum making a show of soliciting votes. Those who did not, from Coriolanus to the younger Cato, were not elected.

2. **contra ea:** 'differently'.

3. **beneficio:** this really means his election.

cogere ad militiam: see note on Ch. LXXXIV 3, *laetus*.

forisque: this is the ablative form (for place where), as *foras* is the accusative (for motion towards), of the obsolete noun *fora* a door; 'outside', 'abroad'; to be distinguished from the third declension *foris* (pl. *fores*) which also means a door; and, of course, from *forum*.

opinione: 'than you think'.

4. **Ad hoc:** this is in effect an adverb.

maiorum fortia facta: there is an interesting sidelight on this pride of ancestors in Plautus, *Persa*, 55–61, where a parasite boasts that he comes of a long line of parasites who for six generations have lived well on other people's food.

cognatorum: relations by blood (*nascor*); *adfines* are relations by marriage.

clientelae: the chief source of strength of the noble was the number of people who regarded him as their patron; when he died they naturally attached themselves to his son.

5. **illud:** this frequently stands for a clause which follows the main verb (here *omnium ora . . . esse*).

procedunt: 'go forward' to the advantage of the state.

invadundi: 'of attacking me'.

6. **capiamini:** 'suffer'.

7. **consueta:** predicate, applying to *labores* as well as *pericula*.

9. **simulavere:** those whose honesty has only been a pretence.

optumis artibus: in Sallust's preface, *bonae artes* is a mark of aristocratic *virtus*. Marius claims that *virtus* for himself, and that even in his youth before he entered public life.

vortit: the balance of the whole sentence would suggest that *bene facere* is the subject and *temperare* the object; but it seems more probable that *bene facere* is the object and the subject has to be found from the sense of the clause *qui . . . egi*. That habit can form character is a notion to be found in Greek philosophy.

10. **iussistis:** as governer of Africa.

id mutare . . . mittatis: 'change your minds and send'.

globo: used of a crowd; here contemptuous. Very likely we have here Marius' own word. *prosapia* is an old-fashioned word by Sallust's time. Marius liked to be considered blunt, but there is no need to think of him as illiterate. The sarcasm of *multarum imaginum et nullius stipendii*, and of the *scilicet* clause, may well be his.

imaginum: the noble Roman kept busts of his distinguished ancestors in the *atrium* of his house, and they were present on family occasions. This right to parade your ancestors, the *ius imaginum*, was the most distinctive privilege of the aristocracy; *imagines* is often the Latin equivalent of 'pedigree'.

12. **Graecorum:** even in military matters, Romans look to Greek instructors; so did the Carthaginians, who put a Spartan mercenary in command of the army which defeated Regulus.

praeposteri: they revised the natural order of things; *gerere magistratus* is the administration of the consulship, and though a man cannot do this until he is elected, he should acquire some practical experience beforehand. No wonder, as Plutarch records, the nobles were angry at this speech.

15. **naturam unam:** there is no intrinsic difference between the nature of one man and another. This is part of a Greek philosophical debate about the nature of nobility, not just the simple remark of a simple Roman.

generosissumum: *generosus* is derived from *genus*; virtue is the real nobility.

17. **faciant idem:** i.e. *despiciant*; *maioribus* may be dative or ablative.

20. **Ne:** 'surely'; this word is nearly always followed by a pronoun; not to be confused with the negative of *ut*.

21. **apud vos:** in the assemblies.

26. **compositam:** a regular word of literary composition – 'well arranged'.

in . . . beneficio: 'in view of your gift'.

in conscientiam duceret: 'mistake it for a guilty conscience'.

27. **vera:** the subject of *praedicet*.

29. **fidei causa:** 'to prove you right'.

militaria dona: like most armies, the Roman had its decorations, only they were more varied than most: there was the *corona*, a wreath for wearing on the head (*corona civica* for saving the life of a *civis*, *corona muralis* or *vallaris* for being first over wall or rampart, etc.); the *phalera*, a medallion for hanging from the horse's bridle; the *torques* for wearing round the neck; there was also the *hasta pura* (*pura* without the metal tip).

30. **Hae . . . haec;** adapting its gender to that of the predicate, as usual.

relicta: *quae* shows that this is neuter plural; it refers to both *imagines* and *nobilitas*.

31. **composita:** compare *compositam* in LXXXV 26 above.

parvi: most of the MSS. read *parum*; either the genitive of value was a little difficult for the copier, or he was used to Sallust's *parum*; a very slight smudge would be enough to put him off.

32. **Neque litteras Graecas:** Plutarch oddly writes that Marius 'neither learned to read Greek nor would make use of that language on any serious occasion'. (The second statement casts some doubt on the first.) Marius seems to have missed the usual Roman higher education; politically too, he was a late starter, and might never have started at all but for the Numantine War.

33. **illa:** the active of *doceo* can take two accusatives, and from *illa me docent* comes the passive *illa . . . doctus sum*.

agitare: Sallust's usual preference for *agitare* over *agere*; *praesidia* is abstract, *not* 'garrisons'.

humi requiescere: the 'soldier's general' shares the discomforts of the troops; he puts this into practice in Africa (C 4) but see Introduction, p. xlix.

34. **arte:** the adverb of *artus*, not the ablative of *ars*.

gloriam meam: *meam* is predicate after *faciam*; so of course is *illorum*.

35. **civile:** suitable for a citizen among citizens.

tute: the suffix *-te* is used to emphasise *tu*.

37. **quis:** *quibus*, i.e. ancestors.

ipsa . . . nos: he is turning the tables on them; he is the real noble.

38. **dono:** a common predicative dative with *dare*, 'for a present'.

39. **exorno:** used of the host; Marius did not give smart dinner parties.

cocum: fashionable cooks were in great demand in Rome; we read frequently of after-dinner performances by actors and dancers.

40. **sanctis:** used often of people, but remains a strong and almost religious word.

mulieribus, viris: this manly morality has a distinguished ancestry, beginning with Hector and Andromache in Homer (*IL* VI).

41. **Quin ergo:** 'well then', this initial *quin* often introduces a command.

42. **non est ita:** 'they wont''.

ereptum: supine.

43. **pessumae artes:** as *optumae artes*, in LXXXV 9, was the practice of virtue.

illis . . . reipublicae: another contrast on the lines of *illos . . . me* in LXXXV 34.

officiunt: as *proficio* is used of going ahead smoothly, *officio* means to block the way.

44. **non illorum flagitia:** their crimes did not really need a long description.

45. **mehercule:** this oath by Hercules belonged to ordinary conversation, not to high rhetoric. Its association is with the altar of Hercules in the cattle market, not with the national shrines on the Capitol.

47. **capessite:** when applied to men who are higher in the social scale, *capessere rem publicam*, means to embark on a career in politics.

    calamitate aliorum . . . imperatorum superbia: the 'chiasmus' order again.

    ceperit: the preceding *neque* contains *ne*, not *non*.

    consultor: for these active nouns see Ch. LXIII 2.

48. **praeda:** now that armies are to be recruited from the very poor (see the next chapter) this becomes an important motive for enlistment, and some generals feel an obligation to provide it.

    decebat: after an unfulfilled condition these verbs of obligation (and *possum*) are normally used in the indicative.

LXXXVI

commeatu: *commeare* is 'to go to and fro'; *commeatus* abstract noun, 'a going to and fro' is therefore a suitable word for the supplying, and then for the supplies, of an army.

legatum: the *legati* usually change with a change of governor.

2. **ex classibus:** the Roman people were divided by wealth into five classes and these classes were the basis for recruitment to the army – the assumption being that, since a man provided his own armour, the richer he was the better he would be armed, and the really poor would not be armed at all. Consequently, the lowest class were not liable to be recruited for the legions. During the second century B.C., as it became more difficult to find qualified recruits (see note on Ch. LXXXIV 3, *laetus* above), the qualification had been lowered, in practice if not in law; but its complete abolition came as a startling novelty.

    capite censos: assessed (on the censors' list), not by their property, but simply as individuals. This use of *caput* corresponds to our use of 'poll' in 'poll-tax'.

3. **alii . . . alii:** Sallust may have had such detailed knowledge of the rumours current in Rome at the time; but this may well be just a literary device – and an effective one – for expressing his own views.

inopia bonorum: this was certainly true, for reasons described above. Marius had realised that if the war was to be won large reinforcements would be necessary. It is interesting to speculate whether he had already formed his plan for recruitment before leaving Africa; if so, he seems to have kept it a secret.

auctus ... erat: they had made him consul, and their reward is the prospect of a new career; the *id genus* is his recruits.

sua: their own property.

cum pretio: see Ch.LXXXIV 4 above. In fact this change in recruitment had far-reaching effects which Marius cannot have foreseen, and was very largely responsible for the fall of the Roman Republic. The proletariat of Rome volunteered in large numbers, and as the need for compulsory recruitment of men with property was therefore diminished, the new soldiers set the tone of the army. In future, whenever a major war is finished, most of the troops have no civilian jobs to go back to, and are ready to follow their commander wherever more booty is to be found; and since the civilian government did not make any provision for demobilised soldiers, they looked to their commander to see that they were settled, preferably with a gift of Italian land. He was therefore, with troops at his back, in a position to dictate to the government in Rome. This loyalty of the troops was the basis of the power of Sulla, Pompey, Caesar and the triumvirs.

4. **decretum:** though a general levied troops by virtue of his own *imperium*, a decree of the senate was considered necessary. In any case, they supplied the money to pay them with.

5. **Rutilio:** one of Metellus' *legati*; for his career see note on Ch. L 1.

LXXXVII

omnia ibi ... militibus donat: this was what they had come for. Booty really belonged to the Roman treasury, but Roman generals were given wide discretion and some distribution to the troops was expected. Distribution on this scale was an abuse of power, and could only whet the appetites of the new recruits.

2. **pugnae:** dative.

4. **posse:** *possum* has no future infinitive.

laxius licentiusque: Sallust elsewhere also uses adverbs with *sum*, where we would expect adjectives.

LXXXVIII

spem: 'expectation'.

plebi patribusque: of all the actors of the *Jugurtha*, Metellus emerges with the greatest credit.

2. impigre prudenterque: a good combination.

3. exuerat: *armis exutus* is used of a soldier who has abandoned his arms in flight.

4. belli patrandi: (a means) of finishing the war.

viris aut loco: places whose garrisons or situation make them conspicuously a help to the enemy and a nuisance to himself.

singulas: one by one.

nudatum: participle, understanding the future infinitive of *sum*. This was also the strategy by which Caesar brought the Pompeians to battle in the campaign which ended at Munda in 45. It has been pointed out by Holroyd (*JRS* xviii 1) that it marks a turning point of this war (but see note on LIV 6). Previously, after the Roman army had passed through, Jugurtha could return to the area; in future the chief towns are either garrisoned or destroyed (Ch. XCII 3 below), and he is gradually excluded from Numidia altogether. Jugurtha would then have to take refuge with Bocchus of Mauretania, on whom everything would depend.

5. ne quid: indirect command.

6. simulaveritne: though *utrum* would here be normal, *-ne* is not uncommon in indirect question; another perfect subjunctive has to be supplied after *an*.

accideret: this compound is used of objects falling from the sky, and as an impersonal verb (*accidit*) of accidents; Bocchus would come 'as a bolt from the blue'.

LXXXIX

4. Capsa: see maps. The narrative shows that the distance was considered too great for a Roman attack. The town therefore had provided Jugurtha with a rallying-point out of reach of the Romans, and its elimination would make Marius' task much easier.

Hercules: in Ch. XVIII (not printed in this edition), Sallust records the African tradition that Hercules died in Spain, and that his army then settled in Africa.

apud Iugurtham: in the reign of Jugurtha.

immunes: free from taxation; in the Roman empire, too, some specially favoured cities were described as *liberae et immunes.*

5. **praeter:** governs *propinqua*; *alia* is nominative.

vasta: this word is connected with *vastare*, and implies desolation rather than size.

aquae: present participles are often treated like adjectives, taking an objective genitive e.g. *patiens laborum.*

ad hoc: 'in addition'.

ipsa: 'by its own nature', even without the thirst.

6. **invaserat:** this verb is often used by Sallust when fear or greed take possession of a man's mind (e.g. Ch.XIII 1, *Adherbalem . . . metus invadit*).

cum . . . tum: 'not only . . . but also'.

usum belli: its usefulness in war.

Thalam: the capture of Thala is described in Chapters LXXV–LXXVI (not printed in this edition); there, too, Sallust describes a desert march, special precautions for the supply of food and water, and the surprise of the enemy.

Capsenses: a new clause begins here, contrasted with *apud Thalam . . . erant.*

iugi: from the adjective *iugis*, 'continuously flowing'.

cetera: ablative singular – the rest (of the water) they used (was) rainwater.

7. **ibique et:** i.e. *et ibi et . . .*

agebat: this use of *agere* is usually confined to people – 'to live'; here *quae* means the Africans rather than Africa.

lacte et ferina carne: Caesar (*B.G.* V 14) says of the inhabitants of the inland of Britain, less civilised peoples than the men of Kent, *lacte et carne vivunt*; this means the absence of corn and wine, the crops of settled Mediterranean agriculture. Sallust is writing of the interior. It is not true of north-east Numidia, the area between Cirta and the Roman province, where, as Walsh has shown (*JRS* LV 154) the production of cereals was encouraged first by the Carthaginians and then by Masinissa. So Cary, *Geographic Background of Greek and Roman History*, pp. 220–9.

non lubidini: this idealising of the simple savages, by inference condemning Roman luxury, is naturally absent from the realistic writings of Caesar; it is a prominent theme of Tacitus' *Germania.*

XC

non poterat: there is no glorification of the people's general.

arvo: the word is derived from *arare*, to plough.

vacuos: nominative singular; the genitive *frugum* depends on it.

tempestate: season; this is the last operation of the year 107.

pro: 'considering'.

exornat: *ornare* regularly means to equip.

2. **equitibus auxiliariis:** the Roman army relied on foreign cavalry.

cohortibus expeditis: these are heavy infantry travelling light.

Laris: accusative plural of the name *Lares*. The exact position of the town is not known, so that we cannot follow this manœuvre.

3. **Tanain:** the river marked on Map 2 is the right distance from Capsa (see next chapter); but there is no certainty.

XCI

in itinere: Sallust's narrative seems to be describing a march over the hills from the upper waters of the Bagradas. This is the march to the Tanais.

ex coriis: as the cattle were killed for food they made leather bottles from their skins. *utres* are also mentioned in Metellus' march to Thala (Ch. LXXVI), and in Caesar *B.C.* I 48 where they are used by Spanish troops.

ignaris omnibus: 'their's not to reason why'.

quae . . . forent: this is the object of *parare*.

cum . . . ventum est: with a temporal antecedent (*sexto die*) *cum* is a relative ('on which'), and naturally is followed by an indicative.

vis: 'quantity'.

2. **levi:** because they will not be staying there for the night.

3. **tertia:** if it was September, the distance from the Tanais to Capsa should be about fifty miles.

duum: genitive; so *deum* for *deorum*.

4. **egressi:** for *egressi sunt*; *multi* is predicate, 'in large numbers'.

intentus: this is explained by *neque . . . sinere*; there were to be no distractions.

5. **res trepidae:** a staccato sentence, even by Sallust's standards; all these nominatives are subjects of *coegere*.

6. **Ceterum:** 'nevertheless'; although they had surrendered.

venum dati: the uncontracted verb *venum dare* is used by the historians for the sale of prisoners of war; its contracted form *vendere* is the usual word for to sell.

divisa: see notes on Chs. LXXXVI 3 and LXXXVII 1.

7. **contra ius belli:** a town which has surrendered should not be sacked. Marius is determined to prevent Jugurtha retreating southwards to a place of security whenever he is defeated in eastern Numidia. *facinus* was a favourite word of Sallust; it was used of a remarkable deed, and often of a crime (the exploit of the Usipi, who killed their centurions and sailed home round the north of Scotland, was described by Tacitus, *Agr.* 28, as a *magnum ac memorabile facinus*).

XCII

maior et clarior: the march to Capsa was considered a remarkable achievement. It raised Roman morale at a time when the war seemed likely to drag on indefinitely. For a comparison with the march to the Muluccha in the next year see note at the end of this section.

2. **bene consulta:** 'deserved successes'.

modesto: *modestus* usually means 'mild', and *modestum imperium* would then mean 'mild discipline'. But *modestus miles* would be a well-behaved, well-disciplined soldier, and Summers draws attention to VII 4 (not printed in this edition), where *modestissume parere* is used of prompt obedience on active service; Caesar (*B.G.* VII 52) uses *modestia* of military discipline. It is possible therefore that *modestum imperium* means not mild discipline but strict (that it is the soldier who is *modestus* not the *imperator*).

simul et: if *modesto* means 'mild', this is an ordinary 'and', since a lavish distribution of booty would naturally accompany mild discipline. If *modesto* means 'strict', then *simul et* is used because Marius is combining two things which do not normally go together – 'and at the same time'.

Our translation of *modestus* will affect, and be affected by, our judgement of the character of Sallust's Marius. It is a difficult decision. See also C 5, *pudore*.

magis quam mortalem: these words are probably to be taken together 'as more than mortal', though the adverb *magis* is then irregular. To take *magis* with *timere*, 'they feared him more than they feared a mortal' may be simpler in grammar, but it is not likely to be what Sallust meant.

portendi: normally used for predictions of inevitable doom; here they believe that the gods tell Marius what will happen, and therefore what to do. *nutus* (like *numen*) is derived from *nuere* 'to nod'.

3. **ad alia oppida:** this is the new strategy in action, the systematic destruction or garrisoning of the towns of Numidia. Jugurtha will eventually have no foothold in his kingdom.

luctu: Sallust does not conceal the human consequences of this strategy. Tacitus found words to describe Roman pacification when he made a Scottish chieftain say (*Agr.* 30) *ubi solitudinem faciunt pacem appellant.*

Capsensium: understand *rem.*

4. **aliam rem:** this is an attack on a hill fort, which is described in the next two chapters. Although they are not printed in this edition a word needs to be said. The fort is said by Sallust to be 'not far from the river Muluccha, which separated the kingdoms of Jugurtha and Bocchus', and it has been assumed that the Muluccha was the modern Moulouya; it is so shown on the map in *CAH* IX 117.

A look at the map and a moment's arithmetic will show that this is absurd. From the Bagradas to the Muluccha is about seven hundred miles, which would mean well over forty days' solid marching each way, even if no enemy were expected. (K. Wellesely, 'The *Dies Imperii* of Tiberius', in *JRS* LVII (1967) 25: 'on good roads within the frontiers Roman infantrymen could march at an average rate of 18–20 Roman miles per day over an extended period'.) It is only necessary to visualise the plight of Marius, attacked when thirty days out from his base by the combined forces of Jugurtha and Bocchus, or the fate of Numidia if they chose to avoid him and march eastwards in force. His would be the rashest march in military history between Alexander and Napoleon. That Sallust ignores the march, and writes of the operation *non eadem asperitate*, is only another nail in the coffin of the Moulouya. Those who accept it are driven to disbelieve Sallust's clear implication (*XCV 1*) that Marius made the outward march without his cavalry.

It follows that the river in our story was several hundred miles east of the Moulouya, and either this easterly river was called

Muluccha, or Sallust has got the name wrong. It has been suggested by Walsh (*JRS* LV 152) that there was some confusion about the western boundary of Numidia, that it had once been the Moulouya, but was now a river much farther to the East; Sallust had transferred the name of the old frontier to the new. See 'Note on the Boundaries of Numidia', p. liv.

Since the map on the frontispiece is meant to illustrate what happened, and is not an accompaniment to a scholarly discussion, I have boldly marked the Muluccha where I think this siege took place.

XCV

ea res: the long drawn-out siege.

quaestor: this was the first important office in the senatorial *cursus honorum;* the holder must be aged 29 or over, and the duties were primarily financial. Sulla would be in charge of the official accounts in the province, including army pay, but in time of war, owing to the small number of *legati* (not more than three, as a rule), the quaestor might be given other tasks.

equitatu: necessary for dealing with guerrilla warfare and African cavalry. Marius is better equipped than Metellus had been. These men will be from the upper classes of the Italian cities, where Marius has many friends.

2. **tanti viri:** this genitive after *admonere* (as if it were a verb of remembering) is not confined to Sallust.

res: the narrative of events.

alio loco: this seems to imply that Sallust has already planned his future work. In fact when he started the *Histories* he began in the year 78, presumably with the death of Sulla, but the surviving fragments indicate that he had found it necessary to write at some length about the dictator's earlier career (Syme, *Sallust*, p. 181).

L. Sisenna: a senator, praetor in 78, he then governed Sicily, and later was a legate of Pompey in Asia. He wrote a history of the Social and Civil Wars and the dictatorship of Sulla. Apart from the bias in favour of Sulla noted here, his work was praised by Cicero and Sallust, and became the standard history of the period; as such in was used by Livy. Badian ('Waiting for Sulla', *JRS* LII (1962) 50) gives a full account. (To look up Sisenna in Syme's index you need to discover that his *nomen* was Cornelius.)

parum . . . libero: he will of course have been elected praetor when Sulla was still influential in Rome.

3. **Sulla:** for the character-sketch as a feature of Roman histories see Introduction, p. xlvi; many of the stylistic tricks are to be found in this passage.

   gentis patriciae: his full name was L. Cornelius Sulla. Many of the most influential families at this time were plebeian, though Sulla himself, and later, Augustus, tried to revive the importance of the patricians.

   nobilis: nominative: for the technical meaning see note on Ch.V 1, *nobilitatis*.

   litteris Graecis: as were most of his upper-class contemporaries.

   remorata: deponent, understand *eum*.

   consuli: impersonal passive.

   uxore: Sulla was married five times, but we do not know exactly what Sallust means. Rolfe translates 'his conduct as a husband might have been more honourable'.

   altitudo: depth, not exaltation.

   largitor: Cato in Livy is *contemptor gratiae*, Catiline in Sallust is *simulator ac dissimulator*: these nouns can supply the lack of a past participle active (*victor* and *victus*).

4. **felicissumo:** Sulla took for himself the name Felix.

   civilem victoriam: he landed in Italy in 83, and his victory was completed by the battle of the Colline gate in 82. This limitation on his *felicitas* is explained by the next sentence *nam postea . . .*

XCVI

   atque in castra: involving, on the traditional view, a march of over 800 miles and a rendezvous in completely unknown country.

   rudis antea: by the time a man is quaestor he has usually had some military service, but of course he might not have been on *active* service. Plutarch, in his life of Sulla, has nothing to say of his career before the quaestorship.

   belli: objective genitive (if *ignarus* was a verb, *bellum* would be its object, *ignorabat bellum*).

   paucis tempestatibus: this really means no more than *brevi tempore*.

2. **milites:** accusative.

benigne: Sulla had seen the importance to an ambitious noble of the personal loyalty of his soldiers. His conduct now is a foretaste of the preliminaries to the march on Rome in 88.

per se ipse: the opposite of *rogantibus*; *multis* and *aliis* are both dative.

invitus: this adjective is regularly used where we should use an adverb.

aes mutuom: the more usual phrase for 'debt' is *aes alienum*.

id: this is explained by the clause *ut illi* . . .

illi: his debtors; *quam plurumi* agrees with it, 'that they should be as many as possible'.

3. **operibus:** in a military context the plural *opera* nearly always means digging, usually for the routine protection of the army when it halts.

multus: adjective for the English adverb again; he was frequently there.

famam laedere: in contrast with the behaviour of Marius described in Ch. LXIV.

consilio . . . manu: between them, these are meant to contain the whole activity of a soldier.

4. **brevi:** understand *tempore*.

XCVII

At: returning to the story of the war, after the digression on Sulla. But there is no attempt to round off the Muluccha campaign, or to describe the march back.

Bocchum: we must assume that Bocchus' territory begins either at or not far from the Ampsaga (See Introduction. Note on the Boundaries of Numidia, p. liv.)

2. **dubium:** agreeing with *Quem*; *belli* depends on *rationes*.

rationes trahere: to calculate, to weigh the pros and cons.

partem tertiam: this would presumably give Bocchus all the territory once ruled by the Syphax.

suis: Jugurtha's – 'with his kindgom intact'.

3. **die:** genitive.

victis: this participle stands for a condition, the opposite of *si vicissent* (which itself represents a future perfect *si vicerimus*).

contra: adverb.

4. **simul . . . et:** 'no sooner had he heard . . . '; so the Greeks wrote ἅμα . . . καί . . .

antequam: no different in meaning from *priusquam* above.

catervatim: 'by individual companies'; similarly *viritim* 'man by man', *ostiatim* 'from door to door'; these adverbs in *-im* must have their origin in an accusative.

conglobaverat: this frequentative pluperfect is usually followed by a main verb in the imperfect, but Sallust's love of the historic present is too much for him.

5. **advorsos:** 'facing', the enemy in front of them.

novi veteresque: the MSS. have *veteres novique*, but, in view of the words which immediately follow, this cannot be right. The cause of the copying error seems to be just plain carelessness.

belli: the same objective genitive as in the previous chapter *locorum scientes*.

orbis facere: a defensive formation, familiar from Caesar and Livy. The equivalent British formation in the Napoleonic Wars was a square.

XCVIII

turma sua: a cavalry word; it is not clear whether this is the same as the *cohors praetoria* – the general's bodyguard – or a part of it. The *cohors* usually contained friends or clients of the commander, and Caesar complains (*B.G.*I 39) that some of those who had come with him to Gaul were not trained soldiers.

manu consulere militibus: if *consulere* can mean 'give instructions to', the sense is clear; *imperare* will mean 'give orders by word of mouth'. But *consulere militibus* should mean 'to look after their interests', and then *manu* must mean 'by fighting'.

conturbatis omnibus: ablative, probably.

3. **ex copia rerum:** 'in accordance with the situation'.

trahit: the usual verbs with *consilium* are *capere* and *inire*.

quaerebat: 'needed'; most of the MSS. have *gerebat*, one has *regebat*; *gerebant* and *regebant* are also found. Once a word has been wrongly written, subsequent copyists often go from bad to worse.

4. **pleno gradu:** a technical term, occurring several times in Livy; not 'double time', but faster than ordinary marching; according to the military writer Vegetius (I 9), it was about four miles an hour,

while *militaris gradus* was about three. Marius is marching to the larger hill.

subducit: this compound is used of leading troops away from the fighting.

6. **fugerant:** some MSS. have *fugere aut*, a copyist having got into the habit of writing historic infinitives.

XCIX

signa: in Livy VII 35 it was a trumpet which marked the time for the relieving of sentries; the verb would naturally be *canere*.

vigiles: presumably they had some method of sounding the alarm. All the MSS. have *vectigales* ('tribute-paying'), but this can hardly be right.

portis: evidently the Romans had strengthened the natural defences of the hill.

C **quadrato agmine:** 'in battle formation'; the phrase is usually applied to an army which is on the march but ready for immediate action. Here the legions are protected on all sides by a screen of more mobile troops. In Caesar *B.G.* VIII 8, where the words are used, the formation appears to be different, but the motive is the same.

2. **dextumos:** a rare superlative of *dexter*; not surprisingly some MSS. have the familiar word *extremos*.

cohortis: accusative; *curabat* is constructed first with *cum funditoribus* and then transitively.

expeditis manipulis: these are legionaries, but they are not now carrying their packs or trenching equipment.

3. **minume cari:** they were considered expendable; *carus* is 'valuable', 'expensive', and the French *cher* is derived from it.

quasi nullo imposito: 'as if he had not put anyone in command'.

4. **item:** 'in the same way' – the soldiers must also be *armati intentique*.

facere: this is subordinate to *secus at ue; munire* is a main verb. This use of a historic infinitive in a clause is rare.

excubitum: supine; it applies to both the objects of *mittere*.

futurum: understand *esse*; not *futura*, though the subject is plural; Sallust is treating the future infinitive as indeclinable.

volentibus: 'to their liking'; this use of the participle is found in Thucydides. This description of Marius and his army may be factually true. It may, however, be a conventional description of the typical behaviour of the Good Commander. See Introduction, p. xlix.

5. **pudore:** this may throw some light on *modesto imperio* (Ch. XCII 2). *malum* is sometimes used for 'punishment'. He shamed them into doing their duty by sharing their hardships; there follow two explanations which belittle his motives.

voluptati habuisset: 'that he took pleasure in it'.

nisi tamen: 'all the same'; *gesta* is probably a main verb, and this is Sallust's judgement. To be a continuation of the reported speech would need *gesta esset* (or *rem publicam gestam*). *decore* is adverb from *decorus*.

CI

quarto . . . die: Holroyd (*JRS* xviii 1) assumes that this is the end of the march back from the 'Muluccha'. But three days' marching at the alert, *agmine quadrato*, would not take an army very far, so that even if this is the return from the west it need not have been the distant west.

speculatores: the next sentence makes it clear that these are Marius' scouts.

2. **nullo ordine commutato:** he is in fact prepared for an attack from any direction.

3. **aeque:** 'if he attacked equally in all directions'.

4. **Sulla:** for the Roman formation see the previous chapter. It gradually becomes clear that Marius himself was commanding the front of the Roman army, while Sulla commanded the cavalry on the right. Jugurtha attacks the Roman front with cavalry, Bocchus the rear with infantry.

turmatim: for a note on these adverbs see Ch. XCVII 4.

6. **convortit:** he came round to join Bocchus. *Numida* is Jugurtha.

Numantiam: when he had served under Scipio Aemilianus in Spain.

oblitum: from *oblinere* to smear.

pedite: this may be one soldier, or it may be used as a collective noun.

8. **aberant:** the Romans.

quos: *advorsum ire* is treated here as a transitive verb.

Mauris: Bocchus' men.

9. **vitabundus:** 'to save his life'; adjectives in *-bundus*, common in Livy, often have a notion of purpose, like the future participle.

10. **equitibus:** Jugurtha had left his own cavalry attacking Marius.

11. **visus:** a noun.

CII

Postea loci: 'after this point of time'.

Cirtam: after what he wrote at the beginning of Ch. C it seems that Sallust is counting Cirta as an *oppidum maritumum*; which goes to show the difficulty of following his geography.

2. **post diem:** this use of *post* as a preposition followed by *quam* is not uncommon.

iterum: the second attack is that described in the last section.

regis verbis: 'in the King's name'. Now that Bocchus has been defeated he is ready to come to terms.

3. **acciti:** summoned (to hear, not to speak).

avorsum: 'if he was hostile'.

4. **facundiae:** for Sulla's abilities see Ch. XCV 3–4.

Manlio: as a *legatus* of Marius he would naturally be older than the quaestor and higher in rank.

CXI

Ad ea: Bocchus has just said that he will retire behind his own frontier (the 'Muluccha', but see p. lv), and cease to help Jugurtha.

multis: understand *verbis*; this is the opposite of *breviter et modice*. The detail in which Sulla's diplomacy is here recorded almost certainly shows that Sallust is using Sulla's memoirs (as, for the battle described in Chs XLIX–LIII, he probably had Rutilius Rufus').

quod polliceatur: this is the object of *habituros*.

retulisse: impersonal, the past infinitive of *refert*; *illorum* and *sua* both depend on it, according to its normal usage – 'in their interests . . . in his own'.

copiam: 'control of . . .'

quam . . . peteret: it was assumed by Last (*CAH* ix 130) that this is the *Numidiae partem tertiam* which he was promised by Jugurtha in Ch. XCVII: also that the Romans subsequently honoured this promise of Sulla. But how near to Cirta this brought Bocchus we do not know.

ultro: this word is used of something done voluntarily, beyond what is necessary.

2. **cognationem**: this is relationship by blood, *adfinitas* is relationship by marriage. Only the second is strictly true here, as Jugurtha had married Bocchus' daughter.

metuere: historic infinitive (if it was indirect statement *erant* should be *essent*).

popularium: his own subjects.

CXII

Asparem: Aspar was mentioned in Ch. CVIII as a close friend of Bocchus and an emissary of Jugurtha; Dabar was also a Numidian whom Sallust goes out of his way to praise for honesty, calling him *sanctus vir*.

poni: that the war could be stopped.

2. **cuncta**: accusative; from the active *eum hanc rem doceo* comes the passive *is hanc rem docetur*.

quae: nominative; *quae imperarentur* is the object of *facere*.

conventam: *convenire* is used as a transitive verb, though not, elsewhere, with the meaning 'to agree upon'.

3. **consultum**: being bracketed with *ratam pacem* this must be the neuter of the past participle, used impersonally: 'to consult the interests of both of them and ratify the peace'.

sua ignavia: understand 'who had come into the power of the enemy'. Fortunately for Sulla, this was never put to the test.

CXIII

comperimus: *comperere* is used of detecting the truth; Cicero, when he had detected the conspiracy of Catiline, bored his friends by the repitition *omnia comperi*.

regiae: another way of saying *regis* (not, probably, *regum* – this is the character of Bocchus, not of kings in general).

3. **inmutata**: *in* before a verb strengthens the meaning, before an adjective contradicts it. *inmutare* is 'to change', and its participle *inmutatus* is 'changed' (the adjective *inmutabilis* means unchangeable).

varius: 'changeable'.

quae: his face and eyes; this is a continuation of the indirect statement; *occulta* is the object of *patefecisse*.

traditur: with the capture of Jugurtha Sallust's interest in the war finishes. We are left to find out from other sources what the Romans did with Numidia. In fact they simply installed another king of the same family, Gauda (see family tree, p. xv). As Badian points out (*Roman Imperialism*, p. 25) no one at Rome had any intention of changing the system.

CXIV

Per idem tempus: this in 105, when Caepio and Manlius were defeated and their armies destroyed at Arausio in Transalpine Gaul by the Cimbri, a German tribe. The Roman people thought that their commanders had been criminally negligent, and both of them were condemned in 103.

2. **Illi:** the Romans of that time.

habuere: 'thought'.

prona: 'easy'.

cum Gallis: the defeat by the Gauls at the river Allia in 390, which was followed by the capture of Rome itself, still ranked as one of the legendary national disasters.

3. **absens:** strictly, all candidates had to be present in the city on nomination day; but the senate could grant exemption, and in view of public feeling they would have no option.

Gallia: as the province had given him the command against Jugurtha, that of Gaul carried with it the war against the Germans.

Kalendis Ianuariis: this is the beginning of 104. According to the Roman custom, Jugurtha was led captive in the triumphal procession and then put to death. We can only conjecture why Jugurtha's death was not mentioned by Sallust.

4. **in illo sitae:** the expected German invasion was delayed, and the Roman took the unprecedented course of re-electing the same man to the consulship for five consecutive years (104–100). With his first consulship of 107, and his final election in the blood-bath of 88–87, this gave Marius a total of seven consulships, unequalled by any Roman before Augustus.

PROLOGUE

I. Falso queritur de natura sua genus humanum, quod imbecilla atque aevi brevis forte potius quam virtute regatur. 2. Nam contra reputando neque maius aliud neque praestabilius invenies, magisque naturae industriam hominum quam vim aut tempus deesse. 3. Sed dux atque imperator vitae mortalium animus est; qui ubi ad gloriam virtutis via grassatur, abunde pollens potensque et clarus est, neque fortunae eget; quippe quae probitatem, industriam, alias artis bonas neque dare neque eripere cuiquam potest; 4. sin captus pravis cupidinibus ad inertiam et voluptates corporis pessum datus est, perniciosa lubidine paulisper usus, ubi per socordiam vires, tempus, ingenium defluxere, naturae infirmitas accusatur; suam quisque culpam auctores ad negotia transferunt. 5. Quod si hominibus bonarum rerum tanta cura esset, quanto studio aliena ac nihil profutura, multumque etiam periculosa petunt, neque regerentur magis quam regerent casus, et eo magnitudinis procederent, uti pro mortalibus gloria aeterni fierent.

II. Nam uti genus hominum compositum ex anima et corpore, ita res cunctae studiaque omnia nostra corporis alia, alia animi naturam sequuntur. 2. Igitur praeclara facies, magnae divitiae, ad hoc vis corporis alia huiuscemodi omnia brevi dilabuntur; at ingenii egregia facinora sicuti anima immortalia sunt. 3. Postremo corporis et

Prologue

SALLUST JUGURTHA I–IV (Translation)

I. Wrongly does the human race complain of its own nature, saying that being weak and short-lived it is governed by chance rather than its own virtues. On the contrary, you could not think of anything greater than human nature or preferable to it, and you would find that men do not so much lack mature strength as application. But the leader and captain of a man's life is his mind; when it fights its way to glory by the path of valour, it has massive power, strength and fame, and is not unblessed by fortune; for fortune cannot give or take away honesty, industry or other such virtuous habits. But if a man is corrupted by base desires and degraded enjoyment of idle pleasures of the body, he for a short time enjoys this destructive hedonism, but then, when sloth has undermined his strength, endurance and mental power, he turns round and finds fault with the weakness of human nature; men who are in fact themselves responsible put the blame for their failure on their environment.

But if men were as enthusiastic about the pursuit of virtue as they are about that of things which are alien, useless and often dangerous to them, they would rule events instead of being ruled by them, and they would rise to such heights that from mortality they would in their glory put on immortality.

II. For as the nature of man is a mixture of body and soul, so, of all our activities and enthusiasms, some follow the nature of the body, others that of the mind. So it happens that distinguished appearance, great wealth, bodily strength, all

fortunae bonorum ut initium, sic finis est, omniaque orta occidunt, et aucta senescunt; animus incorruptus, aeternus, rector humani generis agit atque habet cuncta, neque ipse habetur. **4.** Quo magis pravitas eorum admiranda est, qui dediti corporis gaudiis per luxum atque ignaviam aetatem agunt; ceterum ingenium, quo neque melius neque amplius aliud in natura mortalium est, incultu atque socordia torpescere sinunt; cum praesertim tam multae variaeque sint artes animi, quibus summa claritudo paratur.

III. Verum ex his magistratus et imperia, postremo omnis cura rerum publicarum minume mihi hac tempestate cupiunda videntur; quoniam neque virtuti honos datur; neque illi, quibus per fraudem is fuit, tuti, aut eo magis honesti sunt. **2.** Nam vi quidem regere patriam aut parentes quamquam et possis, et delicta corrigas, tamen importunum est; cum praesertim omnes rerum mutationes caedem, fugam, aliaque hostilia portendant: **3.** frustra autem niti, neque aliud se fatigando nisi odium quaerere extremae dementiae est; nisi forte quem inhonesta et perniciosa lubido tenet potentiae paucorum decus atque libertatem suam gratificari.

IV. Ceterum ex aliis negotiis quae ingenio exercentur, in primis magno usui est memoria rerum gestarum; **2.** cuius de virtute quia multi dixere, praetereundum puto, simul ne per insolentiam quis existimet memet studium meum laudando extollere. **3.** Atque ego credo fore qui, quia decrevi procul a republica aetatem agere, tanto tamque utili labori meo nomen inertiae imponant; certe, quibus maxuma industria videtur salutare plebem et conviviis gratiam quaerere. **4.** Qui si reputaverint. et quibus ego

things of this kind in fact, will be short-lived, while famous feats of the mind, like the soul itself, are immortal.

Finally physical advantages and the gifts of fortune end as they began: they rise and fall, wax and wane; but the mind, incorruptible and eternal, the ruler of the human race, guides and controls all things, and is not itself controlled. All the more remarkable therefore is the wickedness of those who give themselves up to the pleasures of the body, and live lives of luxury and ease, while they allow their intelligence, which is the best and finest part of the nature of man, to lose its vigour for lack of exercise and energy; especially since there are many varied fields in which the mind can gain distinction.

III. However, some of these fields – political office, military commands, in fact all the activities of the state – seem to me at this time undesirable, since office is not given to good men, and those to whom it is given as a result of treachery are neither protected nor made better by it. For even if you can rule your country and your obedient countrymen by force, and even if you can and do correct their faults, it is nevertheless not right to do so. For all changes bring slaughter, exile and other crimes of violence in their wake; on the other hand to struggle in vain, and to gain no reward for your efforts but hatred, is sheer lunacy – unless a man is possessed by a shameful and destructive passion to throw away his own honour and freedom to gratify the tyranny of the mighty.

IV. But of all intellectual occupations the most useful is the recording of past events. I need not sing its praises, since many have already done so, and I do not want anyone to think I am exaggerating the merits of my own studies. I think, too, that since I have decided to abandon public life there will be some who will decry my useful labours and say

temporibus magistratus adeptus sim, et quales viri idem
adsequi nequiverint, et postea quae genera hominum in
senatum pervenerint, profecto existumabunt me magis
merito quam ignavia iudicium animi mei mutavisse,
maiusque commodum ex otio meo quam ex aliorum negotiis reipublicae venturum. **5.** Nam saepe audivi Q. Maxi-
mum, **P.** Scipionem, praeterea civitatis nostrae praeclaros
viros solitos ita dicere, cum maiorum imagines intuerentur,
vehementissume sibi animum ad virtutem accendi; **6.**
scilicet non ceram illam, neque figuram, tantam vim in
sese habere; sed memoria rerum gestarum eam flammam
egregiis viris in pectore crescere, neque prius sedari, quam
virtus eorum famam atque gloriam adaequaverit. **7.** At
contra quis est omnium his moribus, quin divitiis et sump-
tibus, non probitate neque industria cum maioribus suis
contendat? etiam homines novi, qui antea per virtutem
soliti erant nobilitatem antevenire, furtim aut per latrocinia[1]
potius quam bonis artibus ad imperia et honores nitun-
tur; **8.** proinde quasi praetura et consulatus atque alia
omnia huiuscemodi per se ipsa clara et magnifica sint, ac
non perinde habeantur, ut eorum, qui ea sustinent, virtus
est. **9.** Verum ego liberius altiusque processi, dum me
civitatis morum piget taedetque: nunc ad inceptum redeo.

---

[1] *furtim aut per latrocinia* is read by R. Syme in 'Two Emendations
in Sallust', *Philologus*, CVI (1962) 300, who suggests that Sallust has in
mind two particular villains of the triumviral period, Balbus (*furtim*)
and Salvidienus Rufus (*per latrocinia*). The MSS have *et* for *aut*.

that they are nothing but laziness, especially those men who think that the greatest of all activities is to win the favour of the mob and gain influence by dispensing hospitality. But if they reflect on the times in which I gained office, and the quality of the men who failed, and then remember what kind of men subsequently entered the senate, they will surely agree that my change of mind was right, and not the result of idleness; and that my leisure will bring more profit to the commonwealth than the activities of others.

For I have often heard tell that distinguished Romans, including Quintus Maximus and Publius Scipio, used to say that their minds were inspired to good deeds by the sight of the busts of their ancestors. Of course they did not think that the wax or the features had this power in themselves; it is by the recollection of deeds of old that that fire is lit in the hearts of great men so that it cannot be put out until the glory of their own exploits rises to an equal height.

In the temper of our time, on the other hand, who is there who does not rival the wealth and extravagance of his ancestors, instead of their honesty and conscientiousness? This includes the 'new men', who once upon a time outstripped the nobles by their virtues, but now make their way to distinction like thieves or robbers![1] – just as if praetorships and consulships and such-like honours conferred fame and distinction by their own right, and did not depend for their esteem on the qualities of the holder.

But I have strayed far from my path, angered and saddened by the morals of my country. Now I come to my task.

Vocabulary

abdo (3) -didi, -ditum, *hide.*

abicio (3) -ieci, -iectum, *throw away.*

abnuo (3) -nui, -nutum, *refuse.*

abstineo (2) -tinui, -tentum, *abstain.*

abstraho (3) -traxi, -tractum, *remove.*

absum, -esse, -fui, *be absent, distant.*

absumo (3) -sumpsi, -sumptum, *take away.*

abundantia (1), *abundance.*

abundus, -a, -um, *abounding.*

accedo (3) -cessi, -cessum, *approach, be added.*

accendo (3) -cendi, -censum, *set fire to, inflame.*

acceptio, -onis (f.), *acceptance.*

accerso (3) -ivi, -itum, *summon.*

accidit, *it happens.*

accio (4), *send for.*

accipio (3) -cepi, -ceptum, *receive, hear, welcome.*

accuratus, -a, -um, *formal.*

accurro (3) -curri, -cursum, *run to.*

acer, acris, acre, *energetic.*

acerbus, -a, -um, *bitter.*

acriter, *vigorously.*

adduco (3) -duxi, -ductum, *lead in.*

adeo, -ire, -ivi, -itum, *approach.*

adeo, *so much.*

adf..., see aff...

adhibeo (2), *summon, apply.*

adimo (3) -emi, -emptum, *take away.*

adipiscor (3) adeptus, *achieve.*

aditus (4), *approach.*

adiumentum, -i (n.), *assistance.*

adiungo (3) -iunxi, -iunctum, *join.*

adiutor, -oris (m.), *helper.*

administer, -ri (m.), *servant, accomplice.*

administro (1), *administer.*

admitto (3) -misi, -missum, *admit, commit.*

admoneo (2), *remind.*

adnitor (3) -nisus, *strive.*

adolesco (3) -olui, *grow up.*

adopto (1), *adopt.*

adp..., see app...

adquiro (3) -sivi, -situm, *acquire.*

adsum, *be present, help.*

adsumo (3) -sumpsi, -sumptum, *take.*

adulescens, *young; young man.*

adulescentia, -ae (f.), *youth.*

adulterinus, -a, -um, *counterfeit.*

advecticius, -a, -um, *imported.*

advehor (3) -vectus, *arrive.*

advento (1), *arrive.*

adventus (4), *arrival.*

advorsarius, -a, -um, *hostile; enemy.*

advorsor (1), *oppose.*

advorsus, -a, -um, *in the front, adverse.*

advorsus, adversum (prep.), *against.*

aedes, -ium (f.), *house.*

aedificium, -i (n.), *building.*

aeger, -gra, -grum, *ill, corrupt, difficult.*

aegritudo, -inis (f.), *ill health, difficulty.*

aemulus. -i (m.), *emulator.*
aequabilis, -e, *consistent, still.*
aequalis, -e, *equal, contemporary.*
aequos, -a, -om, *just, level*; aequo animo, *calmly.*
aerarium, -i (n.), *treasury.*
aerumna, -ae (f.), *pain, torture.*
aes, aeris (n.), *bronze, copper.*
aestas, -atis (f.), *summer.*
aestivus, -a, -um, *summer.*
aestus (4), heat.
aetas, -atis (f.), *age.*
aeternus, -a, -um, *eternal.*
affatim, *enough.*
affecto (1), *aspire to.*
affinis, -e, *related; relation.*
affinitas, -atis (f.), *relationship.*
affligo (3) -ixi, -ictum, *afflict.*
aggredior (3) -essus, *attack, attempt, approach.*
agito (1), *drive, worry, treat, do, shake, spend.*
ago (3) egi, actum, *drive, treat, do, spend.*
agrestis, -e, *rural, rustic.*
aio (3), *say.*
ala, -ae (f.), *wing.*
alieno (1), *alienate.*
alienus, -a, -um, *alien, someone else's.*
alio (adv.), *to somewhere else.*
aliquis, *someone.*
aliquot, *some, a number of.*
altitudo, -dinis (f.), *height, depth.*
altus, -a, -um, *high, deep.*
altus (alo), *brought up.*
ambeo, -ire, -itum, *approach, canvass.*
ambitio, -onis (f.), *canvassing, ambition.*
ambitiosus, -a, -um, *ambitious, popular.*
ambo, -ae, -o, *both.*
amitto (3) -misi, -missum, *lose.*

amplius, *more.*
amplus, -a, -um, *large, distinguished.*
ancilla, -ae (f.), *servant.*
animadverto (3) -ti, -sum, *notice.*
antecapio (3) -cepi, -ceptum, *take in advance, forestall.*
anteeo (4) -ivi, -itum, *outdistance.*
antefero (3) -tuli, -latum, *prefer.*
antevenio (4) -veni, -ventum, *get in front of, arrive first.*
anxius, -a, -um, *anxious.*
apertus, -a, -um, *open.*
appello (1), *speak to.*
appello (3) -puli, -pulsum, *bring to land.*
appeto (3) -ivi, -itum, *seek.*
appropinquo (1), *approach.*
arbitrium, -i (n.), *will, decision.*
arbustum, -i (n.), *bush.*
arcesso (3) -ivi, -itum, *send for.*
ardeo (2) arsi, arsum, *be on fire.*
arenosus, -a, -um, *sandy.*
argentum, -i (n.), *silver.*
aridus, -a, -um, *dry.*
armo (1), *arm.*
arrigo (3) -rexi, -rectum, *excite.*
arrogo (1), *claim.*
ars, artis (f.), *quality, practice, skill.*
artificium, -i (n.), *artifice.*
artus, -a, -um, *strict, close-packed.*
arvum, -i (n.), *cultivated land.*
ascendo (3) -endi, -ensum, *climb.*
asper, -era, -erum, *hard, harsh.*
asperitas, -atis (f.), *difficulty.*
atrocitas, -atis (f.), *ferocity.*
atrox, *fierce.*
attendo (3) -endi, -entum, *take notice of.*
attero (3) -trivi, -tritum, *wear down.*
attingo (3) -igi, -actum, *touch, border, reach, enter on.*
auctor, -oris (m.), *abettor.*
auctoritas, -atis (f.), *authority.*

audax, *bold.*
audeo (2) ausus, *dare.*
augeo (2) -xi, -ctum, *increase.*
aurum, -i (n.), *gold.*
auxiliarius, -a, -um, *auxiliary.*
auxilium, -i (n.), *help;* auxilia, -orum, *allied troops.*
avaritia, -ae (f.), *greed.*
avidus, -a, -um, *greedy, eager.*
avius, -a, -um, *out of the way, devious.*
avorto (3) -ti, -sum, *turn away.*

bellicosus, -a, -um, *warlike.*
bellicus, -a, -um, *for war.*
beneficium, -i (n.), *good deed.*
benignus, -a, -um, *kind.*
bis, *twice.*

cadaver, -veris (n.), *corpse.*
cado (3) cecidi, casum, *fall.*
caecus, -a, -um, *blind, concealed.*
caedes, -is (f.), *slaughter.*
caedo (3) cecidi, caesum, *kill.*
callidus, -a, -um, *clever.*
capesso (3) -ivi, -itum, *manage, take in hand.*
carcer, -eris (m.), *prison.*
caro, carnis (f.), *meat.*
carus, -a, -um, *dear.*
castellum, -i (n.), *fort.*
casus (4), *chance.*
catena, -ae (f.), *chain, bond.*
catervatim, *in bands.*
caveo (2) cavi, cautum, *take care.*
cedo (3) cessi, cessum, *go, yield.*
celebro (1), *celebrate, frequent.*
censeo (2) censui, censum, *vote, decide, assess.*
centuria, -ae (f.), *century.*
certamen, -inis (n.), *contest.*
certe, *certainly.*
certo (1), *compete, fight.*

certus, -a, -um, *sure, certain.*
ceteri, -ae, -a, *the rest.*
ceterum, *but, and then.*
cibus, -i (m.), *food.*
cicatrix, -icis (f.), *scar.*
circumdo (1) -dedi, -datum, *surround.*
circumeo, *go round.*
circumfundor (3) -fusus, *surround.*
circumsedeo (2) -sedi, -sessum, *surround.*
circumvenio (4) -veni, -ventum, *surround.*
citus, -a, -um, *swift.*
civilis, -e, *civil.*
clades, -is (f.), *disaster.*
clam, *secretly.*
clarus, -a, -um, *famous.*
classis, -is (f.), *fleet, property class.*
claudo (3) -si, -sum, *shut.*
clavis, -is (f.), *key.*
clemens, *merciful.*
clientela, -ae (f.), *supporters.*
coalesco (3) -alui, *grow together.*
cocus, -i (m.), *cook.*
coepi, coeptus sum, *begin.*
coerceo (2), *control.*
cognatio, -onis (f.), *relationship.*
cognatus, -a, -um, *related.*
cognomen, -inis (n.), *name, surname.*
cogo (3) coegi, -actum, *compel, drive together, collect.*
cohors, -ortis (f.), *cohort.*
collega, -ae (m.), *colleague.*
collis, -is (m.), *hill.*
colloquium, -i (n.), *conference.*
comitia, -orum (n.), *assembly, election.*
commeatus (4), *supplies.*
commodum, -i (n.), *advantage, convenience.*
commonefacio (3), *inform.*

commoveo (2) -ovi, -otum, *move, alarm.*

communis, -e, *common.*

commutatio, -onis (f.), *change.*

commuto (1), *change.*

comparo (1), *collect, prepare.*

comperio (3) -eri, -ertum, *find out.*

compleo (2) -evi, -etum, *fill.*

compono (3), *arrange, compare; compositus, -a, -um, elaborate, finished.*

comporto (1), *bring in.*

concedo (3) -cessi, -cessum, *yield, go.*

concido (3) -cidi, *collapse.*

concordia, -ae (f.), *agreement, harmony.*

concubina, -ae (f.), *concubine.*

condicio, -onis (f.), *condition.*

conditor, -oris (m.), *founder.*

condono (1), *present, pardon.*

conduco (3) -duxi, -ductum, *lead together.*

confero (3) -tuli, -latum, *collect, compare.*

confertus, -a, -um, *in a body.*

conficio (3) -feci, -fectum, *complete, destroy.*

confido (3) -fisus, *trust.*

confinis, -e, *neighbour.*

confirmo (1), *strengthen, crown.*

conglobare (1), *throw together.*

coniungo (3) -iunxi, -iunctum, *join.*

conloco (1), *station.*

conscientia, -ae (f.), *consciousness, guilty conscience.*

conscius, -a, -um, *accomplice, conscious.*

consero (3) -evi, -itum, *sow.*

consero (3) -erui, -ertum, *join together.*

consido (3) -sedi, -sessum, *halt, take position.*

consilium, -i (n.), *plan, advice, board of advisers.*

conspectus (4), *sight.*

conspicor (1), *see.*

constat, *it is agreed.*

consterno (3) -stravi -stratum, *strew.*

constituo (3) -ui, -utum, *establish, fix, form up.*

consuefacio (3), *accustom.*

consuesco (3) -evi, -etum, *grow accustomed.*

consuetudo, -inis (f.), *habit.*

consuetus, -a, -um, *accustomed.*

consularis, -e, *consular.*

consulatus (4), *consulship.*

consulo (3) -uli, -ultum, *consult, decree, take thought for.*

consultatio, -onis (f.), *consultation.*

consulto, *on purpose.*

consultor, -oris (m.), *adviser.*

consumo (3) -umpsi, -umptum, *consume.*

contemno (3) -empsi, -emptum, *despise.*

contemptor, -oris (m.), *despiser.*

contendo (3) -endi, -entum, *strive, march.*

contentio, -onis (f.), *struggle.*

contineo (2) -tinui, -tentum, *restrain.*

contio, -onis (f.), *public meeting, speech.*

contra (adv. or prep.), *against, on the other hand.*

contraho (3) -axi, -actum, *contract.*

contremisco (3) -emui, *become afraid.*

controvorsia, -ae (f.), *quarrel, debate.*

contubernium, -i (n.), *service on the staff.*

contumelia, -ae (f.), *insult.*

contumeliosus, -a, -um, *insulting.*

contundo (3) -udi, -usum, *shatter.*

conturbo (1), *disturb.*

convenio (3) -veni, -ventum, *meet,
suit;* convenit, *it is agreed.*

conventus (4), *meeting, association.*

convivium, -i (n.), *dinner party.*

convorto (3) -ti, -sum, *turn.*

copia, -ae (f.), *opportunity, abundance,
circumstances;* copiae, *army.*

coquo (3) -xi, -ctum, *cook.*

coria, -ae (f.), *skin.*

corrumpo (3) -upi, -uptum, *corrupt.*

cotidie, *daily.*

creber, -ra, -rum, *frequent, many.*

credo (3) -didi, -ditum, *believe,
trust.*

creo (1), *create, elect.*

cresco (3) -evi, -etum, *grow.*

criminosus, -a, -um, *disparaging.*

crudelis, -e, *cruel.*

cruento (1), *stain with blood.*

cruentus, -a, -um, *bloodstained.*

cultor, -oris (m.), *cultivator, wor-
shipper.*

cultus (4), *cultivation, way of life.*

cuncti, -ae, -a, *all.*

cunctor (1), *delay.*

cupido, -inis (f.), *desire.*

cupidus, -a, -um, *eager, desirous.*

cupio (3) -ivi, -itum, *desire.*

curia, -ae (f.), *senate house.*

curo (1), *control, look after, take care.*

cursus (4), *running, course.*

damnum, -i (n.), *loss.*

decedo (3) -essi, -essum, *go away, go
down.*

decerno (3) -evi, -etum, *decree,
decide;* decretum, -i (n.), *decree.*

decet (2), *it is fitting.*

declaro (1), *declare.*

decorus, -a, -um, *fitting, dignified.*

decumus, -a, -um, *tenth.*

decus, -oris (n.), *glory.*

dedecoro (1), *disgrace.*

dedecus, -oris (n.), *disgrace.*

dediticius, -a, -um, *surrendered.*

deditio, -onis (f.), *surrender.*

dedo (3) -didi, -ditum, *surrender.*

deduco (3) -xi, -ctum, *lead, post.*

defenso (1), *defend.*

defensor, -oris (m.), *defender.*

defensor (1), *defend.*

defessus, -a, -um, *tired.*

deficio (3) -feci, -fectum, *fail.*

degredior (3) -essus, *go away, go
down.*

dehinc, *after this.*

dehortor (1), *disuade*

deinde, *next.*

delectus, -a, -um, *chosen.*

deligo (3) -egi, -ectum, *choose.*

delinquo (3) -iqui, -ictum, *commit
a crime;* delictum, -i (n.), *crime.*

demissus, -a, -um, *sad, downcast.*

demum, *at last.*

deni, -ae, -a, *ten (each).*

denique, *at last.*

depono (3) -osui, -ositum, *lay aside.*

depravo (1), *deprave.*

derelinquo (3) -iqui, -ictum,
abandon.

desero (3) -erui, -ertum, *desert.*

designatus, -a, -um, *designate.*

desino (3) -ii, -itum, *cease.*

desisto (3) -stiti, *cease.*

despicio (3) -spexi, -spectum, *despise.*

deterreo (2), *frighten, prevent.*

detrecto (1), *belittle.*

detrimentum, -i (n.), *harm, loss.*

devinco (3) -ici, -ictum, *defeat.*

dextumus, -a, -um, *right.*

dictito (1), *say repeatedly.*

diffidentia, -ae (f.), *mistrust.*

diffido (3) -fisus, *mistrust.*

digredior (3) -gressus, *go away.*
dilabor (3) -lapsus, *slip away.*
dilacero (1), *tear to pieces.*
diligens, *careful.*
dimidius, -a, -um, *half.*
dimitto (3) -si, -ssum, *send away.*
diripio (3) -ripui, -reptum, *plunder.*
discedo (3) -cessi, -cessum, *go away.*
discepto (1), *argue.*
disco (3) didici, *learn.*
disiectus, -a, um, *scattered.*
dispar, *unequal.*
dispergo, -si, -sum, *scatter*; dispersus, -a, -um, *scattered.*
dispertio (4), *distribute.*
dissensio, -onis (f.), *disagreement, quarrel.*
dissero (3) -ui, -ertum, *speak at length.*
dissimilis, -e, *unlike.*
distraho (3) -xi, -ctum, *distract.*
distribuo (3) -ui, -utum, *distribute.*
diu, *for a long time; by day.*
diuturnitas, -atis (f.), *duration.*
divido (3) -idi, -isum, *divide.*
divisio, -onis (f.), *division.*
divolgo (1), *spread about.*
divorsus, -a, -um, *separate, in different directions.*
doceo (2) -cui, -ctum, *teach*; doctus, -a, -um, *learned.*
doctor, -oris (m.), *teacher.*
doleo (2), *grieve.*
dolor, -oris (m.), *pain, grief.*
dolus, -i (m.), *trick.*
dominatio, -onis (f.), *rule.*
dono (1), *reward.*
donum, -i (n.), *gift, decoration.*
dormio (4), *sleep.*
dubitatio, -onis (f.), *doubt, hesitation.*
dubito (1), *hesitate, doubt.*

duco (3) -xi, -ctum, *lead, think.*
duritia, -ae (f.), *hardship.*

edictum, -i (n.), *edict.*
editus, -a, -um, *high.*
edoceo (2) -cui, -ctum, *inform.*
effero (3) extuli, elatum, *elevate, reward.*
efficio (3) -eci, -ectum, *achieve, make.*
effringo (3) -egi, -actum, *break.*
effundo (3) -udi, -usum, *spread out.*
egeo (2), *lack.*
egestas, -atis (f.), *poverty.*
egredior (3) -essus, *go out.*
egregius, -a, -um, *remarkable.*
emeritus, -a, -um, *served, retired.*
eminus, *at long range.*
emitto (3) -isi, -issum, *send out.*
enitor (3) -isus, *strive.*
eo, ire, ivi, itum, *go.*
eo (adv.), *to that place.*
epulae, -arum (f.), *banquet.*
equitatus (4), *cavalry.*
equito (1), *ride.*
eripio (3) -ripui, -reptum, *plunder.*
erro (1), *make a mistake.*
eruditus, -a, -um, *learned.*
erumpo (3) -rupi, -ruptum, *break out.*
exaequo (1), *equal.*
exagito (1), *harass, worry.*
excio (4), *excite.*
excito (1), *arouse.*
excubo (1), *keep watch.*
exerceo (2), *conduct, exercise, make use of.*
exigo (3) -egi, -actum, *demand, spend, carry on.*
existumo (1), *think.*
exorior (4) -ortus, *arise.*
exorno (1), *equip, draw up, organise.*
expectatio, -onis (f.), *expectation.*
expedio (4), *unravel, explain.*

expeditus, -a, -um, *lightly equipped.*
expello (3) -puli, -pulsum, *drive out.*
experimentum, -i (n.), *trial.*
experior (4) -ertus, *find out.*
expilo (1), *plunder.*
expleo (2) -evi, -etum, *fulfill, satisfy, fill out.*
exploro (1), *reconnoitre.*
expugno (1), *take by storm.*
exquiro (3) -sivi, -situm, *find out, seek out.*
exstinguo (3) -nxi, -nctum, *put out.*
exstruo (3) -xi, -ctum, *build.*
exsurgo (3) -surrexi, -surrectum, *rise up.*
extenuo (1), *stretch out.*
exulto (1), *exult.*
exuo (3) -ui, -utum, *take off, strip.*

facies (5), *face, appearance.*
facinus, -oris (n.), *deed, crime.*
factio, -onis (f.), *faction, nobility.*
factiosus, -a, -um, *partisan.*
facundia, -ae (f.), *eloquence.*
facundus, -a, -um, *eloquent.*
fallo (3) fefelli, falsum, *deceive, escape notice.*
fama, -ae (f.), *reputation, fame.*
fames, -is (f.), *hunger.*
familia, -ae (f.), *household, family.*
familiaris, -e, *friend, one's own.*
famosus, -a, -um, *notorious.*
fateor (2) fassus, *confess.*
fatigo (1), *wear out, keep asking.*
fautor, -oris (m.), *supporter.*
faveo (2) favi, fautum, *favour.*
felix, *happy, lucky, successful.*
fera, -ae (f.), *wild beast.*
fere, *about.*
ferinus, -a, -um, *wild.*
ferio (4), *strike.*
ferme, *about, almost.*
fero (3) tuli, latum, *bear, say.*

ferox, *fierce.*
fertilis, -e, *fertile.*
ferus, -a, -um, *wild.*
fessus, -a, -um, *tired.*
festino (1), *hurry.*
fidelis, -e, *faithful.*
fides (5), *faith, loyalty, promise.*
fidus, -a, -um, *faithful.*
fingo (3) -nxi, -ctum, *imagine, feign.*
firmo (1), *strengthen.*
firmus, -a, -um, *strong.*
flagitiosus, -a, -um, *criminal.*
flagitium, -i (n.), *crime.*
flecto (3) -xi, -xum, *bend.*
fluxus (4), *a flowing.*
foedus, -eris (n.), *treaty.*
foedus, -a, -um, *foul.*
fons, -ntis (m.), *spring, well.*
forem, *from sum.*
foris, *abroad.*
formido, -inis (f.), *fear.*
fors, fortis (f.), *chance.*
forum, -i (n.), *forum.*
fraternus, -a, -um, *brotherly.*
frequens, *frequent, well-attended.*
frequentia, -ae (f.), *crowd.*
frequento (1), *frequent.*
fretus, -a, -um, *relying on.*
fruges, -um (f.), *crops.*
frustro (1), *frustrate.*
fugo (1), *put to flight.*
funditor, -oris (m.), *slinger.*
fundo (3) -di, -sum, *put to flight.*

gaudium, -i (n.), *joy.*
generosus, -a, -um, *well-born.*
gens, -ntis (f.), *family, nation.*
genus, -eris (n.), *kind, race, tribe.*
gigno (3) genui, genitum, *produce.*
globus, -i (m.), *company.*
glorior (1), *boast.*
gloriosus, -a, -um, *boastful.*
grassor (1), *rage, get to work.*

gratia, -ae (f.), *favour, influence,* (abl.) *for the sake of*; gratiae, *thanks.*

gratuito, *free.*

gravis, -e, *serious.*

gregarius, -a, -um, *in the ranks.*

gula, -ae (f.), *throat, appetite.*

habeo (2), *have, consider, control.*

habitus (4), *conduct.*

haruspex, -icis (m.), *soothsayer.*

hebes (gen. hebetis), *slack, lazy.*

hereditas, -atis (f.), *inheritance.*

hiberna, -orum (n.), *winter quarters.*

hiemo (1), *spend the winter.*

histrio, -onis (m.), *actor.*

honestus, -a, -um, *honourable.*

honor, -oris (m.), *honour, office.*

horribilis, -e, *horrible.*

hortamentum, -i (n.), *encouragement.*

hortor (1), *encourage.*

hospes, -itis (m.), *friend.*

hostia, -ae (f.), *sacrificial victim.*

huc, *hither.*

huiuscemodi, *suchlike.*

humanus, -a, -um, *humane, civilised.*

humilis, -e, *humble.*

humilitas, -atis (f.), *lowliness.*

humus, -i (m.), *ground.*

iaculor (1), *shoot.*

iaculum, -i (n.), *throwing spear.*

ibidem, *in the same place.*

idcirco, *for that reason.*

idoneus, -a, -um, *suitable.*

ignarus, -a, -um, *ignorant.*

ignavia, -ae (f.), *cowardice.*

ignavus, -a, -um, *cowardly.*

ignis, -is (m.), *fire.*

ignoratus, -a, -um, *unknown, unexpected.*

ignosco (3), -ovi, -otum, *pardon.*

illicio (3) -exi, -ectum, *win over.*

illustris, -e, *famous.*

imago, -inis (f.), *picture, bust.*

imbellis, -e, *unwarlike.*

immanis, -e, *monstrous.*

immemor, *unmindful.*

immensus, -a, -um, *immense.*

imminuo (3) -ui, -utum, *diminish.*

immunis, -e, *tax-free.*

immuto (1), *change.*

impedimenta, -orum (n.), *baggage.*

impedio (4), *hinder.*

impello (3) -uli, -ulsum, *incite, encourage.*

impensius, *more eagerly.*

imperitia, -ae (f.), *inexperience.*

imperitus, -a, -um, *unskilled, unknowing.*

imperium, -i (n.), *rule, empire, command, discipline.*

impiger, -gra, -grum, *energetic.*

impono (3) -sui, -situm, *impose, put over.*

importunitas, -atis (f.), *insolence.*

improbus, -a, -um, *wicked.*

improvisus, -a, -um, *unforeseen.*

imprudentia, -ae (f.), *stupidity, lack of foresight.*

impudens, *impudent.*

impugno (1), *oppose.*

inanis, -e, *empty.*

incedo (3) -essi, -essum, *march, occur.*

incendo (3) -di, -sum, *burn, inflame, annoy.*

incertus, -a, -um, *uncertain.*

incipio (3) -cepi, -ceptum, *begin;* inceptum, -i (n.), *undertaking.*

incolo (3) -ui, *inhabit.*

incommodum, -i (n.), *loss, disadvantage.*

incredibilis, -e, *incredible.*

increpo (1) -ui, -itum, *blame.*

incruentus, -a, -um, *bloodless.*

incultus, -a, -um, *crude, wild.*

incurro (3) -rri, -rsum, *attack.*

indicium, -i (n.), *information.*

indignor (1), *be angry.*

indignus, -a, -um, *unworthy.*

induco (3) -xi, -ctum, *lead in, induce.*

industria, -ae (f.), *industry.*

industrius, -a, -um, *industrious.*

indutiae, -arum (f.), *truce.*

inermis, -e, *unarmed.*

iners, *lazy.*

inertia, -ae (f.), *laziness.*

infectus -a, -um, *not done.*

infensus, -a, -um, *hostile.*

infero (3) -tuli, -latum (bellum), *attack.*

infestus, -a, -um, *hostile.*

infidus, -a, -um, *unfaithful.*

infirmus, -a, -um, *weak.*

ingenium, -i (n.), *character, intelligence.*

ingens, *huge.*

ingredior (3) -essus, *enter, attack.*

inhonestus, -a, -um, *dishonourable.*

inimicus, -a, -um, *enemy.*

iniquos, -a, -om, *unequal, unfair.*

initium, -i (n.), *beginning.*

iniuria, -ae (f.), *wrong, harm.*

iniussu, *without the order.*

iniustus, -a, -um, *unjust.*

inmuto (1), *change.*

innocentia, -ae (f.), *innocence.*

innoxius, -a, -um, *innocent.*

inopia, -ae (f.), *want, poverty.*

insequor (3) -utus, *pursue.*

insidiae, -arum (f.), *ambush, trick.*

insidior (1), *lay a trap for, plot against.*

insolens, *insolent.*

insolentia, -ae (f.), *insolence, unfamiliarity.*

insolitus, -a, -um, *unaccustomed.*

insto (1) -stiti, *impend, press upon, pursue.*

instrumentum -i (n.), *instrument.*

instruo (3) -xi, -ctum, *draw up.*

intactus, -a, -um, *untouched.*

integer, -gra, -grum, *upright, unhurt.*

intelligo (3) -exi, -ectum, *understand.*

intendo (3) -di, -tum, *try, pay attention to; intentus, -a, -um, *alert, eager.*

interdum, *sometimes.*

interea, *meanwhile.*

intereo, -ire, -ii, -itum, *perish.*

interficio (3) -feci, -fectum, *kill.*

interim, *meanwhile.*

interimo (3) -emi, -emptum, *kill.*

interpello (3) -puli, *interrupt.*

intervallum, -i (n.), *interval.*

intervenio (4) -veni, -ventum, *come between.*

introduco (3) -xi, -ctum, *let in.*

inultus, -a, -um, *unavenged.*

invado (3) -si, -sum, *attack.*

invenio (4) -veni, -ventum, *find.*

invidia, -ae (f.), *unpopularity, hatred.*

invidus, -a, -um, *jealous.*

inviolatus -a, -um, *undamaged.*

invisus, -a, -um, *hated.*

invitus, -a, -um, *unwilling.*

iocum, -i (n.), *joke, amusement.*

ira, -ae (f.), *anger.*

irritamentum, -i (n.), *incitement.*

irrumpo (3) -rupi, -ruptum, *break in.*

item, *likewise.*

iucundus, -a, -um, *cheerful.*

iudicium, -i (n.), *court, judgement.*

iugis, -e, *flowing (water).*

iugum, -i (n.), *yoke, range of hills.*

iumentum, -i (n.), *pack animal.*

iurgium, -i (n.), *quarrel, abuse.*

ius, iuris (n.), *right, justice*; iure, *rightly.*
iussu, *by order.*
iuvo (1), *help*; iuvat, *it pleases.*
iuxta, *near, equally.*

Kalendae, -arum (f.), *Kalends.*

laboro (1), *struggle.*
lac, lactis (n.), *milk.*
lacero (1), *tear to pieces.*
lacrima, -ae (f.), *tear.*
laedo (3) -si, -sum, *hurt.*
laetitia, -ae (f.), *joy.*
laetor (1), *rejoice.*
languidus, -a, -um, *tired.*
largior (4), *give presents.*
largitio, -onis (f.), *donation, generosity.*
largitor, -oris (m.), *spendthrift.*
lassitudo, -inis (f.), *tiredness.*
latrocinium, -i (n.), *raid.*
latus, -a, -um, *wide*; late, *extensively.*
latus, -eris (n.), *side.*
laus, laudis (f.), *praise, glory.*
laxus, -a, -um, *loose.*
legatio, -onis (f.), *embassy.*
legionarius, -a, -um, *in the ranks, legionary.*
lego (1), *send on a mission, take as a legate.*
lego (3) -gi, -ctum, *read.*
lenio (4), *soften.*
leo, -onis (m.), *lion.*
levis, -e, *light, small.*
liber, -era, -erum, *free.*
liberi, *children.*
licentia, -ae (f.), *licence, freedom.*
licet (2), *it is allowed*; licens, *free.*
lictor, -oris (m.), *attendant.*
lingua, -ae (f.), *tongue, language.*

litterae, -arum (f.), *despatch, letter.*
lixa, -ae (m.), *camp-follower.*
loco (1), *place, station.*
locuples, *rich.*
lubet (2), *it pleases.*
lubido, -inis (f.), *desire.*
ludibrium, -i (n.), *mockery.*
ludifico (1), *baffle.*
lumen, -inis (n.), *light.*
lux, lucis (f.), *light.*
luxuria, -ae (f.), *luxury.*
luxuriosus, -a, -um, *luxurious.*
luxus (4), *luxury.*

machina, -ae (f.), *device.*
maeror, -oris (m.), *sadness.*
magis, *more.*
magistratus (4), *magistrate, office.*
magnificus, -a, -um, *magnificent.*
maiestas, -atis (f.), *dignity.*
maior natu, *older.*
maiores, *ancestors.*
maledictum, -i (n.), *curse, slander.*
maleficium, -i (n.), *crime.*
malitia, -ae (f.), *baseness.*
malo, malle, malui, *prefer.*
mancipium, -i (n.), *property, slave.*
mando (1), *entrust, instruct*; mandatum, *command.*
manipulus, -i (m.), *maniple.*
manus (4) (f.), *hand, band, force.*
mapale, -is (n.), *hut.*
maritumus, -a, -um, *maritime.*
maturo (1), *hasten.*
maturus, -a, -um, *early, ripe.*
medeor (2), *heal.*
mediocris, -e, *moderate.*
mehercule, *by Hercules.*
memini, -isse, *remember.*
memor, *mindful.*
memoro (1), *tell.*
mercator, -oris (m.), *trader.*
merces, -edis (f.), *reward, price, bribe.*

mercor (1), *buy, trade.*

mereor (2), *deserve, serve;* meritus, *deserving;* meritum, *desert.*

meridies (5), *midday.*

metuo (3) -ui, *fear.*

metus (4), *fear.*

militaris, -e, *military.*

militia -ae (f.), *active service, war.*

milito (1), *serve in the army.*

mille passus, *mile.*

minae, -arum (f.), *threats.*

minister, -tri (m.), *servant, accomplice.*

minitor (1), *threaten.*

minumus, -a, -um, *smallest.*

minuo (3) -ui, -utum, *lessen.*

minus, *less.*

mirabilis, -e, *wonderful.*

misceo (2), *mix, cause confusion.*

miserabilis, -e, *pitiable.*

miseret (2), *pity.*

miseriae, -arum (f.), *misery.*

misericordia, -ae (f.), *pity.*

miseror (1), *lament.*

missio, -onis (f.), *leave.*

mobilis, -e, *unstable.*

mobilitas, -atis (f.), *mobility.*

modero, moderor (1), *control.*

modestia, -ae (f.), *moderation, discipline.*

modestus, -a, -um, *moderate, disciplined.*

modicus, -a, -um, *moderate, small.*

modo, *only;* modo . . . modo, *now . . . now.*

modus, -i (m.), *way, limit.*

moenia, -ium (n.), *walls, defences.*

molliter, *softly.*

monitor, -oris (m.), *adviser.*

mora, -ae (f.), *delay.*

morbus, -i (m.), *illness.*

moror (1), *delay.*

mortalis, -e, *mortal.*

mos, -oris (m.), *habit;* mores, *habits, character.*

motus (4), *movement, disturbance.*

moveo (2) movi, motum, *move.*

mulier, -is (f.), *woman.*

multitudo, -inis (f.), *multitude.*

munditia, -ae (f.), *elegance.*

munimentum, -i (n.), *protection.*

munio (4), *protect, fortify, build.*

munitio, -onis (f.), *fortification.*

munus, -eris (n.), *gift, service.*

murtetum, -i (n.), *myrtle bushes.*

muto (1), *change.*

mutuos, -a, -om, *on loan.*

natu, *by birth.*

natus, *son.*

ne . . . quidem, *not even.*

necessarius, -a, -um, *necessary, friend.*

necesse, *necessity.*

necessitudo, -inis (f.), *bond, necessity.*

neco (1), *kill.*

neglego (3) -xi, -ctum, *neglect.*

negotiator, -oris (m.), *trader.*

negotium, -i (n.), *business.*

nequeo, *am unable.*

ni = nisi, *unless.*

nitor (3) nisus, *strive.*

nobilitas, -atis (f.), *nobility, nobles.*

nocens, *guilty.*

nocturnus, -a, -um, *nocturnal.*

nondum, *not yet.*

notus, -a, -um, *known.*

novitas, -atis (f.), *newness.*

novos, -a, -om, *new.*

noxius, -a, -um, *guilty.*

nubo (3) -psi, *marry.*

nudo (1), *strip.*

nutus (4), *nod, will.*

oblino (3) -levi, -litum, *smear.*

obnoxius, -a, -um, *at the mercy of.*

oboedio (4), *obey.*
obscuro (1), *hide.*
obscurus, -a, -um, *obscure.*
obsecro (1), *ask.*
observo (1), *observe.*
obses, -idis (c.), *hostage.*
obsisto (3) -stiti, *resist, obstruct.*
obtestor (1), *beseech.*
obtineo (2), *hold, rank.*
obtrunco (1), *cut down.*
obvenio (4) -veni, -ventum, *fall to.*
obviam, *to meet.*
obvius, -a, -um, *facing, meeting.*
occasus (4), *setting, falling.*
occulto (1), *conceal.*
occultus, -a, -um, *hidden, secret.*
occupo (1), *seize.*
occurso (1), *rush up.*
ocissumus, -a, -um, *fastest.*
octavos, -a, -om, *eighth.*
odi, -isse, *hate.*
odium, -i (n.), *hate.*
odos, -oris (m.), *smell.*
offendo (3) -di, -sum, *offend, meet.*
officio (3) -feci, -fectum, *obstruct.*
oleastrum, -i (n.), *wild olive.*
omitto, -si, -ssum, *neglect.*
omnino, *altogether, at all.*
onustus, -a, -um, *laden*
opera, -ae (f.), *attention, help;*
  operae pretium, *worth while.*
opifex, -icis (m.), *workman.*
opinio, -onis (f.), *expectation, belief.*
oportet (2), *it is fitting, right.*
opperior (4) -ertus, *wait, wait for.*
oppidanus, -a, -um, *townsman.*
opportunitas, -atis (f.), *advantage, suitability.*
opportunus, -a, -um, *useful, suitable, at the mercy of.*
ops, -is (f.), *help, effort;* opes, *resources.*
opto (1), *wish for, choose.*

opulenter, *richly.*
opulentus, -a, -um, *rich.*
orbis, -is (m.), *circle.*
ordo, -inis (m.), *rank, senate.*
orior (4) ortus, *arise.*
oro (1), *ask.*
os, oris (n.), *face.*
ostendo (3) -di, -tum, *show.*
ostento (1), *show.*
ostentus (4), *display.*
otium, -i (n.), *leisure, peace.*

pabulum, -i (n.), *fodder.*
paciscor (3) pactus, *bargain.*
pactio, -onis (f.), *bargain.*
paenitet (2), *repent, be sorry.*
palam, *openly.*
palor (1), *wander.*
panis, -is (m.), *bread.*
par, *equal, right.*
paratio, -onis (f.), *preparation.*
parco (3) peperci, parsum, *spare.*
parens, -ntis, *parent.*
pareo (2), *obey.*
pario (3) peperi, partum, *produce, get, win.*
pariter, *equally.*
pars, -rtis (f.), *part, direction;* partes, *political party.*
particeps, -ipis, *sharer.*
partim, *partly.*
partio (4), *divide, share.*
parum, *too little, not.*
passim, *everywhere.*
patefacio (3) -feci, -factum, *make clear.*
pateo (2), *lie open, be clear.*
patientia, -ae (f.), *endurance, patience.*
patior (3) passus, *suffer, allow.*
patricius, -a, -um, *patrician.*
patro (1), *finish.*
paulatim, *gradually.*
paulisper, *for a short time.*

pavidus, -a, -um, *frightened.*
pectus, -oris (n.), *chest.*
peculatus (4), *fraud.*
pecus, -oris (n.), *cattle.*
pedester, -re, *on foot.*
pello (3) pepuli, pulsum, *drive.*
pendo (3) pependi, pensum, *weigh, pay, value.*
penes, *in the power of.*
penuria, -ae (f.), *lack, scarcity.*
percello (3) -culi, -culsum, *shatter.*
perdo (3) -didi, -ditum, *lose, destroy.*
perduco (3) -xi, -ctum, *lead through.*
pereo, -ire, -ii, -itum, *perish.*
perficio (3) -feci, -fectum, *finish.*
perfuga, -ae (m.), *deserter.*
perfugio (3) -fugi, *desert, take refuge.*
perfugium, -i (n.), *refuge.*
pergo (3) perrexi, -rectum, *go, complete.*
peritia, -ae (f.), *skill, knowledge.*
permaneo (2) -si, -sum, *remain.*
permisceo (2) -miscui, -mixtum, *mix, confuse.*
permixtio, -onis (f.), *mixture.*
permoveo (2) -movi, -motum, *move, trouble.*
pernicies (5), *destruction.*
perniciosus, -a, -um, *destructive.*
perperam, *wrongly.*
perscribo (3) -psi, -ptum, *write out in full.*
persequor (3) -secutus, *pursue.*
pertingo (3), *stretch out to.*
pessumus, -a, -um, *worst.*
peto (3) -ivi, -itum, *attack, aim at.*
phalerae, -arum (f.), *military decorations.*
pietas, -atis (f.), *loyalty.*
piget (2), *vex.*
placeo (2), *please;* placet, *it is decided.*

placidus, -a, -um, *peaceful.*
placitus, -a, -um, *pleasing.*
plane, *completely.*
planities (5), *plain, plateau.*
planus, -a, -um, *level.*
plebs or plebes, -is (f.), *plebs.*
plenus, -a, -um, *full.*
plerique, -aeque, -aque, *many, most.*
pluvius, -a, -um, *rain(water).*
polleo (2), *be strong.*
polliceor (2), *promise.*
pollicitatio, -onis (f.), *promise.*
polluo (3) -ui, -utum, *pollute.*
pondus, -eris (n.), *weight.*
popularis, -e, *popular, of the people, subject.*
porrigo (3) -rexi, -rectum, *hold out.*
porro, *furthermore.*
portendo (3) -ndi, -ntum, *foretell.*
portuosus, -a, -um, *full of harbours.*
posco (3) poposci, *demand.*
possideo (2) -sedi, -sessum, *possess, keep.*
postea, *afterwards.*
posterus, -a, -um, *next;* posteri, *descendants.*
postquam (conj.), *after.*
postremus, -a, -um, *last;* postremo, *finally.*
postulo (1), *ask.*
potens, *powerful.*
potentia, -ae (f.), *power.*
potior (4) potitus, *acquire.*
potior, *better, preferable.*
potissumum, *most of all.*
potius, *rather.*
poto (1), *drink.*
praebeo (2), *provide.*
praeceps, *headlong, steep.*
praecipio (3) -cepi, -ceptum, *instruct;* praeceptum, *instruction.*
praecipito (1), *precipitate.*
praeclarus, -a, -um, *famous.*

praeda, -ae (f.), *booty.*
praedabundus, -a, -um, *bent on booty.*
praedator, -oris (m.), *looter.*
praedatorius, -a, -um, *predatory.*
praedico (1), *proclaim.*
praedico (3) -dixi, -dictum, *foretell.*
praeficio (3) -feci, -fectum, *put in command;* praefectus, *commander.*
praemitto (3) -misi, -missum, *send ahead.*
praemium, -i (n.), *reward. price.*
praepedio (4), *spoil, obstruct.*
praeposterus, -a, -um, *back-to-front.*
praesidium, -i (n.), *protection, garrison.*
praestat (1), *it is better.*
praesum, *am in command;* praesens, *present, in person.*
praeter, *except.*
praeterea, *besides.*
praetergredior (3) -gressus, *go past.*
praetura, -ae (f.), *praetorship.*
pravos, -a, -om, *wicked.*
pretium, -i (n.), *price;* operae pretium, *worth while.*
principium, -i (n.), *beginnings.*
prior, *former, first.*
pristinus, -a, -um, *former.*
priusquam (conj.), *before.*
privatus, -a, -um, *private, commoner.*
probitas, -atis (f.), *honesty.*
probrum, -i (n.), *disgrace, crime.*
probus, -a, -um, *honest.*
procedo (3) -cessi, -cessum, *go on, succeed.*
proditio, -onis (f.), *betrayal.*
prodo (3) -didi, -ditum, *betray.*
proelior (1), *fight.*
profectio, -onis (f.), *start.*
profligo (1), *overthrow, rout.*
profugio (3) -fugi, *run away.*
profundus, -a, -um, *deep, profound.*

prohibeo (2), *prevent, keep off.*
proinde, *equally, therefore;* proinde quasi, *just as if.*
prolato (1), *prolong.*
promitto (3) -si, -ssum, *promise;* promissum, -i (n.), *promise.*
promptus, -a, -um, *quick.*
promptus (4), in promptu, *easy.*
promulgo (1), *promulgate, publish.*
pronus, -a, -um, *inclined, easy.*
propere, *quickly.*
propero (1), *hasten.*
propinquos, -a, -um, *near, related.*
propter, *because of.*
propulso (1), *drive back.*
prorsus, *completely.*
prosapia, -ae (f.), *lineage.*
prospectus (4), *view.*
prosum, -esse, *be of advantage.*
provideo (2) -vidi, -visum, *foresee.*
provincia, -ae (f.), *province (usually Africa).*
proximus, -a, -um, *nearest.*
prudens, *aware, wise.*
puberes, -um (m.), *young men.*
publicus, -a, -um, *public, official.*
pudet (2), *be ashamed.*
pudor, -oris (m.), *shame, modesty.*
pueritia, -ae (f.), *boyhood.*
pulvis, -eris (m.), *dust.*

quadratus, -a, -um, *square.*
quadriduum, -i (n.), *four days.*
quaero (3) -sivi, -situm, *seek, ask.*
quaesitor, -oris (m.), *judge, investigator.*
quaeso (3) -ivi, *ask.*
quaestio, -onis (f.), *enquiry, trial.*
quaestus (4), *gain.*
quamquam, *although.*
quamvis, *however much, although.*
quantus, -a, -um, *how big, how great.*

quartus, -a, -um, *fourth.*
quasi, *as if.*
queo, *be able.*
queror (3) questus, *complain.*
quia, *because.*
quicumque, *whoever.*
quietus, -a, -um, *quiet, still.*
quin, *but that.*
quindecim, *fifteen.*
quintus, -a, -um, *fifth.*
quippe, *because.*
quisnam, *who.*
quispiam, *anyone.*
quisquam, *anyone.*
quisque, *each.*
quisquis, *whoever.*
quivis, *anyone.*
quo, *where (to).*
quocumque, *wherever (to).*
quoniam, *since.*

ramus, -i (m.), *branch.*
rapio (3) -ui, -ptum, *seize, plunder.*
ratio, -onis (f.), *reason, calculation.*
ratus, -a, -um, *ratified.*
ratus, see reor.
receptus (4), *retreat, refuge.*
recito (1), *read aloud.*
rectus, -a, -um, *right, upright.*
recupero (1), *recover.*
recuso (1), *refuse.*
reddo (3) -didi, -ditum, *give back, pay.*
redeo (4), *go back, come back.*
redimo (3) -emi, -emptum, *buy.*
reditus (4), *return.*
refero, ferre etc., *bring back.*
refert, *it matters.*
reficio (3) -feci, -fectum, *mend, refresh.*
regio, -onis (f.), *region.*
regius, -a, -um, *royal.*
regredior (3) -gressus, *go back.*

regulus, -i (m.), *prince.*
reliquos, -a, -om, *remaining.*
remaneo (2) -si, -sum, *remain.*
remitto (3) -si, -ssum, *send back, slacken.*
remoror (1), *delay, keep back.*
removeo (2) -vi, -tum, *remove.*
renovo (1), *renew.*
reor (2) ratus, *think.*
repente, *suddenly.*
reperio (4) repperi, repertum, *find.*
repeto (3) -ivi, -itum, *demand restoration.*
repugno (1), *fight back.*
reputo (1), *think.*
requiesco (3) -evi, *rest, keep quiet.*
resisto (3) -stiti, *resist.*
restituo (3) -ui, -utum, *restore.*
reticeo (2), *keep silent.*
retineo (2) -inui, -entum, *retain.*
rogatio, -onis (f.), *proposed law.*
rogo (1), *ask, propose (law), elect.*
rudis, -e, *untrained, recruit, rough.*
rumor, -oris (m.), *report.*
rursus, *again.*

sacerdotium, -i (n.), *priesthood.*
saevitia, -ae (f.), *savagery.*
saevus, -a, -um, *fierce, savage.*
sagittarius, -i (m.), *archer.*
sal, salis (m.), *salt.*
saltuosus, -a, -um, *wooded.*
sanctus, -a, -um, *holy, honest.*
sane, *at any rate.*
sanguis, -inis (m.), *blood.*
sarcina, -ae (f.), *luggage, baggage.*
satietas, -atis (f.), *satiety.*
satura, -ae (f.), *mixture.*
saucio (1), *wound.*
saucius, -a, -um, *wounded.*
sceleratus, -a, -um, *wicked.*
scelus, -eris (n.), *crime.*
scientia, -ae (f.), *knowledge, skill.*

scilicet, *of course.*
scite, *with elegance.*
scribo (3) -psi, -ptum, *write, enroll.*
scrutor (1), *examine.*
secessio, -onis (f.), *secession.*
secundus, -a, -um, *second, favourable.*
secus, *otherwise, badly.*
sedes, -is (f.), *home.*
seditio, -onis (f.), *rebellion.*
seditiosus, -a, -um, *rebellious, radical.*
segnis, -e, *slow, lazy.*
semisomnus, -a, -um, *half asleep.*
senectus (3), -utis (f.), *old age.*
sententia, -ae (f.), *opinion, vote, decree.*
serius, -a, -um, *serious.*
serpens, -entis (f.), *snake.*
servio (4), *be a slave.*
servitus (3), -utis (f.), *slavery.*
sextus, -a, -um, *sixth.*
significo (1), *indicate.*
signum, -i (n.), *signal;* signa, *standards.*
silentium, -i (n.), *silence.*
simulo (1), *pretend.*
singuli, -ae, -a, *individuals.*
sinister, -tra, -trum, *left, sinister.*
sino (3) -ivi, -itum, *allow.*
sitis, -is (f.), *thirst.*
situs, -a, -um, *placed.*
societas, -atis (f.), *alliance.*
socordia, -ae (f.), *laziness, incompetence.*
socors, *lazy, incompetent.*
soleo (2) solitus, *be accustomed.*
solitudo, -inis (f.), *solitude, desert.*
sollers, *skilful.*
sollicitudo, -inis (f.), *anxiety.*
sollicitus, -a, -um, *troubled.*
solus, -a, -um, *alone, only.*
solvo (3) -vi, -utum, *relax, weaken, pay.*
somnus, -i (m.), *sleep.*
sonitus (4), *sound.*

sordidus, -a, -um, *sordid.*
spatium, -i (n.), *space (time or distance).*
species (5), *appearance.*
spectaculum, -i (n.), *sight, show.*
speculator, -oris (m.), *scout, spy.*
spes (5), *hope, expectation.*
spolium, -i (n.), *spoils.*
stativus, -a, -um, *permanent.*
statuo (3) -uti, -utum, *determine, appoint, set up.*
stipendium, -i (n.), *pay, campaign.*
strenuos, -a, -um, *energetic.*
strepitus (4), *noise.*
strepo (3) -ui, *make a noise, shout.*
studeo (2), *pay attention to.*
studium, -i (n.), *enthusiasm.*
stultitia, -ae (f.), *foolishness.*
subigo (3) -egi, -actum, *drive, compel.*
subsidium, -i (n.), *reserve, reinforcement.*
subvenio (4) -veni, -ventum, *help.*
subvorto (3) -ti, -sum, *overthrow, set aside.*
sudor, -oris (m.), *sweat.*
sumo (3) -mpsi, -mptum, *take, resort to.*
supellex, -ectilis (f.), *furniture.*
superbia, -ae (f.), *pride, arrogance.*
superbus, -a, -um, *proud.*
superior, -ius, *superior, former.*
supero (1), *defeat, exceed.*
supplementum, -i (n.), *reinforcements.*
supplex, *submissive.*
supplicium, -i (n.), *punishment;* supplicia, *tokens of surrender, thanksgiving.*
supplico (1), *pray to.*
supra, *above, earlier.*
suscipio (3) -cepi, -ceptum, *undertake.*

sustento (1), *sustain.*
sustineo (2) -ui, -entum, *sustain.*

taceo (2), *be silent.*
tacitus, -a, -um, *silent.*
tametsi, *although.*
tamquam, *as if.*
tantum, *so much, only.*
tego (3) -xi, -ctum, *cover.*
temere, *rashly.*
temeritas, -atis (f.), *rashness.*
temperantia, -ae (f.), *self-control.*
tempero (1), *restrain, be restrained.*
tempestas, -atis (f.), *storm, time.*
tempto (1), *try, attack.*
tendo, -ere, tetendi, tentum, *go, set, stretch.*
tenebrae, -arum (f.), *darkness.*
teneo (2) -ui, -ntum, *restrain, hold.*
tergum, -i (n.), *back.*
terreo (2), *frighten.*
tertius, -a, -um, *third.*
tibicen -inis (m.), *flute-player, horn-blower.*
timor, -oris (m.), *fear.*
togatus, -a, -um, *wearing a toga.*
tolero (1), *endure.*
tollo (3) sustuli, sublatum, *raise, remove, destroy.*
totus, -a, -um, *all, the whole.*
tracto (1), *handle, govern.*
tractus (4), *course.*
trado (3) -didi, -ditum, *hand over.*
traho (3) -xi, -ctum, *drag, prolong, ponder, plan.*
trames, -itis (m.), *path.*
transfero (3) -tuli, -latum, *transfer.*
transfuga, -ae (m.), *deserter.*
transigo (3) -egi, -actum, *transact.*
transveho (3) -xi, -ctum, *transport.*
transvorsus, -a, -um, *crooked, diagonal, cross-country.*
trepido (1), *panic.*

trepidus, -a, -um, *frightened.*
tribunatus (4), *tribunate.*
tribus (4), *tribe.*
triduum, -i (n.), *three days.*
triplex, *triple.*
triumpho (1), *triumph.*
triumphus, -i (m.), *triumph.*
tugurium, -i (n.), *hut.*
tumulosus, -a, -um, *hilly.*
tumultus (4), *confusion, riot.*
turma, -ae (f.), *squadron.*
turmatim, *by squadrons.*
turpis, -e, *shameful.*
turris, -is (f.), *tower.*
tutor(1), *protect.*
tutus, -a, -um, *safe.*

ubicumque, *wherever.*
ulciscor (3) ultus, *avenge.*
ultro, *freely, of one's own accord.*
una, *together.*
univorsus, -a, -um, *the whole.*
urbanus, -a, -um, *urban, townsman.*
urgeo (3) ursi, *urge, oppress.*
usquam, *anywhere.*
usus (4), *usefulness, resources.*
uter, -tris (m.), *leather bottle.*
uter, -tra, -trum, *which (of two).*
uterque, *each (of two).*
utor (3) usus, *use, hold office.*

vacuos, -a, -om, *empty.*
vagor (1), *wander.*
valeo (2), *be strong.*
validus, -a, -um, *strong.*
vallum, -i (n.), *rampart.*
varius, -a, -um, *varied, changeable.*
vastitas, -atis (f.), *devastation, desolation.*
vasto (1), *lay waste.*
vastus, -a, -um, *deserted, uncultivated.*
vecordia, -ae (f.), *madness.*

vectigal, -is (n.), *tax.*
vehemens, *violent.*
vehementer, *violently.*
velites, -um (m.), *light armed troops.*
velocitas, -atis (f.), *speed.*
velox, *swift.*
venalis, -e, *for sale, corruptible.*
vendo (3) -didi, -ditum, *sell.*
veneo (4) -ivi, *be for sale.*
venio (4) veni, ventum, *come.*
venor (1), *hunt.*
venter, -tris (m.), *stomach.*
venum, *for sale.*
vepres, -ium (m.), *brambles, bushes.*
vereor (2), *fear.*
verus, -a, -um, *true;* verum, vero, *but.*
vesper, -eris (m.), *evening.*
vestio (4), *clothe.*
vetus, *old.*
vetustas, -atis (f.), *old age.*
vexillum, -i (n.), *flag, detachment.*
vigiles, -um (m.), *sentries.*

vigiliae, -arum (f.), *sentries, sleeplessness.*
viginti, *twenty.*
vilicus, -i (m.), *bailiff, agent.*
vilis, -e, *cheap, worthless.*
villa, -ae (f.), *house.*
vincio (4) -nxi, -nctum, *bind.*
vindico (1), *avenge.*
vinea, -ae (f.), *mantlet.*
vinum, -i (n.), *wine.*
vires, -ium (f.), *strength, resources.*
virgultum, -i (n.), *thicket, bush.*
viritim, *man by man.*
viso (3), *visit.*
visus (4), *sight.*
vitabundus, -a, -um, *escaping.*
vitium, -i (n.), *fault, vice.*
vivo (3) -xi, -ctum, *live.*
vivos, -a, -om, *alive.*
volgus, -i (n.), *the people, a crowd.*
voluntas, -atis (f.), *will, wish.*
volvo (3) volvi, volutum, *turn over, roll.*
vorto (3) -ti, -sum, *turn.*

Index of Proper Names

Political and Propaganda Terms

acer, xxviii, lii, 6, 12, 13, 21, 68, 80

amicus, amicitia, inimicus, xxvii, xxviii, 16, 60

amicus populi Romani, amicitia, socius et amicus, xiv, xvi, 2, 7, 9, 34, 36, 52, 55, 61, 66

artes, bonae, xxviii, lii, liii, 13, 19, 21, 32, 69, 79, 81, 91, 100, 120, 124; optimae, 38, 100; malae, 19; pessumae, 41

auctoritas, xxviii, 4, 7, 8, 10, 13, 17, 21, 58

boni, xxviii, 16, 41, 64

contio, 14, 72

dignitas, xxi, xxviii, 20

dominatio, dominor, dominus, xxvii, xxviii, xlv, 15–17, 19, 40, 75, 79

factio, factiosus, xxviii, 5, 12–16, 19, 20, 37, 60, 68, 69, 72, 78

globus nobilitatis, xxviii, 38, 100

gratia, xxviii, 4, 5, 10, 12, 13, 52

imagines, 38, 40, 100, 124

inimicus, see amicus

libertas, xxviii, 14, 16, 17, 20

natio optimatium, xxviii

nobilis, nobilitas, xxvi, xliv, l, li, 4, 5, 12–15, 19, 20, 32–4, 36, 38–40, 46, 55, 73, 79, 92, 100, 124

novitas, novus homo, xxvi, xxix, xxxiii, xliv, l, liii, 32, 34, 38, 91, 92, 99, 124

otium, xxix, 4

pauci (good), 3, 5, 6, (bad), xxviii, 12, 15, 16, 20, 34, 60, 68, 73, 79, 122

partes, 19–21, 33, 78

potentia, xxviii, 12, 14, 15, 20, 42, 68, 122

princeps senatus, 10, 59, 66

regnum, rex, regius, 15, 17, 33, 73

rogatio, rogare, 14, 19, 34, 71, 77, 83

seditiosus, xxviii, xxix, 33, 93

socius et amicus, see amicus

strenuos, lii, 8, 41, 42

superbia, xxviii, l, 1, 15, 16, 20, 32, 33, 36–41, 92

venalis, 6, 17, 61

virtus, xxviii, liii, 2, 3, 32, 34, 38–40, 45, 92, 120–24

Military Terms

capite census, 42, 103

classes, 42, 103

contubernium, 32, 92

dediticius, 16, 71, 75

dona militaria, 40, 101

evocatus, 98

fetiales, 63

funditores, 26, 50

indictio belli, 63

General